Date Due

MAY 1 6 '61			
JAN 1 1 '63			
JAN 2 5 '67			
FEB 8 '67			
MAR 2 2 '67			
MAR 2 9 '67			
APR 2 6 '67			
NOV 1 2 '69			
	PRINTED	IN U. S. A.	

Strindberg's QUEEN CHRISTINA

CHARLES XII · GUSTAV III

Strindberg's QUEEN CHRISTINA
CHARLES XII · GUSTAV III

[August Strindberg]

Translations and Introductions
By Walter Johnson

Seattle · University of Washington Press · 1955
New York · The American-Scandinavian Foundation

44684

Preface

"THE HISTORY of Sweden is the history of her kings," said Erik
Gustaf Geijer, one of the great Swedish romanticists of a century
ago. Obviously an exaggeration, the statement nevertheless has in
it an element of truth: Sweden has had, from the Viking Period
on, remarkably able or colorful monarchs, most of whom have been
highly important in the destinies of the country. In fact, since the
accession of Gustav I in 1523, there have been only three or four
unquestionably incompetent people on the throne—perhaps Queen
Ulrika Eleonora (1718-1720), King Fredrik I (1720-1751), King
Adolf Fredrik (1751-1771), and Charles XIII (1809-1818); and the
incompetence of one of them, Adolf Fredrik, was offset culturally
at least by the brilliance of his consort, Queen Lovisa Ulrika, the
mother of Gustav III. The able or colorful have included Gustav I
Vasa, Erik XIV, John III, Sigismund, Charles IX, Gustav II Adolf,
Christina, Charles X Gustav, Charles XI, Charles XII, and Gustav
III, not to mention the able members of the present reigning Ber-
nadotte dynasty. Even the unfortunate Gustav IV Adolf (1792-
1809) is now being credited with merits that most historians had
been reluctant to grant him before our time.

Many Swedish dramatists, poets, and writers of prose fiction have
exploited the wealth of excellent material available to them in Swedish history and in the history of the Swedish kings. The dramatists
—one of them was Gustav III—have produced an extensive historical dramatic literature. The man who has done more than anyone
else in this field, however, is Sweden's greatest author, August
Strindberg (1849-1912), who planned to write two extensive cycles

v

of historical plays—one dealing with the great figures of Swedish history from St. Erik to Gustav IV Adolf and one with world history. Although he never completed either cycle, he did write some twenty-three historical plays. Several of them rank among his best plays, a significant fact indeed when one recalls that Strindberg is generally recognized as one of the greatest world dramatists.

Strindberg wrote his historical plays for the stage and not for the study. Keenly aware of the contemporary interest in history and of the exceptionally interesting and dramatic raw material in Swedish history, he saw rewarding possibilities in writing plays for the stage about outstanding personalities out of the Swedish past. In doing so, he felt free to select material from such popular but occasionally inaccurate historical sources as Fryxell's *Berättelser ur svenska historien* and Starbäck and Bäckström's *Berättelser ur svenska historien* (referred to as SB in the notes). He also felt free to adapt and compress the material as he saw fit.

In this volume are three of the plays that have, so far as I know, never appeared in print either in an American or a British translation. All of them have had highly successful runs on the stages of various Scandinavian theaters; *Queen Christina* has been played successfully on many occasions in German theaters as well.

As an aid to those who do not know Swedish history, I have presented after each play brief notes on the period, major and secondary characters, and various passages. In these notes, I have presented the material as far as possible from Strindberg's point of view. In the translations, I have used generally accepted English substitutes for some Swedish names (for example, Charles XII for Karl XII) and occasionally an English equivalent when the name has a significance that is concealed if the Swedish original were kept (for example, *Hunger* for *Svält*).

WALTER JOHNSON

Contents

Strindberg's QUEEN CHRISTINA

CHARLES XII · GUSTAV III

Introduction to 'Queen Christina'

In his *Open Letters to the Intimate Theater* (1907 ff.), Strindberg says:

> *Christina.* A woman reared to be a man, fighting for her self-existence, against her feminine nature and succumbing to it. The favorites—translated lovers, frankly speaking—but with forbearance for the daughter of the great Gustav Adolf. Stjernhjelm includes among her lovers even Holm, the tailor, but I did not want to do that. Charge that to my credit, Quiriter!
>
> Christina was so genuine a woman that she was a woman hater. In her memoirs she says frankly that women should never be permitted to rule. That she did not want to get married I think natural, and that she who had played with love was caught in her own net, is, of course, highly dramatic.

When August Strindberg wrote *Queen Christina,* he was interpreting a historical character that both fascinated and repelled him.

His procedure in putting this interpretation into dramatic form was to apply as far as possible the "naturalistic" techniques that he had used in such plays as *Lady Julie* (1888) and *Creditors* (1888) and that he had explained in great detail in the preface to *Lady Julie.* The techniques involved are particularly dialogue, dramatic structure, motivation, and characterization.

The dialogue in *Queen Christina* illustrates what Strindberg says in his famous preface:

> I have avoided the mathematically symmetrical construction of French dialogue and let my characters' brains work irregularly, as

3

they do in actual life, where no topic of conversation is drained to the dregs, but one brain receives haphazard from the other a cog to engage with. For that reason my dialogue too wanders about, providing in the earlier scenes material that is afterwards reworked, taken up, repeated, developed and built up, like the theme in a musical composition.

What may remind anyone who reads the play superficially of the "mathematically symmetrical construction of French dialogue" are the sharpness of repartee and the telling remarks that occur in scene after scene in *Queen Christina*. In people like Christina, Magnus De la Gardie, Oxenstjerna, and Carl Gustav, Strindberg presents characters far more highly sophisticated and intellectually disciplined than either Lady Julie or Jean. Strindberg was fully conscious of the specific individuals he was writing about, and the dialogue is consequently a direct application in terms of each character of what he says in the preceding quotation. Examine, by way of illustration, the passage quoted from the play in the next paragraph.

Strindberg's stage directions—brief though they often are—throw a great deal of light on Strindberg's idea of what sort of person each of his characters was. Take the following lines, for example:

> (CARL GUSTAV *enters, fat and sweaty; soft and bourgeois, but with a certain military and somewhat royal dignity. Falls to his knee, gets up and brushes off the dust*)
>
> CHRISTINA (*takes one of his hands and pats him under his chin with her other hand. Baby talks*): Hello, Carl dear, unshaven as always and careful of your clothes . . . That's the right thing to do! (*Strokes him under the chin*) Double chin, too! But why can't you shave? . . . Come here, my pig, and sit down!
>
> CARL GUSTAV (*good-natured, but a little roosterlike*): My dearest cousin, I've rushed day and night from Öland to tell you how innocent I am in this blessed trial!
>
> CHRISTINA (*darkening a little*): You do not need to tell me that . . .

We have other things to talk about! . . . Sit down! (*Pause*)
(CARL GUSTAV *prepares to hear important questions.*)

CHRISTINA: I'm in a bit of a hurry, so I'll get to the point! . . . Do you understand finances?

CARL GUSTAV: Reasonably!

CHRISTINA: Listen . . . can't a person borrow money . . . Now you're making wry faces as you always do when I talk about money . . . Are you stingy, Carl?

CARL GUSTAV: I haven't anything to be stingy with, old dear.

CHRISTINA: Isn't there something called state . . . deb . . . debent . . .

CARL GUSTAV: Debentures! . . . (*Draws words out, smiling*) Oh, you little . . . (*More hastily*) Yes, there are! But they're government loans!

CHRISTINA: Well-l, can't the head of the government make . . . machines like that?

CARL GUSTAV (*smiles*): No, my dear child, it takes parliament and the National Council.

CHRISTINA (*putting a finger in her mouth*): Oh-h! (*Pause*) What are tax purchases?

CARL GUSTAV (*laughs*): Well, my dear, that's the sort of thing we've been doing for a generation and that's made the whole country uneasy; why, you have signed hundreds of papers like that.

CHRISTINA: Have I? (*Changing her manner*) Oh, you mean those papers with the stamps on them? The ones that look like daler bills and have yellow-and-blue braid on the backs?

CARL GUSTAV (*smiles, but a little seriously*): Most likely that's what all the papers you sign look like . . . but, my dear . . . listen . . . you should avoid revealing to others your ignorance and carelessness in governing the kingdom.

CHRISTINA (*blushes*): What sort of thing is a tax-free grant?

CARL GUSTAV: Now I have to interrupt you! Christina . . . frankly! How much does it come to?

CHRISTINA (*looks down at the floor*): It's a lot, a lot!

CARL GUSTAV: How much?

CHRISTINA: What do you think?

CARL GUSTAV: Millions?

CHRISTINA (*in a weak voice*): Yes!

CARL GUSTAV (*frightened*): How many?

(CHRISTINA *says nothing. Deathly silence*)

CARL GUSTAV (*touched, disturbed*): Oh lord, what have you done, child? It isn't five million, I hope!

CHRISTINA (*childishly*): Five . . . no, of course not; it's three . . . or seven . . .

CARL GUSTAV (*rises, bends—in a friendly manner—over Christina, takes her by the ear, and whispers*): You are joking, aren't you, Kerstin?

CHRISTINA (*hard as steel*): I never joke! I have never joked! . . . Sit down!

Strindberg has provided many hints, all of which give us nuances of the highly complex human being that he thought Christina was. Actors and actresses have apparently perceived the hints and suggestions and have done what Strindberg believed they should do: Interpret Christina's role and all other roles not mechanically but creatively in accordance with leads the dramatist has supplied.

Although quite appropriately Christina is the central and dominant character, Strindberg individualizes the secondary characters— Oxenstjerna, Magnus De la Gardie, Klas Tott, Johan Holm, von Steinberg, Carl Gustav, and Maria Eleonora. The means, as usually elsewhere in Strindberg dramas, are economic, sharp, and distinct. Take as an example, Holm, the queen's tailor, whom she elevated to the nobility as Lejoncrona. The complexity of Holm's character becomes clear bit by bit as we see and hear him with Allerts and his companions before the memorial services for Gustav Adolf begin in Riddarholm Church and his eager attendance upon the queen (Act I). Note his relation with his men at his shop, his calculated behavior toward the queen in the scene at the shop, his honesty about von Steinberg, his unwillingness to talk about Carl Gustav's illegitimate child, the queen's plan to ennoble him (Act III); and his good taste, dignity, and honesty (Act IV), all of which make him far more complex and alive than the ambitious, calculating opportunist and climber one might label him as the result of a cursory reading of the play. Strindberg's technique is here that of the sharp, swift, telling stroke.

The minor or incidental characters are presented in keeping with what Strindberg had said about minor characters in the preface to *Lady Julie* as "mere abstractions . . . ordinary human beings *are* to a certain extent abstract in the pursuit of their calling; that is to say, they are dependent, showing only one side while they are at work. And so long as the spectator feels no need of seeing them from other sides, my abstract delineation of them is fairly correct." Specifically, Allerts the merchant, the farmer from the Västerås district, and the keeper of the Golden Peace are presented as interested spectators, not as active participants in the action; they serve as justified means of supplying exposition and preparation. The journeymen in Holm's shop are likewise seen only from one side—in the pursuit of their calling, and in much the same way, such minor characters as Countess Ebba Brahe and Countess Ebba Sparre are presented only as members of the queen's court and Whitelocke and Bourdelot only in their roles as the English ambassador and the royal physician and favorite, respectively. Each of the minor characters is sufficiently delineated, however, to throw light on the one character Strindberg is particularly interested in presenting in as full detail as possible.

Strindberg's major historical characters are usually dynamic, not static. The queen that appears in Act I is quite different from the woman who walks off the stage at the end of Act IV. A very real development has taken place: "the sleepwalker who had walked so neatly on the roof gutter without falling" has become a thinking, feeling human being who is able to be quite honest with herself. To make this development clear, Strindberg has made use of the techniques of realistic exposition and foreshadowing, every bit of which is neatly sandwiched into scene after scene just as in his great plays of the late 1880's.

Just as he had thought of Julie as a half-woman and a man-hater, he believed Christina had been a half-woman and a man-hater. As he says: "Lady Julie is a modern character; *not that the half-woman, the man-hater has not existed in all ages,* but that she has now been discovered, has stepped to the front and made herself heard." Strindberg was well aware, of course, that Christina, unlike Julie, had had no difficulty in stepping to the front and making herself heard. But he did see in Christina, too, the numerous and complex forces and motivations in heredity and, primarily, in environment that produce the abnormal type that he liked to call "the half-woman, the man-hater."

The Christina that Strindberg presents us upon her first appearance is a queen who varies from moment to moment, from place to place, from person to person, and from situation to situation. These are the elements that stand out: her lack of moral principles or scruples which could serve as a control over her behavior; her relatively little or no respect for anyone or anything unless he or it represents power or distinction; her false ideas of her own nature, qualifications, and standards; her lack of clear-cut goals and reasoned-out plans; her ignorance of official duties, all of which are, for her, parts of a game; her resentment of both her geographical and human environment; her preference for surrounding herself with people whom she can control and manage or who can entertain her; her willingness to play off one person or one group against another—usually to forward her own immediate ends; and her keen desire to be amused.

Strindberg saw Christina's fate as centering in her desperate struggle against her feminine nature. As he understood her, Christina was reared as a man, fought desperately for self-satisfaction in the form of power and intellectual distinctions, types of attention then ordinarily reserved for men. She had been brought up to look upon women and their activities as decidedly inferior to men and their activities. From this fact stems her, for the most part *pretended,* woman-hatred, her distaste and aversion for the marital state, and her frequently unconscious struggle with her masculine competitors—Oxenstjerna, Magnus De la Gardie, and Carl Gustav —for power and place (actual as well as the nominal one which she automatically held). Hence, her development of her acting ability to the point where she acted not only before others but herself as well in order to be the center of attention, the determining factor in her environment, and, in the process, to cover up what Strindberg saw as her very real ignorance of, and lack of interest in, the serious affairs of state. Strindberg shows us that the brilliant queen felt in the occasional moments of honesty with herself that she could not succeed in her hope of competing with such men as Oxenstjerna, Magnus De la Gardie, and Prince Carl Gustav as ruler of a kingdom.

The Strindbergian Christina is a woman without essential inner security. Her emphatic assertion that she is no queen to any king and that she is not to be treated as a woman, her admission that she cannot bear harsh words, and her usually inconsistent and even whimsical behavior are only a few of the many hints that Strindberg gives us of her feelings of insecurity because of the conflict between her nature and what she pretends and tries to be. The inevitable uncontrollable revolt of her suppressed instincts when she falls in love with Klas Tott shatters—as Strindberg sees it—her career as the actress on the Swedish throne. She sees herself as she is by nature, not as she has liked or tried to see herself.

Implicit throughout the play is the central and unifying idea: by the very facts of her environment Christina has been forced to become the Christina "who has innumerable faces" (as Klas Tott says), and "each one gets the Christina he deserves" (as the queen herself puts it), and "the strangest creature God ever created" (as Allerts says).

Just as "Lady Julie's tragic fate has been ascribed . . . to a whole multitude of circumstances," so the defeat of the seventeenth-century queen as queen and woman has been ascribed to a whole multitude of circumstances. Here again are the inherited instincts, the faulty upbringing, the weaknesses of her own character, and the influence of others (an emotionally unbalanced mother, Oxenstjerna, a fawning court, both native and foreign favorites, and her Swedish subjects in general).

Strindberg believed then that Christina was the crowned actress largely because of the faults of her upbringing and environment. He abundantly illustrates what made her what he thought she was. The only child of Gustav Adolf and Queen Maria Eleonora to survive early infancy, Christina was the center of attention not only of her family, the royal court, and the national government but also to a perhaps remarkable degree of the Swedish people. Inheriting the crown at the age of six upon the death of her father in 1632, she was taken from her mother and reared under the direction of Oxenstjerna by her paternal aunt (Carl Gustav's mother) and by carefully selected tutors to be the ruler of a great power. Since women were not highly respected in the seventeenth century, the young queen was exposed to training designed to minimize the effects of what were then considered the defects and weaknesses of the sex. Sensitive, brilliant, headstrong, and egocentric, Christina developed into what Strindberg considered a highly abnormal human being.

The environmental factors that Strindberg believed shaped her into a fundamentally maladjusted person are many. There is first of all the queen mother, Maria Eleonora, an emotionally unstable and in general a pathetic creature who has not only made her daughter suspicious of human feelings and sentiments but who also has inculcated in her a dislike for Sweden and a distaste for most Swedes and most things Swedish. It is Maria Eleonora who says:

MARIA ELEONORA (*old, plain, dignified, warm*): What is it? What's wrong? With my little girl? What have you been up to? Making a mess for yourself? Come and sit here!

CHRISTINA (*places her mother on the sofa, lies down on two chairs*

with her head in her mother's lap): No, sit here, then I can put
my head on your lap! (*Pause*)
>   (MARIA ELEONORA *caresses* CHRISTINA's *hair.*)
> CHRISTINA: You have been a queen, you, too . . . once!
> MARIA ELEONORA: No, my child, I was satisfied with being the great
> *king's* wife, and your mother . . . as long as they let me. (*Her*
> *voice trembles.*) But then they tore my child from me . . . God
> forgive them, if He can! . . . and they reared you to be a
> man! . . . Now they have what they have!

Essentially a good woman with some insight into her daughter and
what has happened to her, Maria Eleonora nevertheless had not
been able to win her daughter's confidence and respect. Christina
had learned early to act in her mother's presence.

Primarily responsible for Christina's education and discipline was
Axel Oxenstjerna, the brilliant and patriotic chancellor who for all
practical purposes ruled Sweden from the death of Gustav Adolf
in 1632 until Christina was eighteen. As Strindberg saw it, Oxenstjerna had little real respect for women, and, when he was called
upon to plan and to supervise the rearing of the child to be the
reigning queen, he resolved to have her brought up as far as possible as a man. It is he who is to a great extent responsible for
giving her her twisted notions of man, woman, and the relationship between them. His handicaps were his unflattering concept of
women, his loyalty and respect for the dynasty, his emphasis on
power and distinctions, his masculine weakness to be affected by a
clever member of the opposite sex, and the conflict between what
he himself wanted to have and what he believed he should train
and have Christina trained for.

As Strindberg understood Christina, she was more than able to
take frequent advantage of, and frequently to control, her great
minister and tutor. She has learned how to manage him:

> CHRISTINA (*coquettish and friendly, pats* OXENSTJERNA *on the hand*
> *that holds the papers*): Thank you very much, good friend, I

take Axel Oxenstjerna's word; no papers are needed with little
Kerstin!
(OXENSTJERNA *remains cold.*)
CHRISTINA: Are you angry with Kerstin, old fellow? Do you re-
member when you used to pull my hair during my history les-
sons . . . (*Takes his hand and puts it on her head*) Caress me
a little; I am so spoiled . . . and I had neither a father nor a
mother . . .
OXENSTJERNA (*half cold*): My child, be honest as you are beautiful,
and you will be both loved and honored!
CHRISTINA (*masters her irritation*): Thanks, Chancellor! Make the
trial short and hush up this unpleasant story quickly!
OXENSTJERNA: Your Majesty, may I have the pamphlet?
CHRISTINA (*gayly*): Yes, when I've received a copy.

Her technique is obvious enough: The appeal to the great man by
means of his own prejudices and masculine pride as well as by her
own pretence. Unfortunate for Christina, however, is the fact that
she does not objectively think through what effect her appeal has.
She does not understand, for example, that it is becoming clear to
Oxenstjerna that she is "Like a cat! . . . a cat . . . It is sad, De la
Gardie, to live long; and to see everything beautiful become ugly,
everything good become evil."

As Strindberg understood him, Oxenstjerna himself wanted to
control Sweden. Hence, he kept Christina, as Allerts says, under
his thumb, and she developed her techniques as an actress and a
coquette to secure what she wanted in spite of the control that he
exercised. He has blinded himself to the facts of her nature as (1)
a child and (2) a woman; he has failed to analyze the educational
program he has set up and the effects of it on her. He feels no
guilt when he says to his twenty-seven-year-old queen:

Christina, little child, get up! . . . I will help you, but you must
never do this again! . . . You see, to rule nations, one has to be
an everyday sort of person. Why, there are farmers and business-

men in parliament! . . . And you are not an ordinary person. You are like an artist—just as careless, just as carefree, just as thoughtless . . . and this . . . does not suit you!

CHRISTINA: It does, no doubt, but it's so boring!

OXENSTJERNA (*smiles*): Yes, it is boring . . . and you want to have a good time above all else . . .

He has, to be sure, moments or flashes of insight into what she has become, but he who above all others is responsible for her upbringing does not see in her seeming carefreeness and thoughtlessness a direct result of the flaws in his own program and its application in practical terms. He has little awareness of the fact that the discipline has been both inadequate and unsuitable.

Strindberg illustrates brilliantly the effect of the attention given Christina by a fawning court who apparently did their best to spoil little Kerstin, the child queen whose keen mind and quick wit fascinated her whole environment. Too early praise on the basis of promise and not of achievement gave her her conviction that she was superior to all or nearly all the people in her immediate environment and certainly far superior to the common people; as she tells Holm: "I don't forget them . . . the little people, Holm . . . I despise them." She assumes that everyone loves her, just as she had most likely been told as a child. Never trained to examine her conclusions about herself critically, she still at twenty-seven allows herself to feel basically superior to everyone, even to the foreigners, who are among her favorites and intimates.

What the whole preparation for her rule of Sweden has become for Christina is clear:

DE LA GARDIE (*sincerely, heartily*): Poor Kerstin, you're involved in . . . something that doesn't befit you!

CHRISTINA: Yes, it is too binding. (*Changes her manner*) But it is interesting! (*Childishly*) And it's fun at times!

DE LA GARDIE: Playing with dolls!

CHRISTINA: Exactly! Big dolls!

For her, ruling a kingdom is a game in which she is the center of attention and is, when she uses her wits and charm, the controlling element for better or (generally) for worse. In still another passage, Christina reveals her attitude in just as striking a fashion:

> CHRISTINA: . . . Holm! I'm tired of the whole comedy!
> (HOLM *silent*)
> CHRISTINA (*as if to herself*): I suspect this is the last act that's on . . .

Governing considered as a game makes Christina only slightly aware of the hard reality of politics and statesmanship. Mastery of such facts was dull and boring for her, but, in some of her rare moments of honesty with herself, she admits to ignorance and other inadequacies. Her honesty does not last long enough to permit her to cease acting to herself or to do anything serious about getting to understand the situations in which she is involved. Granted full authority at eighteen, she has for nine years governed on the basis of whim and impulse without any serious consideration of her actions or of her ignorance. Her ignorance, the result of inadequate training and discipline as well as the dullness of sustained attention to practical and boring problems, leads the libellers to say in their smear: "The queen is a fool who does not understand government in the least." Her "nursery politics," as Prince Carl Gustav tells her finally, have had disastrous effects for both Sweden and herself:

> CARL GUSTAV: And the pages you have written ought to be torn out . . . for they deal only with unlawful acts, embezzlements, scandals, and favorites!
> CHRISTINA: And *you* dare say that?
> CARL GUSTAV: Yes, I dare! . . . And I add . . . your nursery politics have plunged the nation into adventures that I'm to inherit . . . Your insane attack on Bremen has irritated the emperor and Holland.
> CHRISTINA: Hasn't Oxenstjerna straightened that out?

And a little later:

> CARL GUSTAV: You've treated Sweden as your enemy; plundered,
> murdered; above everything, plundered . . .

Christina has not bothered to understand what her country has needed as a ruler, nor has she bothered to understand human beings.

Strindberg has illustrated her sins of omission and commission in one unforgettable scene after the other: Christina's whimsical favoritism, her preference for foreigners, her ignorance of finances, her illegal squandering of national resources, her insistence on having ballets at thirty thousand a night even though the nation cannot afford them, her neglect of the royal navy and army, her careless treatment of both the national council and parliament, and her moral indiscretions.

Yet he was aware that Christina had potentialities that had unfortunately not been allowed to develop. Magnus De la Gardie says: "But she never stays with anything, neither action nor decision" and "She doesn't have any beliefs." The story as Strindberg tells it is the story of a woman who was forced into an impossible situation in which she could not be true to her own nature. That she never stays with any action or decision is the direct result of what her environment has made her; her actions and decisions are based on impulses that are reminiscent of plays in a card game which is to be won in any fashion but not as the result of a carefully considered plan; her lack of beliefs is only superficial. The beliefs that her environment has tried to instill in her are contradictory to what her own nature needs. Her attitude towards the official state religion as opposed to Roman Catholicism and her cultural ambitions for Sweden are illustrations. Strindberg has presented us with an interpretation of Christina, who, if she had been allowed to develop naturally as a woman, could have been far from "the strangest creature that God ever created."

Strindberg shows us Christina's normal behavior. As he said, "she who had played with love was caught in her own net." When she falls in love with Klas Tott, the real and basically sound Strindbergian Christina becomes more and more a natural woman and less and less the crowned actress who acts even to herself. From her first appearance, Strindberg has carefully prepared for just this change: Christina is all along a growing, developing individual who finally becomes emotionally and intellectually an adult. Awakened from her sleepwalking, Christina is a beautiful, charming woman, quite capable of unselfish, considerate actions. She need no longer insist: "If I only knew what I ought to want." Rejected at last by the sensitive Klas Tott largely because of her past and his amazingly sudden Strindbergian insight, Christina is at the end of the play a solitary woman well on the way to being capable of analyzing herself and other people, and a woman who needs no longer to act to herself. It is a characterization that in its insight and wealth of unifying nuances ranks among the best that modern drama has to offer.

The last act is superb. In the Pandora scene, Strindberg presents the crowned actress, the awakened woman, and the human being who at last is beginning to understand herself and her environment. With its modern dialogue—free of all attempts at reproducing the Swedish of Christina's time—and showing the queen in all her major typical moods and forms of behavior, the final act crystallized Strindberg's interpretation of a woman who fascinated him in spite of his personal objections to her record as a ruler. The act serves as an excellent climax to a play that has given Swedish actresses one of their most rewarding roles and drama one of its most interesting characterizations.

Queen Christina · A Play in Four Acts

Characters

CHRISTINA, *Queen of Sweden*
COUNT AXEL OXENSTJERNA, *the Lord Chancellor*
BARON KLAS TOTT
COUNT MAGNUS DE LA GARDIE, *Lord High Treasurer*
ANTON VON STEINBERG
DR. BOURDELOT, *the Queen's French physician*
PIMENTELLI, *the Spanish ambassador*
JOHAN HOLM, *the court tailor*
ALLERTS, *a merchant*
WHITELOCKE, *the English (Cromwell's) ambassador*
PRINCE CARL GUSTAV *(later Charles X)*
MARIA ELEONORA, *the Queen Mother, widow of Gustav II Adolf*
EBBA BRAHE DE LA GARDIE, *mother of Magnus*
EBBA SPARRE, *the Queen's friend*
GENERAL GUSTAV HORN
GENERAL CARL GUSTAV WRANGEL and others

Setting: Stockholm in 1653-1654

ACT I: *Riddarholm Church*
ACT II: *The Treasury*
ACT III: *The Tailor Shop*
ACT IV: *A Pavilion in the Palace Gardens*

ACT I

A section of Riddarholm Church.[1] *At the back to the right is Gustav II Adolf's crypt. To the right in the foreground is the Vasaborg crypt.*

To the right and the left in the foreground are open screens representing entrances.

Soft organ music when the curtain goes up. ALLERTS, *the* FARMER, *and the* KEEPER *of the Golden Peace*[2] *come in slowly from the right.* ALLERTS *is showing the church to the others.*

ALLERTS: And here! Here is the great Gustav Adolf's crypt—it's the anniversary of his death today.[3] The Queen and the whole court are going to bring wreaths . . . in a few minutes.

KEEPER: Heavens, what a lot of banners!

FARMER: Well, well!

KEEPER: Mr. Allerts! May we stay when the Queen comes?

ALLERTS: Yes, if you'll come over here with me . . . Why, there comes my friend, Holm, the court tailor and the Queen's valet— perhaps her chamberlain.

FARMER: Johan Holm? How familiar royalty can be . . . with some people!

ALLERTS (*looks hard at the farmer*): Nils Ersson! Watch out! . . .

(JOHAN HOLM *comes in, carrying a wreath and a cushion.*)

ALLERTS: Holm! . . .

HOLM (*starts*): Mr. Allerts! Hm!

19

ALLERTS: May we stand here and see the Queen?

HOLM (*dryly*): Do you think *you* want to, Allerts?

ALLERTS: Yes, of course I do!

HOLM (*somewhat condescendingly*): Who are these people you have with you?

ALLERTS: This is the keeper of the Golden Peace; and the other one is a farmer from the Västerås district.

HOLM (*indifferently*): Go and stand over there . . . but don't let anyone see you! Her Majesty is coming in from the left!

ALLERTS: Thanks, Holm! (*To the other two*) Come here! (*They station themselves back of a projecting part of the Vasaborg crypt.*)

(HOLM *goes up to Gustav Adolf's crypt and places the cushion on a prayer-stool. The organ music stops.* STEINBERG *comes in from the right, glances about as if he were looking for someone; he is carrying a wreath.*)

ALLERTS (*to the* KEEPER *and the* FARMER): Anton von Steinberg— the one who saved the Queen from drowning in Stockholm Stream—a favorite . . . brilliant future—

KEEPER (*to the* FARMER): But the House of Lords didn't want him!

(KLAS TOTT *enters; with two wreaths; goes up to the* TOTT *tomb with the smaller wreath. He looks pale and highly disturbed.*)

ALLERTS (*to the others*): Klas Tott, the son of Gustav Adolf's Tott —the snow plow . . . a little down at the heels . . . poor boy! A weak strain in his ancestry . . . Erik XIV's great grandson!

FARMER: Erik XIV's?

KEEPER: Yes, not Göran Persson's! [4]

ALLERTS: Quiet, both of you!

STEINBERG (*goes up to* TOTT; *half whispers*): Well, Tott?

TOTT: What do you want, Steinberg?

STEINBERG: *Von* Steinberg, if you please!

TOTT: Do I have a *von* in my name?

STEINBERG (*naively*): I don't know!

TOTT: A person has to be as stupid as you to be that fortunate!

STEINBERG: I can't be blamed for that! And you can be fortunate, Tott, even if you are brilliant!

TOTT: Can I? Tell me then, Steinberg, how I can recover my last thousand ducats, the ones I lost last night! [5]

STEINBERG: Well, I'll tell you, Tott, if you'll meet me at the Golden Peace tonight!

TOTT: Are there any ducats there?

STEINBERG (*ingenuously*): Not there, of course, but I know where you can get them!

TOTT: Why, you are a good man, Steinberg!

STEINBERG: Oh no! Don't say that! Why, everybody is very good . . .

TOTT: You think so, Steinberg? Do you really believe that?

STEINBERG: Yes, of course, I do! And one thing is certain . . . the Queen is an angel!

TOTT: I've never heard the like! . . . I was at the ballet yesterday, and I thought the Queen watched me with eyes more like a hawk's than a dove's!

STEINBERG: Yes, that's her manner! Everybody has his own manner, you see, Tott! . . . Will you meet me at the Golden Peace? Oh yes, do that! Do that, Tott!

TOTT: I will!

STEINBERG: That's really kind . . . of you!

(WHITELOCKE, *the English ambassador, enters, without a wreath, looks over the church.*)

ALLERTS (*to the others*): The English ambassador . . . Cromwell's[6] man . . . saw Charles I beheaded . . . He isn't a nobody by any means!

KEEPER: A king's murderer . . . here?

FARMER: I must get a look at him!

ALLERTS: And he was a member of Parliament when Cromwell closed it and put the keys in his pocket! . . . Sh-h! Now they're beginning to come!

(BOURDELOT and PIMENTELLI *enter, speak inaudibly.* BOURDELOT *with a lorgnette, shows the church to* PIMENTELLI, *a dark, reserved man.*)

ALLERTS (*to the others*): Bourdelot—the French doctor—the Queen's pet monkey, who sneers at everything . . . and who has taught the Queen to sneer, too . . . And the Spanish ambassador, Pimentelli, a Jesuit . . . Look how they're sneering . . . and no wreaths naturally because they're Catholics!

KEEPER: At least they don't conceal their feelings . . . if a person could only understand what they're saying.

ALLERTS: I can understand that much French . . . The Spaniard says: "New saints' chapels . . . and what a saint—Vasaborg— Cabeljau . . ." [7] Now they're looking at the imperial banners . . .

FARMER: And they are the Queen's friends . . . her father's enemies!

ALLERTS: Yes, she! She recently declared publicly that religion during the Thirty Years' War was only a cloak under which they concealed territorial aggression.

KEEPER: Good lord, no!

ALLERTS: Yes, you see she envies her father and his soldiers because she can't wage war. She pretends to despise the old generals, Horn and Wrangel . . .

FARMER: It is hard to be one's father's daughter . . .

KEEPER: Still harder to be under Axel Oxenstjerna's thumb.

ALLERTS: She hates him, too, and wishes that his name were forgotten . . . She's a rare one! Thank heavens for Carl Gustav, the heir to the throne . . . He is a man!

KEEPER: All day, yes!

FARMER: Hope we'll get him then!

ALLERTS: Just wait! Everything's ready to explode here! . . . Sh-h!

(MAGNUS DE LA GARDIE *enters alone, looks depressed and humiliated.*)

ALLERTS (*to the others*): Magnus Gabriel De la Gardie . . . former

favorite—intended King of Sweden—just now in disfavor . . .
great disfavor . . .

KEEPER: Ebba Brahe's son . . .

FARMER: And Gustav Adolf's, eh?

ALLERTS: Talk, gossip . . . there's a lot of it about the Queen . . .
(DE LA GARDIE *greets* BOURDELOT *and* PIMENTELLI *dryly,* TOTT
coldly, STEINBERG *humbly. Stops alone and deserted in the middle
of the floor when everyone draws away from him.*)
(MARIA ELEONORA, *the Queen Mother,* EBBA BRAHE DE LA GARDIE,
and EBBA SPARRE *enter. Differing greetings to different people and
from the various people present.* MARIA ELEONORA *avoids looking
at* DE LA GARDIE.)

ALLERTS: Maria Eleonora, Gustav Adolf's widow . . . Ebba Brahe
De la Gardie. Ebba Sparre, the Queen's friend.
(DE LA GARDIE *kneels at a distance—before* MARIA ELEONORA.)

EBBA BRAHE DE LA GARDIE (*as she passes her son*): Why did you come,
Magnus?

DE LA GARDIE: You may well ask that, Mother!

EBBA BRAHE: The Queen doesn't want to see you, since you wouldn't
be satisfied to be in her court . . .

DE LA GARDIE: Her gang, her pack . . .

EBBA BRAHE: Sh-h, my child!

ALLERTS: Pretty soon the pieces will be set up . . . and then the
game will start . . . I have a feeling that something will happen . . . Look at poor De la Gardie . . .

KEEPER: No one wants to talk to him!

FARMER: They probably want to, but they don't dare to . . .

ALLERTS: Listen to him! He catches on! . . . Now! . . . Now the
Queen's coming! . . . (*General attention directed to the left entrance*) No suite . . . no chamberlains . . . no guards. Doesn't
fear her loyal subjects . . . believes everybody loves her, because
she loves herself!

KEEPER: Does she believe that?

ALLERTS: She believes only what she wants to!

FARMER: But she is majestic, little as she is!

ALLERTS: At the moment, yes, but in the next she's a shopgirl . . . Now you're going to see the strangest creature God ever created . . .

(*During the following scene everyone present should follow and comment on the Queen's actions with looks and facial expressions.* ALLERTS *particularly emphasizes his silent reflections with gestures.*)

(CHRISTINA *enters from the left. Slowly, with dignity, with a certain respect for the church. She is dressed in a black velvet mantle trimmed with black bear fur, a large black felt hat (model of the Thirty Years' War) with a black plume and a diamond aigrette. When she has entered, she opens her mantle, revealing a black dress trimmed with white pearls. Then she pulls off her gloves. She measures everyone present while doing these things. A page with a laurel wreath follows her.* HOLM *approaches her respectfully.* DE LA GARDIE *is near her. When she has nodded to those present and thereby indicated the different degrees of friendship or enmity, she drops her gloves.* DE LA GARDIE *throws himself to his knee, picks up her gloves, and extends them to* CHRISTINA, *whose look makes him step aside.*)

CHRISTINA: Holm!

(HOLM *comes forward, receives the gloves from* DE LA GARDIE *who draws aside, crushed.*)

CHRISTINA: Hold them! . . . Has Chancellor Oxenstjerna come?

HOLM: The chancellor has not come, Your Majesty!

CHRISTINA (*impatient facial expression. Goes up to* MARIA ELEONORA, *pats her vigorously but condescendingly on her arms, and kisses her dutifully on her cheek*): Bless you, Mother . . . (*Greets* EBBA BRAHE *stiffly. Kisses* EBBA SPARRE *on her cheek*) Hello, Ebba dear! . . . (*Nods in a friendly but a somewhat facetious manner to* STEINBERG) My friend, Steinberg . . . (*Greets* BOURDELOT *while she exchanges a look of secret understanding with* PIMENTELLI.

August Strindberg (1849-1912)

Karin Kavli as Queen Christina

Recognizes WHITELOCKE *with a slight gesture*) The regicide among
the tombs of kings! Ha ha!
(BOURDELOT *says something witty to her in French which is inaudible to the audience.*)
CHRISTINA (*first smiles, then says seriously*): Yes, it is a disgrace to
let the Queen wait, but that's the chancellor for you.
(PIMENTELLI *says something in French which can't be heard.*)
CHRISTINA (*looks towards* ALLERTS *and his companions*): Why,
they're only my loyal subjects! They love me! So there's no
danger!
(PIMENTELLI *speaks inaudibly to* CHRISTINA *while he exchanges
passionate glances with her.* CHRISTINA—*her answer cannot be
heard. Speaks to him for only a second.* BOURDELOT *tries to listen,
but in vain.*)
MARIA ELEONORA (*comes down to* CHRISTINA. *Speaks apathetically but
bitterly*): Whom are we waiting for, my child?
CHRISTINA: The chancellor, Mother! Little Kerstin always has to
wait for the great Oxenstjerna!
MARIA ELEONORA: That is thoroughly Swedish . . .
CHRISTINA: Yes, that's right! . . . But I suppose some of the gen-
erals have to be along!
MARIA ELEONORA: The generals? The war's over, isn't it?
CHRISTINA: Yes, but you understand . . . on a day like this the old
fellows want to let the people see them . . .
EBBA BRAHE (*comes up to* CHRISTINA *as if she wanted to ask a favor*):
Your Majesty . . .
CHRISTINA (*hard, with a masculine voice*): We are not granting any
audience in the church . . . least of all by our father's grave!
(*Turns her back, catches sight of* TOTT. *Signals to* STEINBERG *who
comes up to her.* CHRISTINA *half whispers in a friendly tone as if
she were speaking to a harmless person.*)
CHRISTINA (*to* STEINBERG): Tell Tott to come here! Wait . . . Have
you spoken with him?

STEINBERG: Yes, Your Majesty!

CHRISTINA: What did he say?

STEINBERG: He's very kind, but he is having bad luck!

CHRISTINA: Command him to come here!

    (STEINBERG *goes over to* TOTT. PIMENTELLI *tries to get near the Queen and to keep an eye on her.* CHRISTINA *with a look and a half-whispered word makes him draw back.* STEINBERG *comes back without* TOTT.)

CHRISTINA: Well, Steinberg?

STEINBERG (*distressed*): Your Majesty!

CHRISTINA: Why doesn't Tott come?

STEINBERG: He's very strange . . . Poor Tott!

CHRISTINA: What did he say? Is he bashful?

STEINBERG: No, he isn't; but he said only that he didn't want to!

CHRISTINA (*furious*): By God! I've never heard the like! . . . He said he didn't want to!

STEINBERG: Or that he didn't dare!

CHRISTINA (*brightens a little, but smiles grimly*): Go once more, and command him to come at the risk of my disfavor!

    (STEINBERG *goes and gets* TOTT, *who comes along unwillingly.*)

CHRISTINA (*looks daringly at* TOTT *who appears bashful*): You are afraid, Tott?

TOTT: Yes!

CHRISTINA: Of me?

TOTT: Yes!

CHRISTINA (*flattered*): Is little Kerstin that dangerous?

TOTT: Yes!

CHRISTINA (*still flattered but annoyed that* TOTT *could possibly imagine "something"*): That is something! (*Changes abruptly*) You were gambling last night?

TOTT: Yes, Your Majesty!

CHRISTINA: And lost a few thousand ducats? Permit me to cover . . .

TOTT: No, Your Majesty, I can't do that! . . . I can't take money from a woman . . .

CHRISTINA: I am not a woman . . .

TOTT: Well, not even from a queen . . .

CHRISTINA: I am not queen to any king. I was proclaimed king! Do you remember that, Tott?

TOTT: Yes, now I do!

CHRISTINA: Will you be your king's chamberlain?

TOTT: I don't understand the reason for this unexpected favor!

(CHRISTINA *pale and speechless with indignation, but uncertain how she is to interpret his ambiguous words; she does not dare to reveal her feelings and thoughts through an outcry. Pause*)

TOTT (*looks up at* CHRISTINA *and becomes startled by the expression on her face*): If I have expressed myself unhappily, Majesty, forgive the somewhat badly diluted Vasa[8] blood in my veins!

CHRISTINA (*brightens; looks at* TOTT *with pleasure but not yet fully placated*): Vasa blood? (*Changes at first slowly as if she were thinking over what she ought to say now while the words gush out*) Yes, you have a lineage, perhaps a greater one than I, and you seem to be a full-blooded Vasa! (*Changes her manner as if she had happily found the solution*) We're related then, and you can accept anything from a kinsman! (*Cheerful, affectionate, gives him her hand*) Well, welcome to court, Klas Tott! Klas! That is quite nice! . . . Three steps to the side . . . and don't be afraid of little Kerstin!

ALLERTS (*to his companions*): Little Kerstin, over twenty-seven . . . now has Tott on her hook.

KEEPER: And Tott's twenty-three?

FARMER: Why, that's robbing the cradle!

CHRISTINA (*who has noticed that* ALLERTS *has been talking with the others. Turns towards them and speaks softly to* TOTT): Do you see that they love me? What are you afraid of then?

TOTT: I'm afraid of my feelings!

CHRISTINA (*who has not heard him*): I didn't hear you! (*Commotion at the door to the left*) What's that noise? . . . Soldiers, I see!

(AXEL OXENSTJERNA, CARL GUSTAV WRANGEL, GUSTAV HORN *enter.*
Various greetings)

OXENSTJERNA (*comes up to the Queen, bows deeply, and speaks respectfully*): Your Majesty! Please forgive . . .

CHRISTINA (*gayly*): Yes, I forgive you; you know that, Oxenstjerna . . . But . . . (*ironically*) . . . the generals, how can I forgive them?

OXENSTJERNA: Their fault is mine, Your Majesty! Important news . . .

CHRISTINA: Are we at war again?

OXENSTJERNA: No, Your Majesty, but there is trouble . . . Rumors and . . .

CHRISTINA: We won't pay any attention to them!

OXENSTJERNA: Well-founded rumors!

CHRISTINA: May I greet you, Gustav Horn? The best man my father had! . . . and Carl Gustav Wrangel! the Great, our Condé . . .[9] Welcome, my lords . . .

(*All go slowly, group by group, up to Gustav Adolf's crypt, except* DE LA GARDIE, BOURDELOT, *and* PIMENTELLI, *who remain downstage.* BOURDELOT *and* PIMENTELLI *converse and gesture without the audience hearing the words; they finally step to the left where they observe* DE LA GARDIE *with pity.*)

CHRISTINA (*comes back downstage, and calls up to the organ loft which is high up in the left wing*): Düben![10] Let's begin now! (*Waits for an answer which the audience can't hear*) Are you ill, organist? (*Inaudible reply*) We'll have to do without music then! (*To* DE LA GARDIE) Magnus, what are you pouting about?

DE LA GARDIE: I'm mourning . . .

CHRISTINA: Have you lost someone?

DE LA GARDIE: Yes, I've had a great loss!

CHRISTINA: Will you inherit?

DE LA GARDIE: No . . . Tott will!

CHRISTINA (*smiles grimly*): Your answers are superb, Magnus! Say something pleasant . . . these people are all so dull!

DE LA GARDIE: Not today!

CHRISTINA: What day is today?

DE LA GARDIE: Shooting day!

CHRISTINA: What?

DE LA GARDIE: Yes, they shot the late king today!

CHRISTINA (*laughs into her handkerchief*): Magnus, Magnus, you'll be the death of me! (*Turns about and calls*) Let the drapes fall! (*Drapes are let down concealing the upper part of the church*)

DE LA GARDIE: Shall we put out the lights, too?

CHRISTINA: Shame on you!

DE LA GARDIE: But what will the old men say?

CHRISTINA: I had to wait for the generals. Now they can wait for me!

DE LA GARDIE: What's wrong with the music? Doesn't Düben have any wind left?

CHRISTINA (*striking him with her fan*): Magnus!

MARIA ELEONORA (*at the drapes*): Christina, can't we start soon?

CHRISTINA: Yes, my child; you may start.

DE LA GARDIE: You're very pretty today!

(CHRISTINA *puts her finger to her lips.*)

DE LA GARDIE: Poor Tott!

CHRISTINA: Now you are brave, because . . .

DE LA GARDIE: Why? Because . . .

CHRISTINA (*turns*): Can't they start, for Christ's sake?

DE LA GARDIE: How long are we going to keep up this farce?

CHRISTINA (*half furious*): You finish badly!

DE LA GARDIE: I'm already finished! . . . (*with genuine emotion*) When you left me, and I saw you going down, I lost my faith in everything!

CHRISTINA (*touched*): You did love me?

DE LA GARDIE: What a question!

TOTT (*at the drapes*): Your Majesty!

CHRISTINA (*stamps her foot*): Start, damn it!

DE LA GARDIE: Shame!

CHRISTINA (*in a suppressed, soft voice*): Magnus, if you knew how all these dead and half-dead great ones depress me and bind me . . . The great Oxenstjerna, the great Banér,[11] the great Torstensson, the great Wrangel . . . My really great father always has to be used to enlarge their littleness! As plain, as human, as humble as he was, he'd turn over in his coffin if he were lying there! But he is far off, I suspect . . . as far as I wish I were!

DE LA GARDIE (*sincerely, heartily*): Poor Kerstin, you're involved in . . . something that doesn't befit you!

CHRISTINA: Yes, it is too binding. (*Changes her manner*) But it is interesting! (*Childishly*) And it's fun at times!

DE LA GARDIE: Playing with dolls!

CHRISTINA: Exactly! Big dolls!

DE LA GARDIE: Watch out—the regicide is standing back of the curtain!

CHRISTINA: No one will murder me! Everybody loves me!

DE LA GARDIE (*amazed*): You know, Charles I of England said exactly the same thing!

CHRISTINA (*darkens*): Did he?

DE LA GARDIE: "Everyone loves me," he said, and then they cut off his head!

CHRISTINA: Imagine, there are moments when I'd like to be Cromwell . . . and cut off my own head!

DE LA GARDIE: I can understand that—there are moments when I've wanted to hang myself!

CHRISTINA (*smiles*): Crazy! Always crazy! (*Gently but firmly*) Go now!

(DE LA GARDIE *looks questioningly at her.*)

CHRISTINA: Go!

(DE LA GARDIE, *as earlier, shrinks as if collapsing.*)

CHRISTINA: Go, until I summon you.

DE LA GARDIE: Have you been playing with me?

CHRISTINA: Yes! Mayn't I?

DE LA GARDIE: No one plays—unpunished—with a De la Gardie!

CHRISTINA (*furious*): Are you threatening the Queen?

DE LA GARDIE: Yes!

CHRISTINA: Leave the city, bury yourself out in the country—you know where, and if you show yourself again, there are fortresses in Finland! [12]

DE LA GARDIE (*crushed*): Do you mean that or are you joking?

CHRISTINA (*turns her back to him*): I'm serious! On my word! As a woman!

    (DE LA GARDIE *goes to the left.*)

COURIER (*enters, meets* DE LA GARDIE, *falls to one knee, gives him a letter*): Count De la Gardie from Prince Carl Gustav!

    (CHRISTINA, *startled, stops.*)

DE LA GARDIE (*opens a big letter, which contains a smaller one. He reads hastily*): Your Majesty!

CHRISTINA (*uneasy*): My lord!

DE LA GARDIE (*hands her the smaller letter*): To the Queen from Prince Carl Gustav!

CHRISTINA (*accepts the letter coldly, shrugging, with a contemptuous look*): Through De la Gardie! That is courteous!

DE LA GARDIE (*reads his letter*): Oh Lord! Dear God!

CHRISTINA (*reads her letter and shudders*): Now I am afraid!

DE LA GARDIE: Who has written this?

CHRISTINA: They aren't human beings! They're devils.

DE LA GARDIE: It's poison and daggers!

CHRISTINA: What does your letter say?

DE LA GARDIE (*slyly*): The same as yours!

CHRISTINA (*looks hard at* DE LA GARDIE *with hate but with fear too*): Magnus! Be my friend!

DE LA GARDIE: As good a friend as a rejected lover can be!

CHRISTINA: You may not use that word! I cannot bear harsh words.

DE LA GARDIE: Not harsh words, but you can bear harsh deeds . . .

CHRISTINA: Can you guess who the libeler is?

DE LA GARDIE: One of the Messeniuses[13]—if it's the father or the son or both, I don't know.

CHRISTINA: It's terrible; I feel as if I'd been made dirty 'way into my soul!

DE LA GARDIE: Well, that's how they write—in the fortresses in Finland!

CHRISTINA (*weakly*): Don't be unkind, Magnus! Help me!

DE LA GARDIE: If I do help you up, you'll trample me under foot!

CHRISTINA (*uneasy*): Advise me! . . . Or . . . I'll go to Oxenstjerna!

DE LA GARDIE: Go to Oxenstjerna, but not today! Go to Oxenstjerna, but don't let him read the lampoon before you've sounded him out!

CHRISTINA: That's good advice, but what does it mean? Let me think . . . Yes . . . It means: Do not trust anyone! . . . Magnus, don't you believe that my subjects love me?

DE LA GARDIE: You are a child!

CHRISTINA: At this moment, perhaps! . . . And so . . . I'll go to my mother . . . (*Goes along the drapes*)

DE LA GARDIE: Go to your father's grave, too . . . it is good to remember the good sometimes!

CHRISTINA (*back again*): What have I done to make everyone hate me?

DE LA GARDIE: You have played with the destinies of men as if you had been playing with dolls!

CHRISTINA (*amazed*): Have I?

DE LA GARDIE: See, you didn't know! . . . You do not know what you are doing, so God forgive you!

CHRISTINA: You are kind, Magnus!

DE LA GARDIE: Always kind to little Kerstin. Always unkind to the big, nasty Christina!

CHRISTINA: To think that I . . . that I will have to go to Oxenstjerna again!

DE LA GARDIE: You should have done that sooner! He is the greatest and the best!

CHRISTINA: Bourdelot is greater, freer; he soars like a kite over field and horizon, but Oxenstjerna stands like a stork by the rat hole.

DE LA GARDIE: Is Bourdelot *that* great?

CHRISTINA: His spirit . . . Well, I don't want to talk about him, for you wouldn't understand. But if you want to be my friend, you will be Bourdelot's!

DE LA GARDIE: I will try!

CHRISTINA (*notices* ALLERTS *and his company, which has been increased by curious people*): Magnus! . . . I feel as if they hated me!

DE LA GARDIE: Go to your mother!

CHRISTINA (*childishly*): She hasn't any advice to give me, but she has what I don't have . . .

DE LA GARDIE: What is it called—a heart?

CHRISTINA: Yes! (*She goes to the drapes.*)

(WHITELOCKE *comes out between the drapes with a smile surviving a pleasant conversation he has just had.* CHRISTINA *recoils at first, but then goes up.*)

ALLERTS: The regicide!

CURTAIN

ACT II

The treasury room. The walls are lined with shelves filled with blue folios with yellow plates; otherwise, with bundles of gray paper, tied with heavy thread. At the back, a little door to inner rooms.

A door to the right and one to the left.

AXEL OXENSTJERNA *at a large writing desk;* MAGNUS DE LA GARDIE *directly opposite him.*

OXENSTJERNA (*writing*): I'll be ready in a moment!

DE LA GARDIE: No hurry!

OXENSTJERNA (*to himself*): Sixty-five, seventy . . . Let me see . . . Here you have the title to Ekolsund [14]—as a gift from the Queen —that comes a little late, since you are already in disfavor! You still are in disfavor, De la Gardie?

DE LA GARDIE: Yes, in as great disfavor as anyone can be under Christina . . .

OXENSTJERNA: Please speak of our ruler with respect!

DE LA GARDIE: Excuse me, Oxenstjerna! But when the kingdom is on the verge of ruin . . .

OXENSTJERNA: I do not want to hear that!

DE LA GARDIE: I want to remind you that I am a member of the national council and that I am just as great a patriot as you, Oxenstjerna.

(OXENSTJERNA *looks at him with amazement.*)

DE LA GARDIE: Do you know the content of the Messenius pamphlet? [15]

OXENSTJERNA: No! Do you?

DE LA GARDIE: No!

OXENSTJERNA: Do you have an idea of what's in it?

DE LA GARDIE: If I did, I wouldn't tell! . . .

OXENSTJERNA (*sadly*): De la Gardie . . . you are Lord High Treasurer! Do you know what condition the kingdom is in?

DE LA GARDIE: That I don't think anyone can find out!

OXENSTJERNA: I have! I have been checking the accounts for a year . . . Look here . . .

DE LA GARDIE: Well?

OXENSTJERNA (*distressed, rises and walks about*): It is distressing!

DE LA GARDIE: *Claudite libros!* Let's talk about something else!

OXENSTJERNA (*wringing his hands and struggling with himself*): De la Gardie, I have—as you know—always had great reverence for the memory of my great king and for his heir. But I have loved my country as my eye . . .

DE LA GARDIE: Please stop, Oxenstjerna; otherwise, you'll regret it afterwards.

OXENSTJERNA: I know, but I have to speak . . .

DE LA GARDIE: Don't do it; the walls have ears, and Spanish boots tread silently!

OXENSTJERNA (*stops and stares at* DE LA GARDIE): Spanish, you said . . . (*Hastily*) Do you know Pimentelli?

DE LA GARDIE: Yes!

OXENSTJERNA: Who is that man?

DE LA GARDIE: Quite simply . . . a Spanish Jesuit who also happens to be the Queen's favorite!

OXENSTJERNA: A Jesuit! Heaven preserve us! (*Pause*) Do you know, De la Gardie . . . No, I cannot bear anything like that . . . spying and slandering . . . My statesmanship is too old. (*Pause*) Is it true that Holm, the court tailor, is to be ennobled and made a chamberlain?

DE LA GARDIE: That is true!

OXENSTJERNA: Good God! (*Pause*)

DE LA GARDIE: Just as true as that young Tott is going to become a member of the national council!

OXENSTJERNA: Lieutenant Tott, the twenty-three-year-old?

DE LA GARDIE: Yes, he's a favorite!

OXENSTJERNA (*hesitantly*): What is meant by favorite, this word that pursues me, always and everywhere?

DE LA GARDIE: Favorite? . . . It is . . . a favorite, somebody who enjoys someone's favor.

OXENSTJERNA: I wish I were dead! (*Pause*) Is it true . . . God forgive me . . . that the Queen attends Catholic mass[16] at the French ambassador's?

DE LA GARDIE: And makes the sign of the cross? Yes! The whole town knows that!

OXENSTJERNA (*beside himself*): Then I want to be dead! . . . Magnus, in Jesus' name, let me speak. (*Pause*) Reverence, deference, loyalty to the royal house, everything that I have respected, I shall have to throw overboard! I have closed my eyes out of reverence; I have closed my ears out of deference and I have finally become false from pure loyalty. I have become cowardly; I have become a servile toady at court; I have respected meanness; and I am beginning to despise myself. (*Pause*) The kingdom is ruled by a crazy woman, the accounts look as if a mad child had kept them! All the possessions of the crown have been ruined for foreigners; ballets are presented at thirty thousand crowns a night; the army exists only on paper; and the navy is rotting outside Karlskrona;[17] the estates of parliament are treated as a parish council; the national council is recruited with second lieutenants; the palace chapel is a Jesuit meeting place; and the palace is a dance hall. (*Pause*)

DE LA GARDIE: So . . . something has to be done!

OXENSTJERNA: Yes! (*Pause*)

DE LA GARDIE: The Estates have wanted to marry off the Queen!

OXENSTJERNA: Yes, to Carl Gustav of the Palatinate, but that we do not want!

DE LA GARDIE: So—o?

OXENSTJERNA: Carl Gustav is a soldier and can wage war, but he is not a statesman who can rule a country. Besides, we do not want any Palatinate when we have Vasas!

DE LA GARDIE: Do we have Vasas?

OXENSTJERNA: Yes, in Poland! [18]

DE LA GARDIE: That's true! . . . But Carl Gustav has friends!

OXENSTJERNA: More enemies!

DE LA GARDIE: A certain party . . . has wanted to improve conditions by limiting royal power!

OXENSTJERNA: That is my party!

DE LA GARDIE (*delighted, amazed*): And Cromwell's!

OXENSTJERNA: Yes, Cromwell's! . . . Do you know about Cromwell?

DE LA GARDIE: No, not much! . . . They say he decapitated his king!

OXENSTJERNA (*darkens, retreats*): Did he? . . . That was not his fair deed, however! (*Pause*) Think of it, De la Gardie, the five millions[19] we received in the Peace of Westphalia have disappeared!

DE LA GARDIE: Disappeared?

OXENSTJERNA: Stolen!

DE LA GARDIE: By whom?

(*Noise at the right door*)

OXENSTJERNA (*looks to the right*): Her Majesty! (*Both rise*)

(CHRISTINA *enters, dressed in riding clothes. Nods to both. First looks carefully at* DE LA GARDIE'S *face to get information about the situation; then her and* OXENSTJERNA'S *eyes meet.* DE LA GARDIE *brings forward a chair for* CHRISTINA.)

CHRISTINA (*sits down*): Sit down, Oxenstjerna!

OXENSTJERNA (*sits down*): Your Majesty . . .

CHRISTINA (*after a pause*): I have come about the Messenius pamphlet. (*Pause*) Do you know it?

OXENSTJERNA: Not its contents!

CHRISTINA (*takes up a pamphlet*): Then I want to give you only an excerpt from the contents . . . To read it completely would be to demean myself—entirely too much—and you, Chancellor!

(OXENSTJERNA *bows his head.*)

CHRISTINA: The author—if he deserves the name—says . . . to begin with . . . that the Queen is a fool who does not understand government in the least.

(OXENSTJERNA *looks about as if he wanted to discover a traitor.*)

CHRISTINA (*cold-bloodedly*): Further . . . that the resources of the kingdom are squandered on foreigners, of course . . . and then there are the ballets—20,000 a night . . . it was 30,000, I believe, but that doesn't matter! . . . Do you understand?

OXENSTJERNA (*his face becoming hard*): I understand!

CHRISTINA: Then there's something about Jesuit meetings, parish councils, and second lieutenants . . .

(OXENSTJERNA *looks at* DE LA GARDIE *with amazement.*)

CHRISTINA: Then there's an infamous accusation directed at you!

He insists that you are working against Carl Gustav's succession to the throne . . . I would gladly spare you, Axel Oxenstjerna, but it implies that no means will be spared against Carl Gustav —not even poison! [20]

(OXENSTJERNA *makes a movement.*)

CHRISTINA: Genuine poison, which is said to have been mixed at a castle near Stockholm. Guess which castle it is!

(OXENSTJERNA *says nothing.*)

CHRISTINA: Then we shall let that pass! But in all this false meanness there is a point that is dangerous, really dangerous! This says that a certain party that loves Cromwell more than Stuart has made it its aim to use all means to limit our royal power. (*Her voice sharp as a knife*) Did you understand?

(OXENSTJERNA, *ice-cold, bows his head.*)

CHRISTINA: Those were the major points—the still more unreasonable ones I shall pass in silence . . . What do you, Oxenstjerna, say about such an infamous pamphlet? (*Pause*)

OXENSTJERNA: I would not want to attach any significance to it at all, if—among its lies and exaggerations—there were not an expression of fairly general public opinion . . . Yes, I must admit that I heard not very long ago . . . (*Looks at* DE LA GARDIE) . . . statements of the same kind! Your Majesty, this attack is not harmless and cannot be disregarded!

CHRISTINA (*ambiguously, as if lying in wait*): No, that is what I think! And so I have had both the Messeniuses arrested!

OXENSTJERNA: Already?

CHRISTINA (*lashing out*): Don't *you* think that there's no time to waste? (*Slows up*) And when they are examined, I hope to find evidence against all the people who have contributed to forming the opinion, for which the libelers have served as the mouthpiece. I even hope . . . (*Glares at* OXENSTJERNA *who is sitting ready to parry and withdraw*) . . . that new information will be gained about still more important questions through these hearings . . .

(*Stretches her head forward and hisses out*) . . . especially one
question, Oxenstjerna, which concerns me very much!

OXENSTJERNA (*calmly, positively*): Is it the question of the five million?

(CHRISTINA *becomes pale, struggles for her breath, remains in
the pose with head stretched forward.* OXENSTJERNA *does not release her glance.*)

CHRISTINA (*slowly draws her head back and shrinks up*): Which
. . . five . . . million?

OXENSTJERNA: The ones that were stolen! (*Pause*)

CHRISTINA (*slowly*): What money was that?

OXENSTJERNA (*gets up*): The money Sweden got as compensation in
the Peace of Westphalia! I will show you the proof immediately!
(*Goes out through the little door at the back*)

CHRISTINA (*rushes up, takes both of* DE LA GARDIE's *hands and holds
them against her bosom*): Magnus, for God's sake, cancel the
case!

DE LA GARDIE: Too late!

CHRISTINA: Help me! . . .

DE LA GARDIE: Why did you have to play with the lion?

CHRISTINA (*strikes herself with her riding whip*): Why can't I ever
get out of his claws?

DE LA GARDIE: He was not the one who started the clawing . . .

CHRISTINA: Why did I touch this wasp's nest? Help me, Magnus!

DE LA GARDIE: Give in . . .

CHRISTINA: Give in! I?

DE LA GARDIE: All of us have to!

CHRISTINA: I will! But I'll get my revenge afterwards!

DE LA GARDIE: We know that!

(CHRISTINA *puts the riding whip aside and changes her expression.* OXENSTJERNA *comes in with papers.*)

CHRISTINA (*coquettish and friendly, pats* OXENSTJERNA *on the hand
that holds the papers*): Thank you very much, good friend, I take

Axel Oxenstjerna's word; no papers are needed with little Kerstin!

(OXENSTJERNA *remains cold.*)

CHRISTINA: Are you angry with Kerstin, old fellow? Do you remember when you used to pull my hair during my history lessons . . . (*Takes his hand and puts it on her head*) Caress me a little; I am so spoiled . . . and I had neither a father nor a mother . . .

OXENSTJERNA (*half cold*): My child, be honest as you are beautiful, and you will be both loved and honored!

CHRISTINA (*masters her irritation*): Thanks, Chancellor! Make the trial short and hush up this unpleasant story quickly!

OXENSTJERNA: Your Majesty, may I have the pamphlet?

CHRISTINA (*gayly*): Yes, when I've received a copy. (*Looks at her watch*) Now I have to go. Farewell, gentlemen! (*Turns*) Tell me, are there Polish Vasas?

DE LA GARDIE: Yes, Sigismund's descendants!

CHRISTINA: But they are Catholics!

DE LA GARDIE: They can change their faith!

CHRISTINA (*mockingly*): You're right about that! . . . If Vasas are needed, though, I have better ones! . . . Farewell! (*Goes*)

OXENSTJERNA: Like a cat! A cat . . . It is sad, De la Gardie, to live long and to see everything beautiful become ugly, everything good become evil.

DE LA GARDIE: And the pamphlet?

OXENSTJERNA: I will admit that I was amazed. But most likely the authors have heard people talking and have recorded the talk.

DE LA GARDIE: What we all think! . . . And now we have to condemn them to death!

OXENSTJERNA: How cruel life is! . . . But there has to be a change here!

DE LA GARDIE: We can't remove her from the throne, but we can force her to abdicate.

OXENSTJERNA: Can we?

DE LA GARDIE: Yes, we can!

OXENSTJERNA: Will you step in here so that we can talk?

DE LA GARDIE: Is there anyone in there?

OXENSTJERNA: Yes, of course!

DE LA GARDIE: Who is it?

OXENSTJERNA: Come, and you'll see!

DE LA GARDIE (*looks into the rooms*): Allerts, the merchant!

OXENSTJERNA: Yes, do you know who he is?

DE LA GARDIE: He has a daughter . . .

OXENSTJERNA: Who is the mother of a child . . .

DE LA GARDIE: Whose father is Carl Gustav . . .

OXENSTJERNA: Yes!

CURTAIN

ACT III

The lower part of the stage is a splendid salon; to the left, en-closed by a Chinese screen, are a couple of sofas by a large table and some chairs. To the right, a huge walnut cabinet in Dutch style.

The upper part of the stage forms first a walk or a gallery; out-side it, the tailors' work room. To the right, directly in front, a long low window with six ordinary vents. In front of it, a large tailor's table on which sit eight journeymen with their legs under them, sewing beautiful costumes. Nearby stands a journeyman cutting; another is pressing; a third is trying a Pandora's[21] cos-tume on a mannequin.

JOURNEYMAN I (*looking out of the window*): There certainly are people out!

JOURNEYMAN II: Best not to look out!

JOURNEYMAN III: Why not?

JOURNEYMAN II: It takes very little to get pinched . . .

PRESSER: Keep your gab shut then!

FITTER: Are they taking them to the court of appeals?

PRESSER: The Messeniuses, yes! Didn't you know that?

JOURNEYMAN II: I suspect there are still others who'll be brought to court!

PRESSER: Still others?

JOURNEYMAN II: The witnesses!

PRESSER: Keep your mouth shut!

(*The* PRESSER *and the* FITTER *come downstage.*)

FITTER (*to the* PRESSER): It's a devilish trial! Just like a seine; you get both big and small fish in the net when you pull it in! . . . Can you imagine, there's hardly a person of rank who isn't involved . . . not one, from the highest to the lowest . . .

PRESSER: The very highest?

FITTER: Yes! And they suspect each other, all of them . . . all of them!

PRESSER: And . . . the highest?

FITTER: She's scared!

CUTTER (*comes downstage*): Watch out! Watch out!

PRESSER: Huh! We! Tailors? No! . . . Everybody can get into disfavor and go under except us! We're indispensable, and the chancellor calls us the extra council, the one that can't be removed; Holm is our protector . . . Did you know . . . that Holm's going to be ennobled?

CUTTER: Ennobled? Well, what'll that make us?

FITTER: Then we'll be tailors . . .

PRESSER: All the same, those Messeniuses are stout fellows . . . Just think of spewing up all that, every bit of it . . .

CUTTER: That really cleans out the stomach . . . Sh-h, there's Holm!

(*All go back to their work.*)

HOLM (*comes in, with a quill pen back of his ear and wearing a*

*lorgnette; he goes up to the big cabinet, opens the door, and takes
paper out of boxes. He reads and makes entries. Talks to the
journeymen without looking at them)* Quiet, quiet, quiet, quiet!
(JOURNEYMEN *mumble.*)

HOLM: Quiet, quiet, quiet, quiet!

CHRISTINA (*enters, dressed in the traditional Amazon costume with
one side of the skirt fastened high, has a sword and the chain of
the Order of Johannes.*[22] *She looks frightened*): Holm!

HOLM (*fairly courteous*): Majesty!

CHRISTINA: Do you have thirty thousand?

HOLM: Yes, certainly.

CHRISTINA: You have yet to say no to me, Holm! . . . You see, I
have to have the ballet so that the people will get something
beside this blessed trial to talk about!

HOLM: Blessed! Damn the person who set it going!

CHRISTINA (*shrinks back for a single second*): What are they saying
in the city?

HOLM: Oh, there's a lot of talk!

CHRISTINA: Are they angry with me?
(HOLM *gestures towards the journeymen.*)

CHRISTINA: Those fellows? They love me!

HOLM: Your Majesty! The guild, the tailor's guild, is out with its
banners today on the pretext that there's a meeting, but there
isn't any meeting!

CHRISTINA: A trifle! (*Goes upstage and greets the journeymen
gayly*) Hello, boys!
(JOURNEYMEN *prick up their ears, turn, and stare at the Queen
coldly.*)

CHRISTINA (*comes downstage again, dismayed, to* HOLM): I don't
like their eyes!

HOLM: Your Majesty, give them a holiday today, and their eyes will
be beautiful, as yours.

CHRISTINA (*controls her anger and her disgust*): I can't give them
a holiday; I have to have the ballet.

HOLM: Don't forget the little men; many little ones make one big one!

CHRISTINA: I don't forget them, Holm . . . I despise them.

HOLM: Ouch!

CHRISTINA: How does my dress fit?

HOLM (*pokes at the seams*): Oh . . . yes! . . . But when you're willowy . . .

CHRISTINA (*expresses her disgust at a compliment from him*): Do you have Pandora ready?

HOLM: On the modeling stand, as the court painter says!

CHRISTINA (*goes up and examines the Pandora costume on the mannequin*): It looks promising! (*Comes back, nervously*) Some gentlemen are coming soon. Ask them to sit down!

(*Shouts of hurrah outside*)

CHRISTINA (*shrinks*): What's that?

HOLM: The little people!

CHRISTINA (*tries to joke*): Those aren't children's shouts!

HOLM: No, Your Majesty, they're not!

CHRISTINA: Holm! Do I have a single friend among all these people about me?

HOLM: Yes, one!

CHRISTINA: Who?

HOLM: If I except my own humble person that I'd prefer to call slave rather than friend . . . Steinberg!

CHRISTINA (*a little contemptuously*): Steinberg! Who insists on his *von!*

HOLM: Yes, that is his only little weakness; but the good, simple-hearted Steinberg would die for his Queen without demanding *any* reward . . .

CHRISTINA (*reflects*): Do you mean that? (*Pause*) Holm! I'm tired of this whole comedy!

(HOLM *silent*)

CHRISTINA (*as if to herself*): I suspect this is the last act that's on . . . Do you know Allerts, the merchant?

HOLM: Yes, of course!

CHRISTINA: There is a secret about that man that I don't know! Do you know it?

HOLM: No!

CHRISTINA: See to it that you find out!

HOLM: People have become so silent and careful since the trial! . . . There comes Steinberg!

CHRISTINA (*her face changes; she goes up to* STEINBERG): Welcome, Steinberg!

(STEINBERG *on his knee*)

CHRISTINA (*gently*): Don't! . . . Get up! You have saved my life . . .

STEINBERG: Your Majesty, if I could give my life . . .

CHRISTINA: Knowing that your thoughts and good wishes are with me is enough for me, Steinberg . . . Tell me where you have been!

STEINBERG: In the courtroom, Your Majesty!

CHRISTINA (*shudders*): And you heard . . .

STEINBERG: Yes, I heard . . .

CHRISTINA (*afraid to find out but nevertheless curious*): Come in here with me . . . (*Goes out to the left;* STEINBERG *follows.*)

TOTT (*in from the right; looks about; talks to* HOLM): Would you leave for a little while, tailor?

(HOLM *first looks at* TOTT, *then goes up to the back of the stage to left, goes out*)

DE LA GARDIE (*enters from right*): There you are! . . . Let's sit down . . .

TOTT (*points at a chair*): Here?

DE LA GARDIE: Yes-s, this is fine! (*They sit down.*) You're so in the sun now, Tott, that you radiate light!

TOTT: Does it show?

DE LA GARDIE: People in love are always radiant, and anyone who comes near them is warmed . . . You are lucky, Tott!

TOTT: The greatest happiness is always embittered by the thought of the terrible moment that will bring it to an end!

DE LA GARDIE: Why should it end?

TOTT: Why? . . . Before this . . . Why, I have loved other women . . . When we'd be on the verge of breaking up, I used to tear down my idol, trample it in the dust, and I'd be free. That is, I'd weep for a couple of weeks or so!

DE LA GARDIE: I think that's the only time a man does weep and has the right to.

TOTT: This time tears won't help . . . I've placed this one so high and made her so sacred, that if she breaks it off, I'll die!

DE LA GARDIE: Poor Tott!

TOTT: You know, I can already feel the torture in advance . . . Can't the philosophers explain why the grief of love is the most profound? . . . I've seen Johan Banér[23] fall in love . . . that hero was like a child . . . he needed six handkerchiefs a day! But the worst of it is that people laugh at that grief! One thing, Magnus! Do you think she's playing with me?

DE LA GARDIE: Playing? Can a woman do anything else? Why, love is a game!

TOTT: To play with heaven and hell—that's a dangerous game!

DE LA GARDIE: There are people who die!

TOTT: I love her as a youngster would; I worship her like a higher being, and I call her my first love!

DE LA GARDIE: A higher being?

TOTT: Yes, exactly! Don't you see how she hovers above life, how everything is insignificant to her? The crown, which kings place on their heads, she tramples under her feet. I'm almost sure that she'll throw it away some fine day!

DE LA GARDIE (*pricks up his ears*): Do you think so?

TOTT: Yes, she's an eagle, born of air in the air, because she has such a hard time breathing down here! . . . If I only could follow her flight!

DE LA GARDIE: But she never stays with anything, neither action nor decision.

TOTT: That's because she doesn't want to bind herself! Why, that's her greatness!

DE LA GARDIE: She doesn't have any beliefs.

TOTT: Why should she have beliefs when all of them can be disproved? . . . That's why she is always young, always new.

DE LA GARDIE: Good God, you are in love!

TOTT: Yes, I am!

DE LA GARDIE: Doesn't she have any faults?

TOTT: No, because "faults and merits"—that bourgeois concept—doesn't cover her qualities.

DE LA GARDIE: Have you noticed how many faces she has?

TOTT: Holm, the tailor, and people of his kind have only one face; Christina has innumerable faces, because she is not one human being, but a world!

DE LA GARDIE: That's a good one!

TOTT: And the beauty of her countenance only I have seen, and I've been permitted to see it because I love her . . . You others will never get to see it.

DE LA GARDIE: You really can love! Yet you have the reputation of being a misogynist.

TOTT: Woman hater! I still am, but Christina isn't a woman! Besides she's a woman hater herself as you know! So we agree about that, too!

DE LA GARDIE: Watch out for her pretended hatred of women—that's only her device for catching small birds!

TOTT: But she has written that woman is a larva . . .

DE LA GARDIE: She has written! . . . Do you believe what's written? . . . Hasn't she read Euripides[24] aloud to you, too?

TOTT: Yes! How do you know?

DE LA GARDIE: Let's be discreet, Klas!

(CHRISTINA *enters; her face still bears fresh traces of* STEINBERG'S *good personality. She has a note in her hand.* TOTT *and* DE LA GARDIE *get up.* CHRISTINA, *thoughtful, asks* TOTT *with a gesture to withdraw.* TOTT *looks angrily at* DE LA GARDIE *and hesitates.* CHRISTINA *repeats the gesture.* TOTT *withdraws unwillingly.*)

DE LA GARDIE (*radiant, believing that* TOTT *is in disfavor*): Already!

(CHRISTINA, *angry eyes struggling against a smile. She tears the note to pieces and strews them on the floor.*)

DE LA GARDIE (*more courageous*): A final letter?

(CHRISTINA *comes forward; sits down; invites* DE LA GARDIE *to sit; puts her sword between herself and* DE LA GARDIE, *whom she fixes with a sharp, inexplicable look.*)

DE LA GARDIE: The sword between us?

(CHRISTINA *fixing his glance once more ambiguously.* DE LA GARDIE *takes up as if in distraction a jewelry case and fingers it.*)

CHRISTINA: What's that?

DE LA GARDIE: A peace offering!

CHRISTINA: For your wife! . . . For the sake of peace at home! What has she done now?

DE LA GARDIE: Why, she was cross and got out of hand!

CHRISTINA: And now she's to be bribed! Why did you get married?

DE LA GARDIE: You ought to know why you married me to Maria Euphrosyne.

CHRISTINA: Listen, Magnus! Will you sell Ekolsund?

DE LA GARDIE: Why, I've just got the title to it.

CHRISTINA: What difference does that make?

DE LA GARDIE: Is it Carl Gustav who's to have it?

CHRISTINA: No, but that doesn't concern you! . . . How much?

DE LA GARDIE: I don't want to sell it!

CHRISTINA (*angry and haughty, speaks with a masculine voice*): To your king?

DE LA GARDIE: Said the Queen!

CHRISTINA (*lifts her sword*): Are you reminding me I am a woman?

DE LA GARDIE: Is that disgraceful?

CHRISTINA (*scanning*): For me, yes! . . . You know, I'd like to meet you outside sometime with weapons so that you'd learn that I'm your inferior in nothing!

DE LA GARDIE: You mean you want to give me satisfaction . . .

CHRISTINA (*silent, looks to see if he meant something else; thereupon she smiles. Then she changes her manner*): Do you want seventy thousand for Ekolsund?

DE LA GARDIE: That depends on . . . who is going to be my successor!

(CHRISTINA, *humiliated, ashamed, "takes the bit in her mouth and puts down her head." Says nothing*)

DE LA GARDIE: Forgive me, but you're begging for a beating!

CHRISTINA: Is it so delightful to strike someone?

DE LA GARDIE: To strike down idols is delightful, but to hit a woman one has loved . . . that really hurts . . . but it relieves the other pain!

CHRISTINA: You always talk about the pain of parting . . . I don't feel anything like that! I just think it's wonderful to be free again!

DE LA GARDIE: Again! . . . Just wait, you'll find out . . . yes, you will . . . as everybody does who plays with a force of nature, a creative force that has its source at the roots of the tree of life . . .

CHRISTINA (*scornfully, derisively*): What can that be?

DE LA GARDIE: Love! But you don't know what that is!

CHRISTINA: It's a game, I suppose, that one shouldn't take seriously . . . (*Scanning*) "And the one who plays has to bear the game . . ." (*Changes brutally*) Now you may go! Good-bye! . . . Send Tott in!

(DE LA GARDIE *gets up hesitantly.*)

CHRISTINA (*accentuates*): Tott, chamberlain!

(DE LA GARDIE *still hesitates.*)

CHRISTINA (*crescendo*): Tott, member of the National Council!

DE LA GARDIE: Member . . . of . . . the . . . National . . . Council!

CHRISTINA: Perhaps you want to sell Ekolsund now?

DE LA GARDIE: Now I want to sell . . . But the price has gone up!

CHRISTINA (*nonchalantly*): To what?

DE LA GARDIE (*disengaging and falling out*): To five million!

CHRISTINA (*shrinks together; then straightens up and says with a dull voice*): Magnus! Do me a favor!

DE LA GARDIE: My dear cousin, I am always ready to do favors for you, except degrading ones!

CHRISTINA (*softly*): This one isn't degrading . . . for you! Go up to the court of appeals . . . and listen to the proceedings . . .

DE LA GARDIE: Yes, I will . . . if that can help you!

CHRISTINA (*pathetically*): Do you think it's hopeless?

DE LA GARDIE (*caressingly*): Little Kerstin! . . . Poor little Kerstin, you are the one who is on trial and who is being investigated . . .

CHRISTINA: How stupid . . . it is to do stupid things!

DE LA GARDIE: Of course! I certainly know, I who am being whipped for my . . . let us say, stupidities!

CHRISTINA (*sadly*): Why are you always superior towards me?

DE LA GARDIE: Am I? . . . Perhaps I am!

CHRISTINA (*furious, flashes out*): Don't be impudent!

DE LA GARDIE: You won't get out of this mess . . . except in one way!

CHRISTINA: What is that?

DE LA GARDIE: Abdicate!

CHRISTINA: I didn't hear!

DE LA GARDIE: Abdicate! . . . (*Pause*)

CHRISTINA (*pretends not to have heard; cold as ice*): Call Tott!

DE LA GARDIE (*fearlessly*): No! . . . You'll have to do that yourself! (*Goes*)

(CHRISTINA *alone. Stands indecisively; grimaces with her mouth as if she were biting into a sour apple*)

CHAMBERLAIN (*enters*): His Royal Highness, Prince Carl Gustav!

CHRISTINA (*assumes a cheerful, open expression and a friendly tone*

and goes freely and easily to meet CARL GUSTAV): Welcome!
(CHAMBERLAIN *out*)
(CARL GUSTAV *enters, fat and sweaty; soft and bourgeois, but
with a certain military and somewhat royal dignity. Falls to his
knee, gets up and brushes off the dust*)

CHRISTINA (*takes one of his hands and pats him under his chin with
her other hand. Baby talks*): Hello, Carl dear, unshaven as always
and careful of your clothes . . . That's the right thing to do!
(*Strokes him under the chin*) Double chin, too! But why can't
you shave? . . . Come here, my pig, and sit down!

CARL GUSTAV (*good-natured, but a little roosterlike*): My dearest
cousin, I've rushed day and night from Öland to tell you how
innocent I am in this blessed trial! [25]

CHRISTINA (*darkening a little*): You do not need to tell me that . . .
We have other things to talk about! . . . Sit down! (*Pause*)
(CARL GUSTAV *prepares to hear important questions.*)

CHRISTINA: I'm in a bit of hurry, so I'll get to the point! . . . Do
you understand finances?

CARL GUSTAV: Reasonably!

CHRISTINA: Listen . . . can't a person borrow money . . . Now
you're making wry faces as you always do when I talk about
money . . . Are you stingy, Carl?

CARL GUSTAV: I have nothing to be stingy with, old dear.

CHRISTINA: Isn't there something called state . . . deb . . . debent . . .

CARL GUSTAV: Debentures! . . . (*Draws words out, smiling*) Oh,
you little . . . (*More hastily*) Yes, there are! But they're government loans!

CHRISTINA: Well-l, can't the head of the government make . . .
machines like that?

CARL GUSTAV (*smiles*): No, my dear child, it takes parliament and
the National Council.

CHRISTINA (*putting a finger in her mouth*): Oh-h! (*Pause*) What
are tax purchases?

44684

CARL GUSTAV (*laughs*): Well, my dear, that's the sort of thing we've been doing for a generation and that's made the whole country uneasy; why, you have signed hundreds of papers like that.

CHRISTINA: Have I? (*Changing her manner*) Oh, you mean those papers with the stamps on them? The ones that look like daler bills and have yellow-and-blue braid on the backs?

CARL GUSTAV (*smiles, but a little seriously*): Most likely that's what all the papers you sign look like . . . but, my dear . . . listen . . . you should avoid revealing to others your ignorance and carelessness in governing the kingdom.

CHRISTINA (*blushes*): What sort of thing is a tax-free grant?

CARL GUSTAV: Now I have to interrupt you! Christina . . . frankly! How much does it come to?

CHRISTINA (*looks down at the floor*): It's a lot, a lot!

CARL GUSTAV: How much?

CHRISTINA: What do you think?

CARL GUSTAV: Millions?

CHRISTINA (*in a weak voice*): Yes!

CARL GUSTAV (*frightened*): How many?

    (CHRISTINA *says nothing. Deathly silence*)

CARL GUSTAV (*touched, disturbed*): Oh lord, what have you done, child? It isn't five million, I hope!

CHRISTINA (*childishly*): Five . . . no, of course not; it's three . . . or seven . . .

CARL GUSTAV (*rises, bends—in a friendly manner—over* CHRISTINA, *takes her by the ear, and whispers*): You are joking, aren't you, Kerstin?

CHRISTINA (*hard as steel*): I never joke! I have never joked! . . . Sit down. (*Pause*)

    (CARL GUSTAV *looks at her and continues to look at her.*)

CHRISTINA (*tears herself out of the nightmare, and assumes a comradely tone*): Listen, Carl dear, you are going to get me seventy thousand.

CARL GUSTAV (*coldly*): I can't!

CHRISTINA: Then you'll have to sign a note!

CARL GUSTAV (*dryly*): Is it for Ekolsund again?

CHRISTINA: Yes!

CARL GUSTAV: I have paid for it once . . . Am I to pay for it again?

CHRISTINA: Yes! Isn't a crown worth that?

CARL GUSTAV (*brightens*): Yes, it is! . . .

CHRISTINA (*holds out her hand, roguishly*): Give them to me then!

CARL GUSTAV: You'll get them, though I don't have them on me!

CHRISTINA (*still holding out her hand*): Here!

CARL GUSTAV (*takes her hand and kisses it*): Christina, may I say a couple of words? . . . But don't interrupt me and don't laugh!

CHRISTINA: That depends!

CARL GUSTAV (*manfully simple*): I have come to ask for your ultimatum . . . No, I'm not here to demand that you fulfill promises you made as a girl—they're only smoke! But now when we are mature people with an understanding of life, you ought to grasp that your position is just as impossible as mine. You have given me the crown, of course . . . just in case, and when you pass away . . . but I can't go about waiting for you to die!

CHRISTINA (*yawns*): Hurry up; hurry up!

CARL GUSTAV: Well then, do you want me for your husband?

CHRISTINA: No, I don't! I don't want to be a wife! (*Rises and places herself beside* CARL GUSTAV)

CARL GUSTAV: I know that I'm not handsome.

CHRISTINA (*plays with his hair*): You should shave!

CARL GUSTAV: But a more faithful heart . . .

CHRISTINA: Carl Gustav, you are very kind, and you understand finances better than I, perhaps the whole governmental mess, but I will never marry anyone . . . (*Kisses him on the forehead*) I'll give you a kiss because you are a dear! Though you smell of liquor . . . I think!

CARL GUSTAV (*furious, gets up*): Your Majesty! . . . May I go?

CHRISTINA: Yes, indeed! . . . Just so you get me the seventy thousand . . . Wait! One more matter . . . use your influence with the House of Lords and get my friend Holm ennobled.

CARL GUSTAV: Holm, the tailor?

CHRISTINA: The chamberlain, if you please!

CARL GUSTAV: Is that sensible?

CHRISTINA: In our time, in these Cromwell times, when brewers[26] become kings, and regicides become ambassadors . . . Whitelocke is down there, walking freely about in the Swedish royal palace and gets both salutes and beating of drums . . . Do you want to or don't you?

CARL GUSTAV: I don't want to!

CHRISTINA: The crown! The crown!

CARL GUSTAV: I don't want to . . . but I have to!

CHRISTINA: That was a good answer! You have to! . . . And . . . (*Scanning*) . . . so that you won't plague me with further proposals and chatter about your faithfulness and the like, I will ask, at the first opportunity, when you've shaved and don't smell of liquor, to present a particularly good friend of yours, not mine, and who is well known by the name of Allerts the merchant. Do you know that fellow?

(CARL GUSTAV, *silent, crushed*)

CHRISTINA: Father-in-law? Eh? . . . Go, faithful heart!

(CARL GUSTAV *prepares to go.*)

CHRISTINA: Go, but don't forget Tott's seventy thousand!

CARL GUSTAV: Tott's?

CHRISTINA: Yes, Tott's!

CARL GUSTAV: That . . .

CHRISTINA: The crown! The crown!

CARL GUSTAV (*goes, but turns back, comes down like a cat ready to scratch*): How many millions did you say it was?

CHRISTINA (*curtly*): Five! . . . But . . . (*Scanning*) . . . I'll get those from Allerts the merchant when his name comes up next time in the trial . . .

CARL GUSTAV (*amazed*): Has his name? . . . Good God!

CHRISTINA: His name in connection with that of the successor to the throne, Carl Gustav! (*Pause*) Are we quits?

CARL GUSTAV: We are!

CHRISTINA: Yes, say so, otherwise I'll double!

CARL GUSTAV (*goes*): We're quits!

(CHRISTINA *stands for a moment reflecting; then* PIMENTELLI *comes up from in back, puts his arm about her waist and kisses her neck. Thereupon she takes his hand and leads him out into the wing to the left. Then she comes in again and rings.*)

(HOLM *in from right*)

CHRISTINA: Holm, because of your faithful service, I want to raise you to the nobility . . . You may thank me afterwards! Give the journeymen . . . let me see! . . . three hours time off! Keep an eye on all the doors afterwards; I am expecting Baron Tott.

HOLM: Will do, Your Majesty! (*Goes and sends the journeymen away*)

(TOTT *enters unexpectedly.* CHRISTINA *becomes radiant, goes toward him reaching out one hand politely to him; brings him to the table; then they sit down directly opposite each other.*)

TOTT (*looks somewhat uneasy and inquiring*): Who was it that just left?

CHRISTINA: That was Holm!

TOTT: Before him!

CHRISTINA (*looks at him to see if he "knows something" or not*): Before him? There were many!

TOTT: Forgive me, Christina, but I have a hard time finding you again today! They've left so many traces . . . I see a bit of De la Gardie's facetious smiles at the corners of your mouth, and I think Carl Gustav himself has been here bringing wrinkles to your temples.

CHRISTINA: You have sharp eyes!

TOTT: When I'm near you, I can really see, Christina; all my senses come to the surface; contact with your pure flame sublimates my feelings and perceptions so that I . . . I have a hard time associating with other people.

CHRISTINA: You are very handsome today, Klas!

TOTT: If I seem less ugly to you than before, it's because you have entered me . . .

CHRISTINA: Do you still gamble?

TOTT: I don't gamble, I don't drink, I hardly eat, and I can't get an ugly word across my lips!

CHRISTINA: Have you seen any of your friends?

TOTT: I see only you!

CHRISTINA: You are sad!

TOTT: I can't tell sadness and joy apart any more; I am alive, but I am dead! Our evening yesterday was like . . . Christina, now you have my soul in your hand! If you open your hand . . . my soul will fly away and I shall exist no more! . . . I see my image in your eye; you close your lashes; the image is gone, and I am gone!

CHRISTINA: Klas, you are up too high; I can't see you! . . . Come down!

TOTT: When you've taken my soul, this will be only a lifeless body . . .

CHRISTINA: Do you remember the paper dragon? . . . As long as the string binds him to earth he rises. Let the string go and he sinks! . . .

TOTT (*continues in his ecstasy*): I am the one who binds you to earth, but you shall raise me . . .

CHRISTINA (*with genuine feeling*): Klas, you make me unhappy . . . I am not what you believe!

TOTT: You don't know who you are or from where you've come, not any more than a child knows, not any more than you can remember *all* the dreams of the night! When the gods sent you, their daughter, down here, they extinguished your memory . . .

CHRISTINA: Your love is the greatest and the first I have ever encountered, and you are the greatest spirit I have ever run across!

Lars Hanson as Charles XII

Lars Hanson as Gustav III

TOTT: No, I'm nothing . . . I'm a little slate that you're writing on; I was nothing before I saw you; now I am everything . . . through you!

CHRISTINA: Dear God!

STEINBERG (*enters simply, openly, faithfully*): Your Majesty!

CHRISTINA (*stamps her foot on the floor*): Be off with you!

STEINBERG: Forgive me!

CHRISTINA: Go! . . . You have saved my life; yes, you always have to remind me of that . . . Go!

STEINBERG (*delays, sad*): I didn't remind you, but I came to warn you—the city is in revolt!

CHRISTINA: Let it be! Go!

(STEINBERG *goes, depressed.*)

CHRISTINA (*pause*): Klas! Back to earth! . . . You are a member of the National Council!

TOTT: What's that for me? Just so that you won't have to be ashamed of your friend, I have accepted . . . the gift!

CHRISTINA: But . . . I have greater plans for you! Listen, and don't interrupt me! You are a Vasa by blood! The powers that be in this country do not want a Pfalz, but they're looking for a Vasa—from Poland. They will get you, but before that you will become a duke!

TOTT: But I have you!

CHRISTINA (*puts her hand over his mouth*): Sh-h, child! . . . And for that reason I've offered Oxenstjerna the title of duke first . . . I expect his answer at any moment!

TOTT: I am king of the world when you are my queen! Why anything else?

CHRISTINA: Dear child, keep your feet on the ground . . . Kerstin cannot fly! . . . Alas! I shall bring you misfortune . . . Epimetheus! [27]

TOTT: Pandora! You who have given me the first inkling that there is such a thing as happiness . . . You . . . pure, snow-white . . . in your innermost being you are that, even if . . .

CHRISTINA: Even if?

TOTT: Even if the little earth spirit which sets your beautiful figure going . . . (*Shouts from the street*)

CHRISTINA (*up, rushes to the window where the journeymen have sat*): What's happening?

(TOTT *rises and draws his sword.*)

CHRISTINA (*looks out through the window*): It's a riot!

DE LA GARDIE (*enters*): Your Majesty, forgive my audacity, but the city is in revolt . . .

CHRISTINA (*comes downstage*): Why?

DE LA GARDIE: Well, in a word—you! . . . An insane fellow stabbed a woman who he believed was the Queen!

CHRISTINA (*frightened*): Why do they hate me? (*Childishly*) What have I done? Am I not kind to everyone? Haven't I supported the lower estates against the arrogance of the lords? Haven't I . . .

DE LA GARDIE: Child, you have been playing . . . but you mustn't any more. Little Kerstin died long ago, but you insist on reviving her. The chancellor will soon be here. Listen to that wise old man . . . He alone can save you!

CHRISTINA (*sadly*): I suppose I'll have to! (*Goes up to* TOTT, *presses his hand, looks into his eyes passionately*) Wait out there for me until I ring! (*She brings her face close to his as if she wanted to kiss him.*) And don't go! We have to talk about the ballet and your costume.

TOTT: I'll wait for you even if it takes a thousand years, and yet a thousand! (*Goes*)

DE LA GARDIE: Christina, you will have to cancel your ballet, first of all!

CHRISTINA: My ballet? Everything else, but not that!

DE LA GARDIE: Then they'll storm the palace!

CHRISTINA: What's wrong now?

DE LA GARDIE: Everything's piling up! And in the trial . . . the trial . . . everything's being exposed!

CHRISTINA (*wild*): Muzzle them! Execute them without a trial! They were caught in the act, damn it! And have confessed!

DE LA GARDIE: Are they to be sentenced without a hearing?

CHRISTINA: Are we going to let rascals talk, liars lie, libelous writers libel in court? Silence them in the eternal silence . . .

DE LA GARDIE: Poor little girl!

CHRISTINA: Poor Kerstin!

(BOURDELOT *enters with an amused look and happy gestures.*)

CHRISTINA (*to* DE LA GARDIE): Drive him out! He's an ape, not a human being!

DE LA GARDIE (*goes up to* BOURDELOT *and takes him by the shoulders*): Out, sir!

(BOURDELOT *grins.*)

CHRISTINA: Hit him, Magnus!

DE LA GARDIE (*shoves* BOURDELOT *out*): That was number one . . . That was the greatest one! The great spirit!

CHRISTINA: Don't be unkind, Magnus!

DE LA GARDIE: Forgive me, but you set him above Oxenstjerna!

CHRISTINA: I didn't know Tott then!

DE LA GARDIE: Klas?

CHRISTINA: Yes, there's a head for a crown!

DE LA GARDIE: You love him?

CHRISTINA: Yes, I do love him; I am in love for the first time in my life, and . . . for ever!

DE LA GARDIE: You played with him, lured him, and now you're caught!

CHRISTINA: Yes, I am caught, and I love the dear bonds! He alone can lift me out of this filth.

DE LA GARDIE (*genuinely touched*): Christina, I have had a hard time forgiving you when you have been cruel and faithless; and I have been faithless to you; but when I see what a delightful woman Klas Tott has been able to create out of your false, crude nature, I blush . . . (*with tears in his voice*) . . . and I see that it was my fault that you couldn't . . . become anything else through my love . . . and I hope you will be happy—sincerely, believe me—in having found a love like that—and a man like him!

CHRISTINA (*brushes her hand over her eyes to conceal a tear that she is ashamed of*): Magnus! . . . (*Forces back her tears*) You have been frank. I want to be! . . . With this love the Queen is dead; now the woman is born! . . . (*Changing her manner*) Usch, I am ashamed! . . . Listen!

DE LA GARDIE: The chancellor!

CHRISTINA (*collapses inwardly*): Now the Queen is needed, but she doesn't exist! Magnus . . . ask my mother to come up in a little while! . . . And try to find Steinberg . . . I was cruel to him a while ago . . . Ask him to forgive me . . . (*She lets down the side of the dress that has been pinned up.*) And don't be angry with me!

DE LA GARDIE: *There* you do have a friend! . . . (*Changing his manner*) Shall I say something to Pimentelli, too?

CHRISTINA (*flares up*): Go, I despise you . . . and your sarcasm . . .

DE LA GARDIE (*honestly*): Thank you, for that, Christina; I do, too! . . . So . . . to your mother, first! Mother first . . . and last!

CHRISTINA: Yes, mother! . . . (*Without thinking*) Why can't one be a mother without having to get married?

DE LA GARDIE: Christina! (*Pause*) The chancellor!

(CHRISTINA *draws herself erect again, becomes the Queen.*)

CHAMBERLAIN (*enters*): The chancellor, Count Oxenstjerna!

(CHRISTINA *nods affirmatively.* DE LA GARDIE *goes.*)

(OXENSTJERNA *enters, dark, looks as if he were ready for a struggle. Bows, coldly*)

CHRISTINA (*firm, dignified*): I have had you summoned! (*More gently*) Thank you for coming!

(OXENSTJERNA *looks up in amazement.* CHRISTINA *points to a chair.*)

OXENSTJERNA (*sits down*): Your Majesty! (*Wearily*) No doubt you know people are rioting in the city!

CHRISTINA (*warmly, reasonably*): I know, and I know why. So I have decided to have *one* die for the people!

OXENSTJERNA (*ambiguously*): There are two Messeniuses!

CHRISTINA (*smiles*): You are terrible! (*Changes*) Have you received my offer?

OXENSTJERNA (*indifferently*): Oh, about the title of duke? Yes, but that is not for me!

CHRISTINA (*dully*): That's true . . . When one is Axel Oxenstjerna . . .

OXENSTJERNA: May I ask a personal question?

CHRISTINA (*briskly*): Is it about the five million again? Well, I have remitted them partly, and the rest I've disposed of, as it was so aptly termed, after my great father's death!

OXENSTJERNA (*crushed*): Remitted?

CHRISTINA (*gayly*): Yes, of course, in return for remunerations, because no one gives anything without payment in cash. Isn't that so?

OXENSTJERNA (*looks at the floor*): Another question . . . Does Your Majesty know that Sweden is at war?

CHRISTINA (*horrified*): War? No! . . . With whom?

OXENSTJERNA: That is extremely strange! Your Majesty does not know, and the council, that ought to have been informed, has no knowledge of it.

CHRISTINA: With whom are we at war?

OXENSTJERNA: With the Free City of Bremen! [28]

CHRISTINA (*embarrassed*): Bremen?

OXENSTJERNA: Doesn't Your Majesty know anything about the matter?

CHRISTINA: No! . . . That is to say, Königsmarck wrote a letter complaining about the people of Bremen . . . so . . . so I answered, naturally! I always answer letters!

OXENSTJERNA: What did Your Majesty answer?

CHRISTINA (*frightened*): Is it dangerous then?

OXENSTJERNA (*sternly*): What did Your Majesty answer?

CHRISTINA: I said naturally that he was . . . to beat them or whatever the generals call it!

OXENSTJERNA: Good God!

CHRISTINA: What? What is it?

OXENSTJERNA: It is this: Königsmarck has built forts illegally, has besieged the city . . . and flooded the whole area . . .

CHRISTINA: Can't that be changed?

OXENSTJERNA: Good heavens, yes; this won't do!

CHRISTINA (*childishly*): But help me, Oxenstjerna. You understand this sort of thing!

OXENSTJERNA (*heartily*): Well, my child, when I wanted to help you, you would not let me, and now, when I may, it's too late!

CHRISTINA: Why, what's happened?

OXENSTJERNA: Holland and the emperor have allied themselves with Bremen!

CHRISTINA: The emperor! (*On her knees*) Help us! Help us! Help us!

OXENSTJERNA: Christina, little child, get up! . . . I will help you, but you must never do this again! . . . You see, to rule nations, one has to be an everyday sort of person. Why, there are farmers and businessmen in parliament! . . . And you are not an ordinary person. You are like an artist—just as careless, just as carefree, just as thoughtless . . . and this . . . does not suit you!

CHRISTINA: It does, no doubt, but it's so boring!

OXENSTJERNA (*smiles*): Yes, it is boring . . . and you want to have a good time above all else . . . Everyone to his taste!

CHRISTINA (*interrupting*): So! I'll abdicate!

OXENSTJERNA: Not so fast!

CHRISTINA: Yes, I want it quickly!

OXENSTJERNA (*teasing*): Is someone waiting?

CHRISTINA: That, too! I'll abdicate!

OXENSTJERNA (*rises*): In this case, your will is above the law of the land, Your Majesty, but in this question, which you can only answer with your own conscience, I do not want to be your councillor.

CHRISTINA: Why not?

OXENSTJERNA: Because I cannot calculate the consequences of such an act . . . And now I'll go, with an insignificant little request!

CHRISTINA: What is it?

OXENSTJERNA: Cancel the ballet! . . . The people are excited, and their sympathy is with the Messeniuses!

CHRISTINA: I suppose I'll have to!

OXENSTJERNA: Thank you, my child! . . . And live well! (*Shakes her hand warmly*) God bless you and keep you! (*Goes*)

(CHRISTINA *alone; recovers from her overexcited state, and again becomes a graceful woman with a gentle manner and languorous movements. She rings.*)

(HOLM *enters.*)

CHRISTINA: Is that you, Chamberlain? Light the lamps, please; It has become dark!

HOLM (*lights two oil lamps*): There's a disturbance in the city!

CHRISTINA: So I have heard, my friend! . . . But it will soon be over . . . (*Rings again, three times*)

(TOTT *in.* HOLM *out*)

CHRISTINA (*up to* TOTT, *passionately*): Klas, we won't get a ballet, but you're to come down in the pavilion by the lion's den[29] this evening, and I'll have a feast for you alone! A Roman one!

TOTT: You and I are the world—no one else is needed for a feast!

CHRISTINA: And you will see Pandora, just the same!

TOTT: Are you playing with evil?

CHRISTINA (*softly*): Strict!

TOTT: Yes, you have made me good; I do not want to become evil again!

CHRISTINA: My mother is coming! (*She kisses him on the mouth.*)

TOTT (*staggers, shyly*): You gave something, and you took something. What you gave me, I don't know, but you took my soul . . . Christina, do not slay me . . . I am very young!

CHRISTINA: Yes, you are young! Very young! A young god! . . . Go now!

(TOTT *out.* CHRISTINA, *alone for a moment, walks over and turns down one lamp.*)

MARIA ELEONORA (*enters, without being observed by* CHRISTINA *over by the lamp*): Are you here, my child?

CHRISTINA (*throws herself in her mother's arms*): Dear mother!

MARIA ELEONORA (*old, plain, dignified, warm*): What is it? What's wrong? With my little girl? What have you been up to? Making a mess for yourself? Come and sit here!

CHRISTINA (*places her mother on the sofa, lies down on two chairs with her head in her mother's lap*): No, sit here, then I can put my head on your lap! (*Pause*)

(MARIA ELEONORA *caresses* CHRISTINA's *hair.*)

CHRISTINA: You have been a queen, you, too . . . once!

MARIA ELEONORA: No, my child, I was satisfied with being the great *king's* wife, and your mother . . . as long as they let me. (*Her voice trembles.*) But then they tore my child from me . . . God forgive them, if He can! . . . and they reared you to be a man . . . Now they have what they have!

CHRISTINA: Go on talking; it does me good to hear someone be sorry for herself!

MARIA ELEONORA: Little clown! But you were the one who was going to pour out your troubles!

CHRISTINA: Let me rest for a while first—I am so tired, so tired—then I'll pity myself afterwards! Brush your hand over my forehead! I'll close my eyes . . . marvelous . . . for only a minute! . . . one single minute! . . . to be a child again, innocent, without worries! . . .

MARIA ELEONORA: Poor little Queen!

CHRISTINA (*begins talking with a slippery, honey-sweet tone*): Mother dear, wasn't the Pfalz count Johan Kasimir a Calvinist? [30]

MARIA ELEONORA: You mean Carl Gustav's father. Yes, he was.

CHRISTINA: When did Carl Gustav become a Lutheran?

MARIA ELEONORA: I don't know, darling! (*Pause*)

CHRISTINA (*priming herself again*): Is it true, mother dear, that your father was a Calvinist?

MARIA ELEONORA: Of course!

CHRISTINA (*fires her shot*): When did you become a Lutheran then?

(MARIA ELEONORA *remains silent.*)

CHRISTINA (*enjoys her victory*): Have you heard that Oxenstjerna and his party are trying to get the Polish Vasas back?

MARIA ELEONORA: Yes, I've heard something like that, and rather that than Pfalz.

CHRISTINA (*looks like a demon, kicking her feet with delight*): But the Vasas in Poland are Catholics! So the great Oxenstjerna counts on their renouncing their faith and becoming renegades.

MARIA ELEONORA: Darling, I never interfere in religious matters, and I . . . really believe that each and every person becomes saved by his own faith!

CHRISTINA (*jumps up like a cat*): Thank you for those words, mother!

(MARIA ELEONORA *looks without understanding and with amazement at* CHRISTINA.)

CHRISTINA (*takes the sword and breaks it across her knee*): Done!

CURTAIN

ACT IV

The scene is the interior of the pavilion in the section of the palace gardens known as the lion park.[31] *To the right is a section with cloisonné walls painted with scenes from Greek mythology on softly colored fields. There is a table with a white cloth, flowers, wine carafes in ice, gold and silver dishes, fruits of all kinds, and so forth.*

In front of the table stands a Roman tripod on which a sacrificial fire is burning.

To the right in the section stands a throne under a canopy.

To the left an anteroom with a gallery for musicians with a door at the back.

(CHRISTINA *in from the right; dressed as Pandora in a one-piece, low-necked white, tight-fitting dress which ends in a border at the ankles. On her feet, white sandals. Her hair hangs loose over her shoulders; she has a garland of roses on her head; she is radiantly beautiful. She carries an engraved box.*)

DE LA GARDIE (*comes toward her from the right, takes a step backwards when he sees her, and covers his eyes with his hands as if blinded by light*): Christina! Beautiful! Beautiful in a way you never let me see you!

CHRISTINA: The one who loves me sees me! Everyone has the Christina he deserves!

DE LA GARDIE: What do you have in the box? Pandora?

CHRISTINA (*opens it and shows him a royal crown*): All the misfortunes of the world enclosed in one!

DE LA GARDIE: Surely it isn't the . . . royal crown!

CHRISTINA: Mere paper, darling!

DE LA GARDIE: Is it true that you want to give up the crown?

CHRISTINA: Want to? If I only knew what I ought to want!

DE LA GARDIE: They say you have already signed your abdication!

CHRISTINA: They don't know that! (*Pause*)

DE LA GARDIE: Do you believe that the man you love will love you as warmly and tenderly when you're not wearing that becoming headpiece which is crowned by the globe, the symbol of power?

CHRISTINA (*hesitantly*): I have not thought about that! . . . Do you believe that it . . . is . . . the Queen he loves . . . the Queen alone?

DE LA GARDIE: I don't know! We are just as strange as you! . . .

Besides, is it important to you to be loved as a woman . . . a woman alone?

CHRISTINA: Yes, this time!

DE LA GARDIE: You, who are a woman hater!

CHRISTINA: I . . . who . . . am . . . a . . . woman hater!

DE LA GARDIE (*strikes like lightning*): Where are you going to go?

   (CHRISTINA *looks up, as if* DE LA GARDIE *has discovered her secret.*)

DE LA GARDIE: To Paris, naturally . . . the center of the world, the modern Delphi,[32] where the oracles still speak!

   (CHRISTINA *silent, her lips compressed with anger*)

DE LA GARDIE: You've arranged things badly for yourself then . . . The Spanish minister, Pimentelli, is the worst enemy of the government of France.

   (CHRISTINA *gives a start.*)

DE LA GARDIE: And if you travel in his company, you won't be received at the French court.

   (CHRISTINA *places the box on a tripod in front of the sacrificial fire.*)

DE LA GARDIE: And you have dismissed Bourdelot in an insulting fashion! That's not a recommendation either! (*Pause*)

   (CHRISTINA, *by the stairs of the throne, places one foot on a step and reties her sandal, in order to conceal her emotional disturbance.*)

DE LA GARDIE: Christina! I will help you!

CHRISTINA (*turns to him*): Do . . . you . . . want to help me?

DE LA GARDIE: I will help you! You! You see, that's how great my little love was, how unselfish! . . . You won't find a dismissed lover every day who wants to help his rival!

CHRISTINA: When we were friends, Magnus, we were always enemies . . . It looks as if love grows the farther apart we are . . .

DE LA GARDIE: As the square of the distance, Descartes[33] would have said!

CHRISTINA (*smiling*): Clowning, always clowning!

DE LA GARDIE: Wasn't that how you wanted me? You wanted me to play the fool to make the princess laugh. And with Tott she wants to weep!

(*Roaring outside can be heard*)

CHRISTINA (*pricks up her ears*): What was that?

DE LA GARDIE: The tame lions in the den, I suppose!

CHRISTINA (*pulls off two rings from her hand and gives them one at a time to* DE LA GARDIE): Magnus, go to Pimentelli with this ring . . . at once!

DE LA GARDIE: That means: Cut your throat!

CHRISTINA: And to Bourdelot with this one!

DE LA GARDIE: With the inscription: Not without hope! . . . I will go . . . Will I see you again this evening? (*Looks about*)

CHRISTINA (*shyly, softly*): No!

DE LA GARDIE (*sadly*): I suppose I'll have to go home . . . to my . . . wife . . . my vulture, and let her hack away at my liver! I can't afford to buy her bribes any more . . .

CHRISTINA (*sorrowfully*): Poor Magnus! Is she so very difficult?

DE LA GARDIE: I loved her . . . at first . . . as a gift from you! Everything that came from you was dear, even your cruelty . . .

CHRISTINA (*touched*): *Perhaps* it is the last time we'll see each other . . . Take me in your arms!

(DE LA GARDIE *embraces her with warmth but with respect.*)

CHRISTINA: A kiss on my cheek!

(DE LA GARDIE *kisses her cheek.*)

CHRISTINA: Say: Poor Kerstin!

DE LA GARDIE (*with suppressed emotions*): Poor Kerstin!

CHRISTINA (*tears herself free, draws herself up*): Done!

(DE LA GARDIE *goes out hastily.* CHRISTINA *strikes her hands together.*)

(STEINBERG *enters from the right.*)

CHRISTINA (*goes toward him in a friendly way*): My dear Steinberg! You aren't angry with me . . .

STEINBERG (*blinded by her beauty, gripped*): Your Majesty . . .

CHRISTINA: You see, I'm giving a feast . . . and I need a dependable friend . . .

STEINBERG: I am at Your Majesty's service, but . . . (*looks at his clothes*) . . . I believe I'm not dressed so . . .

CHRISTINA: That doesn't matter!

STEINBERG: It's too great an honor, Your Majesty . . .

CHRISTINA: The honor is slight . . . Come, and look at this! (*Takes him by the hand and leads him to the compartment*)

(STEINBERG *misunderstands the situation and shows himself flattered by her attention but does not become ridiculous.*)

CHRISTINA (*takes a flower from a vase*): Look at this flower! Isn't it as pretty as a young girl? (*She kisses the flower.*)

(STEINBERG, *intoxicated with pleasure, still does not understand, but never becomes ridiculous.*)

CHRISTINA: When I take this flower . . .

(STEINBERG, *stretching out his hand to take the flower*)

CHRISTINA (*fixing his glance*): When I take this flower, you are to go out . . . and . . . (*Stops*)

(STEINBERG *inclines his head and begins to understand.*)

CHRISTINA (*a little impatiently*): Understand what I'm saying . . . There is going to be a surprise for . . . the guests . . . the guest; and, you see, Steinberg, this wall is movable . . . (*Points at the back wall of the section*) When I give you the sign, you, as I said, are to go out . . . and give your signal . . . Then the wall will be drawn up . . . Back of it in the garden a tableau will be revealed and the fireworks display will be lighted!

(STEINBERG *crushed*)

CHRISTINA (*looks at him with loathing mixed with pity*): Do you understand?

STEINBERG (*sadly; tries to smile*): Yes, now I understand!

CHRISTINA: That was all!

STEINBERG (*throws himself to his knees*): Queen!

CHRISTINA (*turns her back to him*): Now leave. (*Pause*) And stay out there until I call! (*Walks away from him*)

(STEINBERG, *distressed; gets up and goes out to the left.* CHRIS-
TINA *alone; goes over to the fire and warms her hands*)

(KLAS TOTT *enters from the right. Just as he enters, the stage is
lighted by concealed lights; exquisite string music* is played, and
from a basket of flowers suspended in the ceiling a rain of flowers
falls at* TOTT's *feet.*)

TOTT: Pandora with all the gifts, Eve, the first and only woman!
You, who give life to the children of men, when you have given
life to a man!

CHRISTINA: Prometheus, bringer of light, who stole all kinds of skills,
arts, and beauty from the wealthy gods and gave them to poverty-
stricken human beings!

TOTT: And, as a punishment, Zeus created you, Pandora, so that
through you he could rule over rebellious men and force them
into humility and goodness!

CHRISTINA: All the misfortunes of the world he concealed in the
treacherous wedding box, and with woman came evil times!

TOTT: And good through evil!

CHRISTINA: But at the bottom of the box he placed the gift that
never perishes, that never betrays—hope, ever faithful hope! Son
of the gods, embrace me, and I will bring you a sacrifice!

TOTT: No, I do not want to embrace you!

CHRISTINA: Tell me why. Quickly!

TOTT: I love you too much! I love you as a work of art; I want to
look at you, but I do not want to touch you!

CHRISTINA: Touch me! I am clay of this earth. In your hands I can
be molded into an immortal work of art!

TOTT (*on his knees*): Rule over me, Zeus; I bow before your power,
under woman! Your woman!

CHRISTINA (*on her knees*): Rule over my will, Zeus, so that I may
will only what is good.

* A string octet (with double basses)—only modulation, no distinguishable melodies.

TOTT: Woe unto you, woman, if you misuse the power Zeus—no, God in heaven—has placed in your little hand! (*Takes her hand and kisses it*)

CHRISTINA: You have taken my hand! Keep it!

TOTT (*rises*): I could have your hand only if you were my wife!

CHRISTINA (*rises*): I want to be your wife!

TOTT: That cannot be!

CHRISTINA: What is in the way?

TOTT: A crown, a mantle, and a scepter!

CHRISTINA: Say a crown! The rest will follow! . . .

TOTT: I say a crown!

CHRISTINA: Well, then! . . . (*Goes to the box, takes out the crown, and places it on the sacrificial fire*) Receive my sacrifice, the greatest and the only man I have ever seen, the man who has made me a woman!

TOTT: I can't accept your sacrifice!

CHRISTINA: You shall! What do you fear?

TOTT: I fear happiness—it is deceptive.

CHRISTINA: Coward! . . . Don't you dare to accept a lifetime of anguish for one moment of bliss?

TOTT: Now I dare! . . . But not here, not in this country!

CHRISTINA: No, abroad! . . . You will go with me!

TOTT: Around the world!

CHRISTINA: We have said it! May Heaven hear us! (*They can hear someone weep so loudly and uncontrollably that it sounds like laughter.*) What? What was that?

TOTT: They're laughing!

(CHRISTINA *strikes her hands together.*)

(HOLM *enters, dressed as a chamberlain; he wears his costume with good taste and dignity.*)

CHRISTINA (*without anger*): My dear Holm, how are you watching the doors?

HOLM: Your Majesty?

CHRISTINA: Who is laughing out there?

HOLM: Laughing! . . . I saw only Baron von Steinberg standing out there . . .

CHRISTINA: What is he doing?

HOLM: Weeping! Weeping like a child . . .

CHRISTINA: Good old Steinberg! . . . (*To* TOTT) Laughter or tears . . . they're not far apart! (*To* HOLM) Tell Steinberg he is free! . . . He may go home!

HOLM: It's raining, Your Majesty!

CHRISTINA (*goes up to* HOLM *and whispers to him. He goes out. Then she takes* TOTT *by the hand and leads him to the throne*): I don't give you a crown, my master, but a throne, a throne in my little kingdom . . . my kingdom in which there is no difference between people! Hail to thee, my king! (*She takes a flower. The roaring can be heard again.*) Whatever . . . Who is disturbing my feast? (*Strikes her hands together*)

(HOLM *comes in again.*)

CHRISTINA: What is happening out there?

HOLM: Why do you ask, Your Majesty?

CHRISTINA: Because it makes me uneasy . . . as everything unknown does!

HOLM: Well, it's the people who have heard that you have abdicated . . .

CHRISTINA: Drive them out!

HOLM: That will be difficult . . . since the Messeniuses are just being taken to their execution!

CHRISTINA: God in heaven! (*Draws herself up*) We will not let ourselves be disturbed! (*Whispers to* HOLM, *who goes out again*) Now give to Epimetheus Paphos'[34] homage that Pandora received! (*She strikes her hands together.*)

(*The wall in the section at the back is drawn up. One sees instead of the expected tableau a crowd of strange people, all of them motionless, silent, pale-faced.[35] At the very front of the*

crowd stand ALLERTS *the merchant,* THE KEEPER, *and* THE FARMER
from Act I.)

(CHRISTINA *screams—prolonged.* TOTT *comes down from the
throne and puts his arm about her waist.*)

CHRISTINA: Are they specters from Hell?

TOTT: I don't know! But I feel as if I were awakening from a long
sleep! (*Looks about*) What sort of game is all this?

CHRISTINA: What did I hear? Klas Tott!

TOTT: Yes, my Queen!

CHRISTINA: I am no longer the Queen! I am only your . . .

TOTT: What?

CHRISTINA: Your queen of hearts!

TOTT: Whore, you mean!

CHRISTINA (*staggers backwards*): Good God, now you really hurt
me! (*Puts her hand over her heart*) You killed me . . . Why
did you use that word? . . .

TOTT: Why? Well, I felt I needed to murder you!

CHRISTINA: What have I done to you?

TOTT: I don't know, but in all these faces just now I read a terrible
judgment . . . of you!

CHRISTINA: You have never loved me.

TOTT: Loved?

CHRISTINA: Yes!

TOTT: If that means being out of one's mind, I have loved as no
one else!

CHRISTINA: Are you going to desert me now?

TOTT: Of course!

CHRISTINA (*wild*): I have given up a crown for you, and you . . .
you swore you would follow me into exile!

TOTT: Oh, one says a lot of things . . .

(PIMENTELLI *enters, comes forward, sits down self-confidently
on a chair with his arms akimbo and looks at* CHRISTINA *and*
TOTT.)

TOTT: How does that man dare . . . Are you used to his presumption?

CHRISTINA: What can I do about it? I suppose he hasn't received my message yet and thinks he's my guest!

TOTT: May I tell him?

HOLM (*comes in with a letter for* TOTT): From Ambassador Pimentelli!

CHRISTINA (*senses the contents of the letter and wants to snatch it away from* TOTT): Don't read it! It's poison! Don't read it!

TOTT: Poison? (*Reads, becomes pale, looks at* PIMENTELLI, *staggers backwards and falls*)

CHRISTINA (*throws herself down over* TOTT): God help us! (*To* PIMENTELLI) See your work, you poisoner!

TOTT (*raises himself with an effort*): Forgive me! I fell, but I'm going to raise myself again! . . . Christina, now I am done.

CHRISTINA: And I, I'm sinking, down, down, down, since you awakened me. Why should you awaken the sleepwalker who had walked so neatly on the roof gutter without falling, without soiling a hem?

TOTT: All beauty perishes; ugliness alone survives.

(*The music has come to an end; one lamp after the other goes out. One can hear noise at the doors and commotion outside. On the musicians' gallery appears* WHITELOCKE, *stern, pale, looking about in amazement.*)

CHRISTINA: Give me my coat! . . . Quickly! I'm freezing! Why, I'm naked!

TOTT: Let me leave you, Christina!

CHRISTINA: Then I'll die!

TOTT: You?

CHRISTINA: Yes, this time it was I who loved!

TOTT: Poor girl! We're both to be pitied! A week of tears will not wash this away!

CHRISTINA (*takes him by the arms*): Don't leave me . . . don't go! (*Her whole body trembles.*)

TOTT: I must . . . You have soiled my soul that I gave into your keeping . . . You have brought me into a whirlpool of unknown desires . . . you have led my thoughts into paths they must not go . . . and to break off I must kill my body to release my spirit into purer air.

CHRISTINA (*on her knees*): Let me follow you! Out, upwards!

TOTT: No, you are the one I must flee from! . . . Pandora! Do you have anything left in your box? You said "faithful" hope, but in the story it says "false" hope! I didn't want to correct you—you were so beautiful when you said it!

CHRISTINA: Poor us! When the gods are playing, the children of man must weep!

TOTT (*looks about*): Do you see that our love has become public property?

CHRISTINA: I see, but no one cares about what I say! They know the Queen is done . . . How I regret it! Give me my coat! Why, I am naked! My coat! (*She tries to cover herself with her long, loose hair. A window is opened in the compartment;* BOURDELOT's *head can be seen.*)

TOTT: This insulting intimacy . . . No, I can't stay . . . Farewell, my bride, my one great love! Queen of my heart! . . . Farewell! . . . forever! (*Exits to the right*)

(CHRISTINA *falls to her knees.*)

STEINBERG (*enters hastily looking for the Queen; he has her ermine mantle, which he places over her shoulders*): Your Majesty! (*Whispers the rest*)

CHRISTINA: Steinberg, don't desert me, even though I have been ungrateful! Go away with me!

STEINBERG: Wherever Your Majesty commands! Around the whole world!

CHRISTINA: Come with me! But don't demand any reward . . . like the others . . .

STEINBERG: That is my reward . . . that I may go with you!

HOLM (*enters*): His Majesty, the King!

CHRISTINA: The King! . . . And here is the Queen! (*To* HOLM, *now Lejoncrona*) Holm! Lejoncrona! I am leaving tomorrow . . . Report my debt to you to the treasury . . .

HOLM: Oh! Well? . . . Is . . . Your Majesty leaving? . . . May I ask you for something in writing?

CHRISTINA: Shame! You have my word!

HOLM: Words are words, but writing is money!

CHRISTINA: You speak of money now . . . at this moment . . . Shall I think about money now? . . . And you whom I raised from the dust and placed in the House of Lords! . . . Churl! Go!

(HOLM *wants to say something, but* STEINBERG *forces him out.*)

(CARL GUSTAV *in field attire; dignified.* CHRISTINA *has seated herself on the throne. They look at each other for a moment. Then* CARL GUSTAV *motions to* STEINBERG *that he is to leave them.*)

CARL GUSTAV: Christina!

CHRISTINA: Carl Gustav! Carl the Tenth Gustav!

CARL GUSTAV: Yes, tomorrow!

CHRISTINA: Are you sure?

CARL GUSTAV: Yes, since you have abdicated . . .

CHRISTINA: There are other pretenders . . .

CARL GUSTAV: So-o-o!

CHRISTINA: The Polish Vasas . . . for example!

CARL GUSTAV: That wasn't what I wanted to talk about!

CHRISTINA: What is it you want then?

CARL GUSTAV: I was going to . . . wanted to settle your accounts before I take over . . .

CHRISTINA: . . . the tenancy! Talk with the inspector!

CARL GUSTAV: That is De la Gardie, your lord high treasurer! You've made a financial mess . . .

CHRISTINA: What tone is it you're taking?

CARL GUSTAV: The King's!

CHRISTINA: Don't forget I have made you King!

CARL GUSTAV: No, the Estates have, and my right of succession! . . .

I am even Gustav Adolf's nephew, and so I'm closest to the throne, after you!

CHRISTINA: That is new! . . . Is Sweden an elective monarchy?

CARL GUSTAV: It must be, since Gustav Adolf was elected instead of the lawful Duke John,[36] the son of King John III . . .

CHRISTINA: Who says anything about him?

CARL GUSTAV: Carl IX speaks particularly of him in his last will and begs that his rights be respected! (*Pause*) Yes, you should have read Swedish history a little better before you set out to make Swedish history!

CHRISTINA: Don't you have any shame?

CARL GUSTAV: And the pages you have written ought to be torn out . . . for they deal only with unlawful acts, embezzlements, scandals, and favorites!

CHRISTINA: And *you* dare say that?

CARL GUSTAV: Yes, I dare! . . . And I add . . . your nursery politics have plunged the nation into adventures that I'm to inherit . . . Your insane attack on Bremen has irritated the emperor and Holland.

CHRISTINA: Hasn't Oxenstjerna straightened that out?

CARL GUSTAV: Not yet! . . . But, what is worse . . . you have expelled the Portuguese ambassador[37] from Stockholm to please Spain, to please the Spanish ambassador, to please your lover Pimentelli! But you've forgotten the trouble you've caused your own country . . . when Swedish ships lie loaded in Portuguese harbors . . . and are sure to be held! You've treated Sweden as your enemy; plundered, murdered; above everything, plundered . . . You have pillaged[38] the palace in Stockholm down to the wallpaper; you have fleeced Uppsala Castle so that there is only one bed left for the King . . . You have emptied the national treasury so that the government employees do not get their salaries . . .

CHRISTINA: Nemesis!

CARL GUSTAV: What? Nemesis?

CHRISTINA: Yes, because you have plundered my country; you, too, were along with Torstensson . . .[39]

CARL GUSTAV: My country?

CHRISTINA: Yes, mine! because I am a German as my mother is; I am a Brandenburger as you are a Pfalz! . . . were a Pfalz when you fought against your own country! I have never felt that I was Swedish,[40] and I have hated Sweden as my mother has hated it! I wanted to end the Thirty Years' War because I knew Sweden had no business out there . . . and in fifty years, believe me, you won't own one stone in Germany; instead, I wanted my new country to make conquests in other areas where greater honors could be reaped, honors that would be less perishable; that's why I tried to educate this crude nation and awaken its interests in something other than war! . . . But you don't understand that! You say I have plundered! . . . That's a lie! I've restored . . . what was stolen! When I saw those ships with goods hauled home from Germany, art treasures that can't be separated from their native soil, libraries that should be read where they were written . . . then I was seized with a boundless desire once to . . . Once I thought of marrying the great prince . . . of Brandenburg . . . so I . . . could have been what I am . . . because the future lies by the Spree[41] . . . and not by Stockholm's Stream! (*Pause*)

CARL GUSTAV: Have you really had any meaning in your meaningless actions, or are you improvising?

CHRISTINA: It's possible that now when I'm first attacked my need for self-defense helps clear up the darkness in my intentions . . .

CARL GUSTAV: Perhaps this country was too limited for you?

CHRISTINA: Who knows? Perhaps that's it!

CARL GUSTAV: And what do you intend to do now?

CHRISTINA: That does not concern you! And no other mortal, either! . . . Anything else?

CARL GUSTAV: There's a lot more, but I'll have to bear that burden along with the rest!

CHRISTINA: You see, that goes with the crown! I had to struggle along with the debts left by my guardians . . .

CARL GUSTAV: That isn't what I wanted to talk to you about . . .

CHRISTINA: No! But what I do not want to talk about, you may not talk about! (*Pause*)

STEINBERG: The royal chancellor!

CHRISTINA: See! Now he came at the right time . . . for once! . . . Sit down, Carl Gustav! It's only a farewell call!

(CARL GUSTAV *sits down unwillingly.*)

(OXENSTJERNA *enters, looks about, observes* CHRISTINA, *then* CARL GUSTAV.)

CHRISTINA: How can I be of service?

OXENSTJERNA: Only with a frank answer to a direct question.

CHRISTINA: Ask it!

OXENSTJERNA (*with a great effort*): I have been sent by the Council and the Estates! . . . It's the question of Your Majesty's allowance after your abdication . . . It is even a question of certain conditions . . . I have been commissioned to . . .

CHRISTINA: Go on!

OXENSTJERNA: Your Majesty, it is extremely painful to state a question which in a moment can destroy my own and the nation's dearest hopes!

CHRISTINA: Go on!

OXENSTJERNA: Well, then . . . There are rumors that Your Majesty has accepted the Roman Catholic faith! Is that true?

CHRISTINA: It is not true . . .

OXENSTJERNA: God be praised!

CHRISTINA: Wait! It is not true, but it may possibly become . . . One never knows where one will end.

OXENSTJERNA: Would it be possible for Gustav Adolf's daughter to desert her forefathers' faith?

CHRISTINA: It is very possible that she will return to her forefathers' faith,[42] to St. Erik's, Engelbrekt's, Stures', and the first Vasas' faith . . . from which you are apostates. (*Pause*)

OXENSTJERNA: And I should hear this before I close my weary eyes! But, since you have not done it yet . . . I beg you, on my knees, if you demand that!

CHRISTINA: No, don't beg! Because my faith will not let itself be bribed . . . and isn't to be sold either!

OXENSTJERNA: Then I shall have to speak in another tone!

CHRISTINA: Are you threatening me? Then I appeal to the spirit of my great father; I, too, for he gave his life, not for a faith forced upon anyone, but for freedom of faith, for tolerance!

(OXENSTJERNA *and* CARL GUSTAV *bow their heads and are silent.*)

CHRISTINA: Have you anything to add?

OXENSTJERNA: No! . . .

CHRISTINA (*rises*): Then we shall say merely . . . farewell!

OXENSTJERNA: Farewell! . . .

(CHRISTINA *exits.*)

CURTAIN

Notes on 'Queen Christina'

THE THIRTY YEARS' WAR which raged from 1618 to the Peace of Westphalia in 1648 involved directly or indirectly almost every European country. The causes were many and complex, but the struggle between Protestantism and Catholicism, conflicting commercial interests, and the political ambitions of the various rulers and nations were the most outstanding. Under the inspiring leadership of its brilliant king, Gustav II Adolf, Sweden entered the war in 1630 to protect itself from unfriendly neighbors, to deliver fellow Protestants from oppression, and, perhaps as Strindberg's Christina says, to win territory and power for Sweden. The motives may very well have been both idealistic and selfish.

For Sweden, the war was eminently successful in that all three of the cited purposes were achieved: The country in 1648 was one of the most powerful in Europe; it had gained recognition as the leader of Protestantism, strengthened itself against its three most dangerous neighbors—Poland, Russia, and Denmark—and had expanded its territories on both the eastern and southern shores of the Baltic. Perhaps Sweden's greatest loss was the death of its king in the Battle of Lützen on November 6, 1632. Fortunately, however, Sweden had not only exceptionally able civil and international leaders such as Axel Oxenstjerna, but a large number of the greatest military men of the time—men such as Gustav Horn, Johan Banér, Lennart Torstensson, Åke Tott, and Gustav Wrangel.

The financing of Sweden's participation in the war and the rewarding of the Swedish heroes and other participants led to unfortunate practices such as the sale or mortgaging of crown property and the

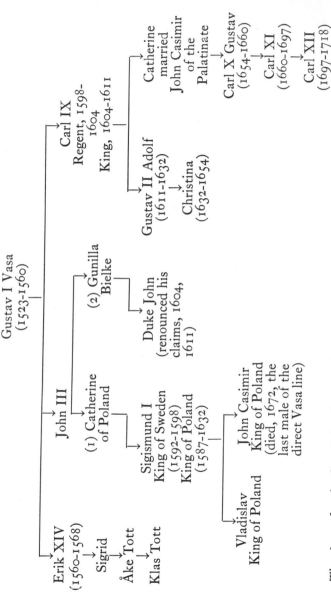

Gustav I Vasa
(1523-1560)

Erik XIV
(1560-1568)
Sigrid
Åke Tott
Klas Tott

John III
(1) Catherine of Poland
(2) Gunilla Bielke

Sigismund I
King of Sweden
(1592-1598)
King of Poland
(1587-1632)

Vladislav
King of Poland

John Casimir
King of Poland
(died, 1672, the
last male of the
direct Vasa line)

Duke John
(renounced his
claims, 1604,
1611)

Carl IX
Regent, 1598-1604
King, 1604-1611

Gustav II Adolf
(1611-1632)
Christina
(1632-1654)

Catherine
married
John Casimir
of the
Palatinate

Carl X Gustav
(1654-1660)
Carl XI
(1660-1697)
Carl XII
(1697-1718)

The dates for the Swedish rulers are for their reigns.
The Polish Vasas were Sigismund and his descendants, specifically, in the play, John Casimir and his younger brothers.
The Palatinate = Pfalz. See note 30. Carl = Charles.

creation of fiefs during the regency (1632-1644) but even more during Christina's reign (1644-1654). Christina's generous "gifts" and reckless expenditures emptied the treasury; she did encourage the development of education and the arts in Sweden, however.

THE HOUSE OF VASA

The diagram on the facing page may help to make clear the relationships of the royal characters mentioned in the play.

THE CHARACTERS

Christina (1626-1689) was the only child of Gustav II Adolf (1594-1632) and Queen Maria Eleonora to survive infancy. Upon the death of her father at Lützen on November 6, 1632, Christina was proclaimed queen but did not become actual ruler until 1644. A highly gifted woman, Christina assembled a brilliant court of learned men, artists, and aristocrats; consequently, she attracted attention throughout Europe somewhat as Elizabeth of England had done. Unfortunate for Sweden were (1) her extravagant award of royal and national property and money to her many favorites, (2) other financial extravagance, and (3) her boredom with and neglect of her official duties as ruler. Converted to Roman Catholicism and apparently not too much interested in straightening out the financial chaos of the Swedish government for which she was at least partially responsible, she abdicated in 1654 after having assured herself of an adequate income for life. Her career as a queen had made her the object of both admiration and gossip, and her career as a queen without a throne was no less colorful.

Axel Oxenstjerna (1583-1654), generally considered Sweden's greatest statesman of all time, was Gustav II Adolf's right-hand man and, after the king's death in 1632, supervised Christina's training, became the actual ruler of Sweden at least until 1644, and brought the Thirty Years' War to what was a successful conclusion for Sweden.

Klas Tott (1630-1674), the son of Field Marshal Åke Tott ("the snowplow" and one of the ablest Swedish generals during the Thirty Years' War) and the great-grandson of Erik XIV, was extraordinarily handsome, lively, and good-mannered; during the closing years of her reign, the queen heaped one honor and one gift after the other upon him and even tried to have him declared heir apparent. Gossip declared him her lover.

Magnus Gabriel De la Gardie (1622-1686), Queen Christina's first favorite, was the fourth son of Count Jacob De la Gardie and his countess, Ebba Brahe, the noblewoman that Gustav II Adolf had loved as a young man. By 1647, the young queen had heaped so many honors on and granted so many other favors to the handsome and talented Magnus that the public suspected that she intended to marry him; instead, she arranged for his marriage to her cousin, Princess Maria Euphrosyna. That he ultimately lost the queen's favor resulted partly from her tendency to change her mind and partly from his envy of other favorites and his accusations and intrigues against them. What the relationship between the queen and her favorite and exfavorite had been still remains largely in the area of gossip and idle speculation. One bit of contemporary gossip, incidentally, as Strindberg suggests on page 23, was that Magnus' actual father was Gustav Adolf.

Anton von Steinberg (died, 1675), a German by birth, gained the queen's favor when he rescued her in May, 1652, from drowning at a naval inspection on Stockholm Stream. Accompanied by Admirals Herman Fleming and Gustav Wrangel, General Wachtmeister, and Steinberg (then her equerry), the queen had set out for Ship's Island (*Skeppsholmen*) to inspect the fleet. Just as Admiral Fleming was conducting the queen across a temporary bridge of loose boards to one of the ships, a board slipped and both queen and admiral fell into the water. Steinberg jumped in and saved the queen. Among the rewards for Steinberg was his being made a baron (*friherre*) in 1653 and a count in 1654. The members of the House of Lords were not enthusiastic. When Christina left Sweden in 1654, von Steinberg went along as a member of her retinue. Strindberg has chosen to disregard what his major source has to say about Steinberg's quarrelsomeness and incompetence.

Pierre Bourdelot, a French physician who came to the Swedish royal court early in 1652, succeeded not only in improving Christina's physical health (there had been a great deal of public concern about her suffering from malaria) but in affecting her attitudes towards her position and towards life. As her doctor, Bourdelot prescribed less attention to her learned studies and greater attention to amusements and pleasures. A libertine in his views, Bourdelot was addicted to ridiculing what he considered pedantic learning (Queen Christina had been widely known for attracting great European scholars to her court and for her own serious interest in learning); a freethinker, Bourdelot made the church and religion butts of ridicule. The change that took place in Queen Christina's thinking and behavior between her coronation in 1650 and her abdication in 1654 may well be the result of the influence of Bourdelot, whom she considered a genius, a genius above all others as Strindberg suggests on page 32. Bourdelot, incidentally, became so generally unpopular that he had to leave Sweden in June 1653.

Don Antonio Pimentelli de Parada was the Spanish ambassador who appeared in Stockholm in August, 1652. A handsome, cultured man of the world, Pimentelli quickly became a favorite of the queen and, according to gossip, her lover. Until he left Sweden in May, 1654, Christina heaped such costly favors and gifts upon him, says SB (V, 466), that "he had cost Sweden more than if his king had sent over a hostile army of 50,000 men." The queen's enthusiastic attention to the Spaniard, his frequent sojourns at various palaces while she was in residence, their far from restrained conduct in other people's presence, and his departure from her rooms as late as four o'clock in the morning are only a few of the details given by SB.

Johan Holm (died 1687) became the court tailor in 1642 and the queen's valet shortly afterwards. In 1649, the queen sent him to Paris to buy her coronation wardrobe. In 1653, he was ennobled under the name Lejoncrona. A wealthy man, Holm lent large sums of money to the queen, debts which were never fully paid (SB, V, 601-603). The lords' resentment about Holm's elevation to their social level and the general public's view of tailoring as a menial vocation are stated by Starbäck.

Clas Allerts was a Stockholm merchant, whose daughter became the mother of Carl Gustav's illegitimate child in 1647. Starbäck says that his affair with the Allerts girl had attracted a great deal of attention and implies that it may have been one reason why the queen no longer took his suit seriously.

Bulstrode Whitelocke, Cromwell's able and admirable chancellor, came to Stockholm in 1653 to try to secure an alliance with Sweden. A treaty of friendship and peace was concluded in April, 1654. Whitelocke's diary, *A Journal of the Swedish Embassy in the Years 1653 and 1654,* is one of the major sources of information about the closing months of Christina's reign.

Carl Gustav (1622-1660), the son of Count Johan Casimir and the Swedish princess Catherine, Gustav II Adolf's half-sister, was encouraged by Christina as her suitor in her teens but discouraged from then on in spite of his strenuous attentions. She did manage to provide him with opportunities to make a distinguished military career in the Thirty Years' War and had him declared heir apparent in 1649. As king (1654-1660), Carl X Gustav extended the boundaries of Sweden proper to include Skåne, Blekinge, Halland, and Bohuslän and did much to undo the results of Christina's unfortunate financial and political acts.

Maria Eleonora (1599-1655), a princess of Brandenburg and the dowager queen, loved and adored her husband Gustav Adolf but disliked both Sweden and the Swedes. An exceptionally beautiful and devoutly religious woman, Maria Eleonora was a difficult problem for her husband, her daughter, the Swedish government, and herself because of her lack of control over her emotions, her whimsicality, extravagance, and strange eccentric behavior. Because of her shortcomings, Gustav Adolf provided that Christina was to be reared by others. Christina apparently had neither love nor respect for her mother.

Ebba Brahe De la Gardie (1596-1674), the woman that Gustav II Adolf loved and intended to make his queen, was married off by the king's mother to Jakob De la Gardie in 1618. Known for her beauty, charm, and intelligence, Ebba Brahe became the mother of many children and one of the most admirable women of the seventeenth century. Her marriage proved a happy one.

Ebba Sparre (1626-1662), Queen Christina's only woman friend, belonged to one of the most distinguished families of the aristocracy and until 1653 served as one of the queen's ladies-in-waiting. In 1653, Ebba Sparre's marriage to Count Jakob Casimir De la Gardie, a younger brother of Magnus, was celebrated at the royal palace. She was famous for her beauty, charm, and good character.

Gustav Horn (1592-1657), field marshal and national councillor, was one of the leading Swedish generals in the Thirty Years' War.

Carl Gustav Wrangel (1613-1676) was from 1644-1648 the field marshal over the Swedish armies in Germany.

Strindberg's major historical source was the semipopular *Berättelser ur svenska historien* by C. Georg Starbäck and P. O. Bäckström. In the notes, SB represents this work as it appeared in the 1885 edition (F. & G. Beijers Förlag, Stockholm).

ACT I

1. Riddarholm Church, built during the late thirteenth century, serves as the burial place of Swedish kings and queens. The Vasaborg crypt is the burial place of Gustav Gustavsson (1616-1653), Count of Vasaborg and half-brother of Queen Christina. See note 7.

2. The Golden Peace (*Gyldene Freden*) is one of Stockholm's oldest and most famous restaurants.

3. Gustav II Adolf was killed in the Battle of Lützen on November 6, 1632. The action of the play opens then on November 6, 1653.

4. Göran Persson (*ca.* 1530-1568), Erik XIV's favorite and adviser, was considered Erik's evil genius but was an exceptionally able man. He was imprisoned, tortured, and executed shortly after Dukes John and Charles forced Erik to abdicate.

5. Tott was an enthusiastic and unlucky card player. SB, V, 593: "During one evening alone, he lost 2,400 ducats, at that time a very large sum."

6. SB, V, 495: Queen Christina proposed declaring war on Cromwell's government when the news of Charles I's execution in 1649 reached Sweden, but the national council succeeded in preventing such an action but not Christina's personal support of Prince Charles Stuart, whom she recognized as king of Great Britain and Ireland. Cromwell's ability and genuine achievements as well as his friendly gestures toward Sweden led to the Swedish recognition of his government in 1651. See the note on Whitelocke above.

7. Margareta Slots Cabeljau, daughter of a Dutch resident of Sweden, became for a time in 1615 the mistress of Gustav II Adolf. Their illegitimate son was Gustav Gustavsson, who was made a baron (*friherre*), count, and a member of the national council by his half-sister. See note 1.

8. One of Klas Tott's grandmothers was Princess Sigrid, daughter of Erik XIV. See the House of Vasa, page 82.

9. Louis de Bourbon, Prince of Condé (1621-1686), was one of the greatest of French generals.

10. Anders Düben, a German by birth, was Queen Christina's organist and music director as well as organist in the German Church (*Tyska kyrkan*) in Stockholm.

11. Johan Banér (1596-1641) was one of Gustav II Adolf's ablest generals. See note 23.

12. Finland was until 1809 part of Sweden. The threat of imprisonment in a fortress in Finland was not an idle one as many Swedes had discovered.

13. Arnold Johan Messenius (1608-1651) and his son Arnold (1629-1651) belonged to a gifted family which for three generations had succeeded not only in displaying their ability but also in getting into trouble with the Swedish government and with other people. The grandfather, Johannes Messenius (1579-1636), was a historian and a professor at Uppsala. Accused of treasonous correspondence with the Polish Vasas, Messenius was sentenced in 1616 to life imprisonment at Kajaneborg Fortress in Finland; while there, he wrote *Scandia Illustrata,* a history of Scandinavia. In 1651, the younger Arnold Messenius wrote a pamphlet attacking the queen, her extravagance, her mismanagement of the government, the higher nobility, and other factors and people he felt would ruin Sweden; he sent a copy to Carl Gustav, who in turn sent it to Christina through Magnus De la Gardie. On the queen's order, both the pamphleteer and his father were arrested and brought to trial, condemned after extraordinarily unfair hearings, and executed. Even Strindberg's main source, SB, V, 438-453, condemns the father's sentence and execution as a political murder.

ACT II

14. Ekolsund, the birthplace of Klas Tott, was the Tott family estate in Uppland which at Christina's request was purchased by Carl Gustav to be presented by the queen as a gift to Magnus Gabriel De la Gardie. After Magnus' fall from favor the queen persuaded Carl Gustav to buy the estate from De la Gardie to be given by her to Klas Tott. SB, V, 592.

15. Act II presents Arnold Messenius' (and the general public's) ma-

jor complaints against Christina and her reign as stated in his pamphlet. See note 13.

16. Christina did not officially become a Roman Catholic until December, 1654, in Brussels, but she had long before become antagonistic toward the Church of Sweden, its doctrines and clergy. The queen's conversion was naturally shocking to the Swedes whose king Gustav II Adolf was generally regarded as the defender and savior of Protestantism.

17. Karlskrona, the major base of the Swedish fleet, is in Blekinge, one of the provinces acquired in 1658, four years after Christina's abdication! King Carl XI founded the city in 1680 in order to have a convenient and ice-free base for the navy, which since then has had its headquarters there.

18. Sigismund (1566-1632), the son of John III and his queen Catherine of Poland, became king of Poland in 1587, and, upon his father's death, king of Sweden as well. He was dethroned in Sweden in 1598. The legal claims of the "Polish" Vasas to the Swedish throne were in fact stronger than Gustav II Adolf's had been.

19. The Peace of Westphalia, signed October 14, 1648, concluded the Thirty Years' War and brought Sweden, in addition to territorial gains, cash compensation to the extent of five million *riksdaler*.

20. SB, V, 445, says that the Messenius pamphlet asserted that Countess Ebba Brahe De la Gardie and her son Magnus Gabriel not only worked against Carl Gustav's succession to the throne but were prepared to poison him at Jakobsdal Castle.

21. The Greek myth of Pandora (all gifts), the first woman in the world, suited Strindberg remarkably well in his interpretation of the queen, who not only was interested in drama and theater but who was also well-versed in classic mythology. The legend is, briefly: Furious because Prometheus had stolen fire from heaven for the use of mankind, Zeus or Jupiter avenged himself on man by having Vulcan fashion a godlike being from earth and water and by having the gods endow her with good and evil qualities. Among these gifts were beauty, artistic qualities, artfulness, and cunning. When Prometheus saw her, he rejected her, but his gentler brother, Epimetheus, married her. Their union was happy until Mercury put into her care a box which he forbade her to open. Overcome with curiosity, she opened it, releasing the

sufferings, vices, sins, and other afflictions of mankind. In her terror, Pandora closed the box and thereby saved Hope for mankind. Strindberg's major source, SB (V, 563 ff.), in discussing the dramatic entertainments of various kinds popular at Christina's court says that in some of these mythological characters were impersonated and that Christina occasionally was a participant.

22. The Order of Johannes is the Maltese order.

23. Johan Banér (1596-1641), one of Gustav II Adolf's most brilliant and colorful generals, had a reputation for emotional outbursts and affairs with women. SB (V, 82 ff. and 191 ff.) tells about several of these as well as about his three marriages. SB (V, 84): "Wine and women were his weaknesses."

24. Euripides (*ca.* 480-406 B.C.), one of three great Greek writers of tragedies, has been considered a woman hater by some people because of his realistic treatment of many of his woman characters.

25. When Carl Gustav was officially made crown prince in 1649, he was granted an annual income of fifty thousand *riksdaler* and in 1651 he was given governmental control over Öland, the island province off the southeastern coast of Sweden. The younger Arnold Messenius, the author of the libelous pamphlet, in 1648 was Carl Gustav's personal servant; at the time he wrote the pamphlet, he was a government employee in Stockholm, and was actively involved in intriguing in behalf of the crown prince, apparently without the latter's knowledge. As Strindberg says, he sent a copy of the pamphlet to Carl Gustav who sent it to the queen in care of Magnus Gabriel De la Gardie along with his declarations of: (1) innocence in the matter and (2) loyalty to the queen.

26. Some of the earlier Cromwells had been brewers.

27. Epimetheus. See note 20.

28. In 1653, Christina approved without consulting the national council Governor General Hans Christofer von Königsmarck's proposal to build forts near the free city of Bremen, which had refused to acknowledge itself in any way under the control of Sweden in spite of the provisions of the Peace of Westphalia. Resulting hostilities were concluded to Sweden's advantage shortly after Carl X Gustav's accession to the throne. Neither the emperor nor Holland participated directly in the brief war, contrary to what the Swedes had feared.

29. Lions were kept in part of the old palace moat. Hence, *Lejonkulan* or the lion's den.

30. The Palatinate Count Johan Casimir of Zweibrücken-Kleeburg, a miniature German county, married Gustav II Adolf's half-sister, Princess Catherine, in Stockholm on June 11, 1615. When the Thirty Years' War broke out, the Swedish king offered Johan Casimir and his wife asylum in Sweden. Their oldest son, Carl Gustav, was born in Nyköping on November 8, 1622. Until her death on December 13, 1638, Princess Catherine was entrusted with the care of young Queen Christina. Johan Casimir was, as Strindberg suggests, a Calvinist, but his son was reared as a Lutheran.

ACT IV

31. *Lejongården* or the lion park was a section of the palace gardens. See note 29.

32. Delphi in ancient Greece, where the Greek gods were said to reveal their purposes as well as knowledge which worshippers sought.

33. René Descartes (1596-1650), the French philosopher and mathematician, was one of the many foreign scholars who were attracted to Sweden by Queen Christina's genuine interest in, and support of, learning and scholarship. He died in Stockholm.

34. Paphos, the ancient town on Cyprus and the seat of worship of Aphrodite or Venus, goddess of love. Venus' gift to Pandora was beauty.

35. The old royal palace in Stockholm which was destroyed by fire in 1697 was, as Strindberg points out in *Svenska folket,* p. 91, not only a royal residence but the center of most governmental affairs and hence fairly readily open to the general public.

36. Duke John (1589-1618) was the son of John III and his second queen, Lady Gunilla Bielke. When the Estates in 1599 deposed King Sigismund I (the son of John III) who was also king of Poland (1587-1632), they acknowledged that Sigismund's oldest son, Crown Prince Vladislav, would be crowned king if he came to Sweden within a year and were reared a Lutheran. In 1600, when the young prince had not appeared, the Estates declared that Sigismund's heirs were ineligible for the Swedish crown. The crown was offered to Duke Charles of Södermanland, the regent and brother of John III, in spite of the far

stronger claims of young Duke John. In 1604, the young duke renounced his claims to the throne; thereupon, Duke Charles became King Charles IX. In 1611 on the accession of Gustav II Adolf, Duke John again renounced his claims.

37. King John IV of Portugal had been officially recognized as king by the Swedish government shortly after his accession in 1640; yet, shortly before her abdication in 1654 and without consulting the national council, Christina notified Don Antonio da Silva e Sousa, the Portuguese minister, that his presence in Stockholm was superfluous and that she no longer recognized John as King of Portugal. The queen's strange action which could have had serious results for the flourishing Swedish trade with Portugal was remedied by Axel Oxenstjerna and King Carl X Gustav shortly afterwards.

38. According to SB and to most Swedish histories, most of these charges are accurate. For her own purposes the queen deliberately shipped out of Sweden national treasures not all of which by any means were continental booty from the Thirty Years' War.

39. Field Marshal Lennart Torstensson (1603-1651) was the highly successful commander of the Swedish forces on the continent and in Denmark from 1641 until 1646. Carl Gustav served under Torstensson in 1645, and, in 1648, was named "generalissimus" over the Swedish armies in Germany. The victorious Swedes sent home many shiploads of booty, as Christina says.

40. Christina's attitude towards Sweden and the Swedes was like her mother's. See the note on Maria Eleonora, page 86. Christina did, however, make serious attempts at improving Swedish schools and Swedish cultural life in general.

41. Berlin lies on the Spree, a river in Burgundy, the home of Queen Maria Eleonora.

42. St. Erik, the patron saint of Sweden, was the twelfth-century king who is supposed to have done much to secure Christianity in both Finland and Sweden proper. Engelbrekt Engelbrektsson was the fifteenth-century hero and liberator who freed the Swedes from Danish oppression for several years until his assassination in 1436. The Stures, leaders in the fifteenth- and sixteenth-century struggle against the Danish overlords, were, like St. Erik, Engelbrekt, and the Vasas before the reformation in the 1520's, Roman Catholics.

Introduction to
'Charles XII'

In *Open Letters to the Intimate Theater*, Strindberg had this
to say about *Charles XII*:

Charles XII, the man who ruined Sweden, the great criminal, the
champion fighter, the idol of the ruffians, and the counterfeiter, was
the one I was going to present on the stage to my countrymen.

Well, everyone does have motives for his actions, every criminal
has the right to defend himself, so I decided to plan my drama as
a classical tragedy of fate and catastrophe. The end of a life that
was a big mistake. A strong will that struggles against the course
of historical development, forgivable because he did not understand
what he was doing. Charles XII did not understand that Czar Peter
of Russia was right when he wanted to Europeanize his country,
just freed from the two-hundred-year domination by the Mongols;
he did not understand that Europe needed Russia to defend its
borders against the Turks and other Asiatics now that Poland had
collapsed of itself. Charles XII is the barbarian when he stirs up
the Turks against Czar Peter; he is the betrayer of Europe when
he allies himself with Asiatics; Charles XII is a "gengångare," a
ghost who walks the earth, who is given form by the smoke of
powder, and who fades away as soon as the cannons are nailed
down, the cannons with which he intended to keep world history
from taking its course. Ruined even then by the revelation of his
inner disharmonies and awakened doubt, he falls in his struggle
against the powers. The problem of the bullet at Fredrikshald has
not yet been solved; I let it come from "above," which Swedenborg, Charles XII's last friend, interprets in his elevated fashion,
while the public believes it came from the fortress. Let that be as

it may. It came when it should—and places the period after the last act of the tragedy.

As Strindberg saw it, only in the last few years of Charles XII's life did the real tragedy of his life become evident to his people and to the king himself. The Charles we meet therefore is not the young hero king that Tegnér and other romanticists had idealized but the weary defeated king who, though still in his thirties, feels and *is* old and almost exhausted. It is the last period in the life of the tragic human being whose "life has been one big mistake" that interested Strindberg most. For that reason Strindberg concentrates his attention on Charles XII as he approaches his final defeat and fall as a hero and as a man of destiny.

In *Charles XII,* Strindberg has used a technique decidedly different from that in *Queen Christina.* Instead of a technique reminiscent of the naturalistic one explained in the Preface to *Lady Julie* and illustrated not only in *Queen Christina* and *Lady Julie* but even more thoroughly in *Creditors,* Strindberg has—except in the fourth act—used in *Charles XII* the impressionistic-expressionistic techniques he had used very effectively in *The Road to Damascus* I and II in 1898. In *Charles XII* are the seemingly disjointed structure, the strange and striking mixture of reality and the dream experience, the fairly extensive use of symbolism, the stress on emotions and feelings, the melancholy mood, and the use of music to help set the mood. Many of the characters, moreover, are expressionistic rather than realistic types. The primary concentration falls on the subjective inner experiences of the king rather than on external realistic events; the major emphasis then is on the conflicts within Charles himself.

All that remains for Strindberg's Charles is the twilight of a career that should have ended long since. What Strindberg wanted primarily to do was to give his audience insight into the king's character and actions during the last three years of frustration, waiting, indecision, and inner defeat. By means of carefully selected and chronologically arranged representative scenes from those three years, Strindberg gives us, first and foremost, a synthesis and, secondly only, an analysis. Note also Strindberg's emphasis on his themes, the preliminary exposition of the themes, their varied development, and the final recapitulation. It is the sort of thing that Strindberg had already done in *The Road to Damascus*.

The combination of realistic and expressionistic elements has resulted in a new type of historical play so far as technique goes. Unlike the symbolists in so many of their plays of the 1890's and after the turn of the century, Strindberg retains an intense preference for reality but combines it with poetic fantasy. He tries successfully to penetrate into the very core of the human being he is concerned with and presents a synthesis of the essentially human in Charles. That rather than the heredity and environment that produced Charles and made him what he was is Strindberg's major concern.

As in *The Road to Damascus,* Strindberg is primarily interested in the relationship between Charles and the Powers, the forces back of the material world that control man and interfere in nature and with the human individual. Strindberg had come out of his Inferno experiences in the 1890's with a very vivid faith in a Providence who was concerned about everything and everyone, a Providence who did not hesitate about interfering in the life of any man. This Providence with whom he identifies the term *the Powers* is interested in every man's destiny, and chastens those who are guilty of pride and arrogance by making them suffer blow upon blow until they either attain humility and resignation or go under. The use of his own concept of the Powers in dealing with the tragedy of Charles XII was a happy idea: Charles XII's extremely orthodox Lutheranism stressed the vengeful, jealous God of the Old Testament rather than the gentle forgiving Saviour of the New. Charles himself would not have found the idea of a watchful, punishing Deity interested in his every act and thought inaccurate.

The mood in *Charles XII* is heavily depressing in much the

same way as in *The Road to Damascus*. The winter setting of the first act when the king returns to Sweden under anything but happy circumstances, the weariness and the hopelessness of most of the characters, and the silence of the king are further enhanced in Act II by the barely audible mumbling of the king, his subjects' embarrassment and fear in his presence, and are further developed in Act III by the people who are forever waiting for the king to do something. In fact, all through the play except in the episodes with the three women in Act IV, the silence and the sense of everyone's waiting are constantly present. For example:

> FEIF: What do Polhem and Swedenborg think?
> KING: They don't say anything! (*Pause*) The whole city says nothing; the whole country says nothing! A silence as of death is beginning to close about us! (*Pause*) And besides I am sick! (*Pause*) The streets are empty; no one comes to call! No one protests! . . . No one says anything! (*Pause*) Say something!
> FEIF: I have nothing to say, Your Majesty!

In the last act (again the time is winter) when Charles in the desperation of inner defeat has marched against Norway, i.e., "against . . . the enemy . . . whoever wants to be . . . toward a victory . . . or certain defeat," the emphasis on silence and waiting reaches its climax. Feif says, significantly, "See, if he only turns his back, everything will break up."

The mood is strengthened by Strindberg's use of Sebastian Bach's saraband. Luxembourg, the court dwarf, plays the saraband, about which Gyllenborg and Horn comment:

> GYLLENBORG: What is that infernal music that I've been hearing all morning?
> HORN: It sounds like a grasshopper . . .
> GYLLENBORG: I think it sounds like the autumn wind blowing between double windows, or like the crying of children.

Later on:

> MAN: Why do you always play that sad piece?
> DWARF: Because I used to play it for my King when he was sorely afflicted.
> MAN: Listen to that fellow!
> DWARF: And a king composed this song of sorrow—Sebastian Bach, the king of the Land of Sorrows and Pain . . .

The accentuation of the mood by means of the stately but melancholy saraband is reminiscent of the effective use of music in *The Road to Damascus*.

Note Strindberg's effective use of symbols. For example: the ruined village beside the dark sea on a windy cold day with its pale gray dawn represents the Sweden which in the course of fifteen years has sunk from a position as the greatest power of the North to that of a ruined land at the mercy of its enemies. The one wind-ravaged apple tree represents Sweden as well; the tree is not dead, however; it may yet bear good fruit when sunlight and warmth return. The single rotten apple on top that hangs stubbornly on but that his people feel ought to be shaken down represents Charles himself. The wind that cannot dislodge the rotten apple represents in turn the ineffective spoken protests and complaints of a people kept from the plucking of the apple directly because of the crippling effects of absolutism. Briefly put—they can talk, but they cannot feel free to act.

In keeping with all this is the nameless man in rags who searches among the ruins of the home he does not have any more; he and the malcontent, the poverty-stricken woman with the petition, and the other for the most part unidentified minor characters represent the people who look like ghosts and who inhabit a country that is a ruin and a scrap heap and whose position is almost hopelessly desperate. There is, to be sure, one ray of hope—symbolized by the pale gray dawn, which is given concrete human expression in Horn and Gyllenborg, the men of a better future.

There are characters who are presented realistically—Horn, Gyllenborg, Hultman, Luxembourg, Feif, Emerentia Polhem, Princess Ulrika Eleonora, the former queen Katarina of Poland, Swedenborg, and Görtz. Strindberg refrains from diverting attention from Charles XII, by making no attempt to characterize them any more fully than is needed to clarify their respective relationships with the king and to throw light on him. In spite of this, Strindberg has succeeded amazingly well in individualizing them with economy and a sure touch.

As in *The Road to Damascus,* many of the characters are merely expressionistic types: The Man, the Malcontent, the Woman, and the whole array of ghostlike, silent figures who appear and disappear in the manner of many of the characters in the somewhat later *Dream Play.* The strange, dreamlike figures serve as a sort of chorus that not only provides exposition but also foreshadows the inevitable defeat and fall of Charles. Even the "widows," though they are identified by name, belong to this chorus of lamentation and foreboding.

Strindberg's chief concern of course is with the character of the king. He speaks of him as "a ghost who walks the earth, who is given form by the smoke of powder, and who fades away as soon as the cannons are nailed down." There is something dreamlike in most of the scenes in which the king appears. The silent king in Act II is not certain that his experience with Hunger (*Svält*) was reality or a dream. Horn regards Charles as a dead man, whose spirit is walking the earth. When Feif says, "Are you aware that we are talking as if he were dead?" Swedenborg, the seer, replies very simply: "He *is* dead."

In Act IV, the presentation of Charles XII is primarily realistic. One of the outstanding facts about Charles XII that any Swedish school child knows is that he was not attracted to women and that he never seriously planned to marry. Strindberg had to deal with this fairly unusual characteristic, and he does so in a thoroughly realistic fashion by having Hultman and the professor discuss the matter briefly, by presenting Swedenborg and his fiancée Emerentia Polhem in a conversation that tells a great deal about the young woman who has sworn to bring the king to her feet, and then in three episodes presenting the king—in turn—with the young coquette, his sister who hopes to inherit his throne, and the former queen of Poland who insists on the conventional prerogatives of women. The whole sequence of lively episodes reveals Charles's attitude towards women and provides a welcome relief from the depressing mood and tension of the first three acts.

This tension has its basis in a striking mixture of love and hate, of admiration and contempt for the monarch by his people who, it should be noticed, represent every class in the Swedish community —the commoners, the burghers, the clergy, and the nobles. The Man calls him a villain and says he ought to be shot, but, when he gets the opportunity to kill him, limits himself to saying what he thinks and adds, "It has been marvelous to speak out for once! And now we can be just as good friends all the same . . ." (p. 131). Malcontent echoes the thought, "Think of it, I can't get really angry with that man!" (p. 141.) The national councillor and the speakers of the Estates, to take one more illustration, agree that they will not kneel when the king enters, but they do, nevertheless. The speaker of the Farmers' Estate says, "So he does have something different!" (p. 113). The mixture of fear and admiration, of hatred and sympathy, of resentment and pity which appears in scene after scene provides a great many nuances of a highly complex character.

Two characters in particular are eminently suited to analyze Charles realistically—the brilliant statesman Count Arvid Horn and the genius Emanuel Swedenborg. Both have the intellectual gifts, the integrity, and the opportunity to observe and study the king. It is Horn—who was to succeed Charles as the man of power in Sweden—that provides the most detailed summary of the character of Charles; for, in characterizing Görtz, Horn says what his

auditors—and Horn himself to his embarrassment—find applicable
to the king himself:

HORN: Well then; according to everything I've heard, Baron Görtz
. . . (*Tries to discover with his eyes what the* KING's *opinion of*
GÖRTZ *is, and to compare it with the expressions on* FEIF's
face) . . . that man is . . . an exceptionally unusual personality,
and his desire to be unusual can only be measured . . . in its
strength . . . by his desire for power.
(KING *draws—without looking up.*)
HORN: They say that he thinks he's the center of the world, that
he looks in the papers every morning to see if the destinies of
Europe have undergone any change while he has been sleeping,
and the learned Swedenborg . . .
(KING *pricks up his ears.*)
HORN: . . . assures us that if Görtz died today, he'd set the king-
dom of the dead against the heavenly powers.
(KING *quits moving his pen, but does not look up.*)
HORN: This overwhelming desire for honor he conceals . . . tries
to conceal beneath a simple exterior, and a condescending manner
towards his inferiors . . .
(GYLLENBORG *shows his uneasiness.* KING *becomes red in the*
face)
HORN: Inferiors, whom he actually despises, just as he despises all
humanity.
(KING *inclines his head towards his chest.*)
HORN: These outstanding characteristics of Baron Görtz, coupled
with his most exemplary insensibility to the sufferings of others,
would seem incompatible with a religious spirit, but Baron Görtz
is not without religion. One could say that he fears for God,
without fearing God.
(FEIF, *until now inscrutable; fixes his eyes with horror on*
HORN. KING *puts his fingers to his throat as if he were choking.*)
HORN (*goes on without noticing anything, completely unaware of*
the unconscious hints): The learned and pious Swedenborg believes Baron Görtz uses religion as a sort of magic, through
which he secures support and power for himself, even in his

purely criminal activities . . . for example, in extorting funds, in getting revenge on enemies . . . because he also has the peculiarity of never being able to forgive anyone.

(KING *fixes* HORN's *glance as if he wanted to read his innermost thoughts and to see if he has any mental reservations. His mouth is open, and his upper lip quivers.*)

HORN: In a word, a great weakness . . . disguised so that it seems like a tremendous strength; a convulsive stubbornness that cannot break down his own wilfulness . . .

(KING—*there is a noise from his spurs.* HORN, *as if awakening from a dream and realizing the infernal aspect of the situation, becomes silent with horror. All look at each other with mutual embarrassment, without anyone's quite being able to break the silence. . . .*)

The arrogant egotist who believes he is the man of destiny and the center of the world; who conceals his inordinate desire for honor beneath extremely simple speech, attire, tastes and manner; who despises his fellow men to whose sufferings he is insensible; who is not religious in any ordinary way but who uses religion to get power and support; who is unable to forgive anyone; and who is wilful and stubborn—basically, this is Strindberg's interpretation of Charles XII.

And yet Strindberg makes it abundantly clear that that is not the complete Charles. Appropriately enough, it is again Horn, who speaks even more pointedly:

HORN (*carried away by his eloquence*): That man, who is lying there, waiting for his journey to the grave—for he is dead—was once the man of destiny . . . and success upon success attended him as long as he walked the paths of justice. But after that, when he wanted to walk his own paths eighteen years ago and to control the destinies of people and nations . . . then destiny took him by the ear and played blindman's buff with him! And now he stands . . . or lies divided against himself! He has wasted eighteen years to keep one vow—that Peter of Russia and

August of Poland be exterminated from the earth! His whole life
has revolved about these two poles! And now . . . now he's negotiating to get related by marriage to the Russians . . . one
day, and for friendship with Poland, the next . . . all this while
he has lain down in Norway! In Norway! . . . And this paradox
that looks like a colossal hoax. He wanted to raise a strong
Poland against Russia, but then he broke up Poland and did the
work of Russia! Wanted one thing and did another! That is how
destiny plays with those who want to play the part of destiny!

But it is Swedenborg, the seer and philosopher, who says the final
word (p. 165):

> SWEDENBORG: . . . That strange man!
> FEIF: Have you ever understood his destiny?
> SWEDENBORG: No, and we'll probably never understand it! I have
> never understood *one* human destiny, not even my own insig-
> nificant one.

What Strindberg reveals about Charles XII is distinctly reminiscent of what he says about his own Inferno experiences in *The Road
to Damascus*. Success attends the man of destiny as long as he walks
the path of justice, but when the king in his arrogance decides to
walk his own paths, the Powers or Destiny chasten him.

"And now he stands . . . or lies divided against himself!" In this
statement is the core of Strindberg's characterization of Charles.
The pale, cold, silent king of Act I seems unhesitant but isolated.
In Act II, his lack of inner certainty and security becomes evident
in the undecided facial expressions and his embarrassment when he
recognizes himself in Horn's characterization of Görtz; his reactions reveal plainly his self-doubt and inner questioning. As the act
proceeds the inner struggles become more and more evident. The
man who has believed himself self-sufficient and right has come to
the point of presenting his defense.

FEIF: The country is impoverished . . . and the people!
KING: And that is my fault! Did I cause the plague? Did I cause the crop failures? Did I cause the fires? . . . Have I declared the wars? . . . No, I have only defended myself, my country, my royal inheritance!

The king does not appear in Act III, but in Act IV, weary and ill, he admits that he has lost his self-confidence and his will to live. Irritated, he bursts the limits of his abnormal efforts at self-control with a continuation of his self-defense:

KING: "The moments of life are over, smiling I want to die!" Do you remember what that is? . . . Ragnar Lodbrok in the snake-pit! (*Pause*) They thought I was impenetrable because I did not talk; and I did not talk because I did not drink; because I alone protected my senses among drunkards, they thought I was a fool. (*Pause*) Ulla! Put your hand on my forehead! Now you are like my mother! The only woman I have ever loved, because she was my mother, and so . . . was not a woman to me! (*Pause*) There isn't an act that I cannot defend, but I do not take care of myself! (*Pause*) The apprentice calls the journeyman a tyrant, and the journeyman calls the master a despot. All people in power seem to be despots. They would all like to have power, all of them, if they might, if they could! (*Pause*) Yes, you women! I have stood outside windows and looked into homes; that's why I saw more than others, because the ones who are inside see only their own . . . The most delightful, the most bitter! . . . Love is almost identical with hate! (*Pause*) Now I shall go to sleep! Sleep, the best there is! The next best!

The inner struggles become gradually such that he is constantly waiting for something to bring an end to a life that Strindberg felt was "one great mistake." The struggles end not in bending before or yielding to the powers but in stubbornly clinging to his arrogance until he fades away, as Strindberg says, when the cannons are nailed down. Charles does not bow to Destiny in humility; therein, lies his tragedy.

How sympathetic Strindberg was to the Charles near the end of his life is clear. Charles in spite of all his flaws is a tragic human being who has had "a great rich life" and whose measure cannot be given with a few small words. To be sure, he is proud, obstinate, and hard-hearted, but he is, says Strindberg, to be pitied because as a great man he is isolated and lonely, and as a great man he has felt he had to have an almost abnormal self-control and self-reliance. The masks which he assumes to conceal his feelings and emotions drop only on rare occasions to reveal his real nature: the great man with human frailties and the great man who is thrown in upon himself to excess.

Charles XII · A Play in Five Acts

Characters

CHARLES XII
PRINCESS ULRIKA ELEONORA
GÖRTZ
ARVID HORN
KARL GYLLENBORG
FEIF, *the King's secretary*
HULTMAN, *the King's steward*
KATARINA LECZINSKA, *formerly Queen of Poland*
EMERENTIA POLHEM
EMANUEL SWEDENBORG
LUXEMBOURG, *the dwarf*
THE MAN
THE WOMAN
A MALCONTENT
THE ROYAL COUNCILLOR
SPEAKERS OF THE FOUR ESTATES
THE SAILOR
THE COASTGUARD and others

Settings

ACT I: *On the coast of Scania*
ACT II: *In the King's audience room in Lund*
ACT III: *The market square outside the house in which Görtz is living in Lund*
ACT IV: *In the garden of the same house*
ACT V: *Before Fredriksten Fortress in Norway*

ACT I

It is a windy morning on the Scanian coast in December 1715.[1]
*At the center is a cottage, beyond repair; deserted in the plague
of 1710; its foundation imbedded in the drifting sand. The windows
are broken; the roofing tiles ripped off; the door is gone. The
sooty stove and the chimney can be seen through the collapsed
front of the house. Outside the cottage is a leafless wind-ravaged
apple tree with one lone apple, which is being shaken in the
wind. Next to the tree is a scrap pile with withered burdocks on
it. To the right of the cottage can be seen the burned remains of
a church and several houses. Beyond, the sea lies dark; on the
horizon can be seen a pale gray ray of dawn.*

A MAN *dressed in rags is walking about searching among the
ruins.*

A COASTGUARD *comes in.*

COASTGUARD: Halt! Who goes there?

(MAN *conceals himself behind a pillar among the church ruins.*)

COASTGUARD: Halt! Who goes there?

MAN: Who am I? . . . I used to be a soldier; there used to be a
village here!

COASTGUARD: What are you looking for?

MAN: I'm looking for a home I once had, but that I don't have
any more!

COASTGUARD: Talk louder! The wind's blowing your words away!

107

MAN: Wasn't there a village here that was called Stavstorp? [2]

COASTGUARD: Yes, of course! You see the ruins; the church was here; the school was here!

MAN: Where was the soldier's cottage?

COASTGUARD: There!

MAN: There! Why isn't it still there?

COASTGUARD: The plague killed all the people, and then the enemy burned the buildings.

MAN: When did the plague strike?

COASTGUARD: Right after the Battle of Poltava! [3]

MAN: Where did the plague come from?

COASTGUARD: From Russia . . . that's where Poltava is . . . from Russia that swallowed our King and our army. Were you in the army?

MAN: Yes, at Poltava and in Russia and in Siberia!

COASTGUARD: What were you there for? You should have stayed home!

MAN: Oh! (*Examines the cottage*) That's absolutely right! My cottage was here, my home was here, my wife and my two children were here! My oatmeal used to be cooked on this stove, my children played by this window, my wife used to sit in this doorway waiting for me and mending our clothes. That's fifteen years ago! . . . Fifteen! . . . I planted this apple tree before I left; I never got to see its fruit . . . Now I do, but it's rotten! (*Shakes the tree without getting the apple to fall off*) That's obvious. (*Stirs in the scrap heap*) See, there are my broken household goods, the earthenware plates, the iron spoons, the salt barrel . . . and the sole of a shoe . . . That's my wife's . . . She had such a pretty little foot that walked so gently and quietly . . . here! Well, what's the use of lamenting! . . . I suppose the whole country looks like this! . . . A ruin, a scrap heap . . . with a rotten apple on top . . .

COASTGUARD: That ought to be shaken down!

MAN (*flaring up*): By whom?

COASTGUARD: By a man who has a heart in his body!

MAN: See! Here's my soldier's plate that hung just above the door: Number seventy-three, Southern Scanian Regiment. That was I! . . . What are you looking for out at sea?

COASTGUARD: Don't you know? Don't you understand?

MAN: No!

COASTGUARD: Haven't you heard that Stralsund has fallen? [4]

MAN: No—o! And the villain?

COASTGUARD: Has fled!

MAN: Just as at Poltava! The villain always flees except when he wins! Once he fled because of a woman! [5]

COASTGUARD: *Once?* He has always fled from women!

MAN: Why has he always fled from them?

COASTGUARD: Because the villain has never thought that he could manage women!

MAN: That's it, most likely! . . . What do you see out there at sea?

COASTGUARD: I see a Danish frigate pursuing a brigantine! [6]

MAN: Brigantine! Doesn't brigant mean a villain?

COASTGUARD: Yes, it does!

MAN: Then the villain is on the brigantine!

COASTGUARD: Right!

MAN: Aren't there any reefs or shoals or currents here?

COASTGUARD: Yes, but the one who's to be hanged won't drown.

MAN: Isn't there any rope left in all Sweden?

COASTGUARD: There's rope at Karlskrona,[7] but there's no one who dares to hold on to it!

MAN: No?

COASTGUARD: Do you know anyone?

MAN: Yes, I do! . . . Is he going to land here?

COASTGUARD: That's the idea! . . . What did you do in Siberia? [8]

MAN: First I went to school . . . then I became a teacher.

COASTGUARD: So that's why you know what *brigant* means! By the way, can you see those men riding along the shore?

MAN: I see them!

COASTGUARD: Then you see a member of the national council and the speakers of the four estates!

MAN: Don't you think if one fired a shot here, right here, it would remove both the frigate and the brigantine from the world of the living and the kingdom would be saved?

COASTGUARD: Strange that you and I who run across each other for the first time should both have the same thought!

MAN: Maybe there is only one thought in the whole country! Shall I fire?

COASTGUARD: Fire! But I don't think it will help. Up to now neither point nor edge, neither fire nor water, has had any effect on him; and nothing will have any effect until his time has come!

MAN (*lights a fire in the stove in the cottage*): When the villain sees this fire, he'll say to himself: See the fire of joy over there! . . . Yes, it can become a fire of joy, but it isn't that yet!

COASTGUARD: Why do you always call him villain?

MAN: You know why as well as I and the whole people . . . the whole—no . . . half—because the other half is dead . . . But tell me, what are those men doing . . . down on the shore?

COASTGUARD: Well, they're afraid for their heads, since they've summoned parliament in his absence and have demanded his—what do you call it—suspension.

MAN: Suspension? You suspend a drunken clergyman, an incompetent official, a cowardly officer . . . That's a good word!

COASTGUARD: See! . . . The fire's doing it! The brigantine is tacking . . . The Danish frigate is withdrawing and going on for fear of shallows . . . A boat's putting out from shore . . . He's saved!

MAN: Then it's time for us to save ourselves, too!

COASTGUARD: Give me your hand first, countryman!

MAN: Here!

COASTGUARD: Where will you go?

MAN (*sadly*): Who can tell? . . . Farewell! The rulers are coming!

COASTGUARD: The rulers . . . on the highway! The King on the wrong road! . . . Poor, poor country! (*Each of them goes his way.*)

(*A distant shot is heard; the wind and the rain increase. The national* COUNCILLOR *and the* SPEAKERS *of the four estates come in; they are dressed in wet capes and are pale from sleeplessness, rain, cold, and anxiety.*)

COUNCILLOR: The King is coming?

LORD: God be gracious unto us!

CLERGYMAN: What have we done?

BURGHER: Our duty!

FARMER: More than our duty—we made sacrifices!

COUNCILLOR (*takes up a paper, which he shields from the rain*): I have written this: The nation, which has been deserted by its king for fifteen years, welcomes him home, and pleads for peace . . .

LORD: He'll never want to hear that!

CLERGYMAN: Pity the nation whose king is a madman!

BURGHER: Pity us, that are to be judged by a madman!

FARMER: Pity the country, whose king is a villain!

(*Applause from off stage can be heard. The* COUNCILLOR *and the* SPEAKERS *draw close together in horror.*)

COUNCILLOR: What did you say, farmer?

FARMER: Villain, I said!

COUNCILLOR: Quiet! The wind can carry your word to the ear which heard in Turkey what was whispered in Sweden! [9]

FARMER: The ear that could deafen itself to the prayers, the just complaints, and the cries of anguish of a whole people. Lord, hear us from your heaven; Lord, punish him; Lord, have mercy upon us!

ALL: Amen!

ADJUTANT: The King! . . . Make way, people!

COUNCILLOR: The government is not the people!

ADJUTANT: Government? Are you the government? (*Makes a gesture with his arms: "out of the way!"*)

COUNCILLOR (*comes forward*): Do you know me, adjutant?

ADJUTANT: The royal councillor? . . . Why are you here?

COUNCILLOR: To get an audience with the King and present the nation's . . .

ADJUTANT: We've been hearing all that for a long time . . .

FARMER: Hear it once more then!

ADJUTANT: Behave yourself, farmer! . . . On your toes . . . the King is coming!

LORD (*to the others*): No one on his knees!

FARMER: No kneeling!

BURGHER: Agreed!

(DÜRING[10] *enters from the right at a tremendous speed; sees the fire; goes into the cottage and adds wood to the fire.*)

ROSEN[10] (*enters from the right*): Out of the way, farmers! . . .

(HULTMAN *enters from the right with a box under his arm.*)

LORD: That's the King's suite!

CLERGYMAN: The steward!

FARMER: The plate licker!

(LUXEMBOURG, *the dwarf, enters with a violin under his arm.*)

BURGHER: The court fool! . . . What companions!

FARMER: With a government like that you can go far! . . . The giant seeks the dwarf . . .

(*Two* GUARDSMEN *with drawn swords keep back the* COUNCILLOR *and the* SPEAKERS, *who back up to the left, fall to their knees, and stretch out their hands to the right.*)

(KING *enters from the right, pale, very cold, wet, with a cape; goes quickly by the* COUNCILLOR *and the* SPEAKERS, *who are concealed by the* GUARDSMEN, HULTMAN, *and* LUXEMBOURG. *The* KING *enters the cottage, takes off his cape, and stations himself, calm, motionless, before the fire.* ADJUTANT *goes up to the* KING, *who softly gives him an order; whereupon the* ADJUTANT *goes out to the* COUNCILLOR *and the* SPEAKERS, *from whom he receives letters, which he turns over to the king immediately. Respectful silence prevails while the* KING *opens the letters. He glances through*

them and throws them into the fire. Thereupon he summons the
ADJUTANT *with a gesture. Seems to counsel with him about which
road to take. Then he tightens his belt; presses his hat down on
his forehead.* ROSEN *helps him get into his cape, whose collar is
turned up. The* ADJUTANT *goes out; commands: Attention! and
signals toward the right foreground. The* GUARDSMEN *go out in
that direction, in front of the ruined church. The* KING *follows
with quick steps. Then* ROSEN *follows, but gestures to* HULTMAN
and LUXEMBOURG *to stay.* DÜRING *follows the* KING.)

LORD (*to* BURGHER): Why did we kneel?

BURGHER: I don't know! Couldn't do anything else!

FARMER: Was it the King? . . . So he does have something different
from other people. Just as if someone had preceded him and
cleared . . . I cannot understand . . . (*Brushes his knees*) . . .
It was as if someone had knocked my legs from under me
. . . that is to say, it wasn't I who fell to my knees . . .

LORD: So I imagine!

COUNCILLOR: It's the conqueror and the Lord's anointed! Do you
understand that now? . . . No! . . . But you see, that's the difference between us and you!

DWARF (*comes up with an open snuffbox*): While the weather's
improving, we'll take a pinch on that! (*Offers the* FARMER *first*)

FARMER (*takes snuff with pleasure*): Thanks!

DWARF: That's not bad snuff, that! (*Offers the* BURGHER)

BURGHER (*takes snuff*): Thank you!

DWARF: Will it do? (*Offers the* CLERGYMAN) Get your questions
ready!

CLERGYMAN (*pretends to take snuff*): Are you in court service,
dwarf?

DWARF: No, I'm only the court dwarf! He despises me like all others,
but I amuse him! It isn't everyone who does! (*Offers the* LORD)
Help yourself!

LORD: No, thank you!

DWARF: That was a fine fellow; I like that one! We should have more like him! If I offer the councillor some, according to the laws of nature and the rules of precedence, he'd toss the whole box into my eyes, and I don't want that . . .

HULTMAN: What's the idea? Are we to live in this burned-out spot or what?

DWARF: Hultman! Don't ask, but live; live your life minute by minute! No one knows what tomorrow will bring, and after death comes no pleasure.

HULTMAN: Cynic! Epicurean! I ask only where I'm to set the King's table next time; I'm asking neither about tomorrow nor the pleasures of death . . . My lord and King, the very greatest of men and conquerors, is the most perfect of all people born of woman and his slightest wish is my command; his satisfaction is my gospel . . . Now I'm asking where my king commands me to put this table silver that I've dragged about in the cities of Saxony, the countryside of Poland, the plains of Russia, and the pleasure gardens of Turkey . . .

DWARF: Hultman! The sun will soon rise! Save the wear on your tongue . . .

HULTMAN: This silver that I've saved from the siege of Stralsund, from the Danish frigate, from . . .

DWARF: Put on the brakes, Hultman! Put on the brakes, for God's sake, or you'll never get to an end!

HULTMAN: See, the adjutant is back!

ADJUTANT: The King commands the national councillor and the speakers of the estates to return without delay to their posts in the capital and there await His Majesty's further decisions! . . .

COUNCILLOR: Even this!

ADJUTANT: What's that? Any criticism? Has the King the legal right to govern the kingdom as he wishes?

COUNCILLOR: He has! . . . but . . .

ADJUTANT: Did you break your oaths, when you wanted to depose him? Your silence admits it! . . . Go then, and thank God in heaven that he didn't take your heads! *Allez!*

HULTMAN (*to the* DWARF): That was a real man at talking! So these are the traitors who wanted to depose our king because he had reverses! Well, that's what the world is like and the people in it!

ADJUTANT (*to the* COUNCILLOR *and the* SPEAKERS): Go quickly, gentlemen, because other traitors are to be executed here!

DWARF (*to* HULTMAN): That's the skipper of the brig *Snap-Up*,[6] who's to be shot, because he didn't show up at the meeting place.

ADJUTANT: Yes, it is! And the crew are to be flogged!

HULTMAN: And they complain that there isn't law and justice in this country!

(COUNCILLOR *and* SPEAKERS *draw back towards the wing, shaking each other's hands.*)

SKIPPER (*brought in, tied up, by two soldiers*): Let go of me, for Christ's sake, I say; it wasn't my fault that ice delayed me . . . Let me go; I haven't done anything! Let go of me!

DWARF (*tuning his violin*): Don't scream, fellow!

SKIPPER: They want to kill me!

DWARF: Well, are you going to scream about anything as trifling as that?

SKIPPER: I haven't done anything; I don't control the weather and the wind; I can't be an icebreaker. Let me go!

ADJUTANT: Out with him, quick!

SKIPPER (*taken out*): Let go of me! I haven't done anything!

HULTMAN (*to the* ADJUTANT): Have you perceived, sir, if our gracious King has uttered a wish concerning quarters, food, and such things?

ADJUTANT: Yes! You have horses in the next village that will take you into the city, Hultman!

HULTMAN: Fine! Just so I'm told!

DWARF: How about me?

ADJUTANT: You? Who cares about you?

DWARF: Is that my dismissal? Does he have a new dwarf? Am I to be tossed aside? Am I not a deserving man? Wasn't I top dwarf in the kingdom? Luxembourg, the one and only? . . .

ADJUTANT (*as he goes*): There are horses for you in the next village, Hultman!

DWARF: Yes, Hultman, the big liar and the indispensable . . . That's life! Don't depend on princes . . . (*Plays a melancholy saraband by Sebastian Bach.*)

HULTMAN (*as he leaves*): Shame!

DWARF: The one is taken up, the other is left behind . . . Go, steward, and tell your lord that you have seen Luxembourg cast up on a shore where no roses grow . . . (HULTMAN *is now outside. The* DWARF *is alone; looks about; gets up in fury*) Just wait! I am small, and I can only play the violin! But I will play . . . and then, by my life and knife, you will get to dance! You'll get to dance!

CURTAIN

ACT II

The KING's *audience room in Lund.*[11] *To the right a large stove; next to it, a clothes tree; to the left a large table with paper and writing equipment; a large easy chair with a crown and ermine mantle. Two very low and soft armchairs in the center of the floor turned towards the* KING's *place. A tabouret alongside the* KING's *chair. Farthest down to the left an army bed with a blue silk cover.*

*   GYLLENBORG and* HORN *are standing by the fire warming themselves.*

GYLLENBORG: Do you know why we've been summoned?

HORN: No! But then there are new people every day.

GYLLENBORG: Do you think anyone knows the King's plans?

HORN: Does he have any plans?

GYLLENBORG: What a question!

(*Creaking in the beams of the wooden house can be heard. The two men jump and look about.*)

HORN: What was that?

GYLLENBORG: The cold . . . it's getting colder! (*Pause*) Have you ever lived through anything as horrible as this?

HORN: Never!

GYLLENBORG: Have you seen him since he came home?

HORN: I saw him yesterday!

GYLLENBORG: Wel-l-l?

HORN: A dead man, whose spirit is walking the earth. (*Now, from a distance, can be heard the* DWARF's *saraband.*)

GYLLENBORG: What is that infernal music that I've been hearing all morning?

HORN: It sounds like a grasshopper . . .

GYLLENBORG: I think it sounds like the autumn wind blowing between double windows, or like the crying of children. Do you know sixty thousand children have died in the latest children's plague?

HORN: Lucky for them!

(PROFESSOR *steals in from the back. Looks about uneasily; goes up to the stove and examines the damper*)

GYLLENBORG: Who's that?

HORN (*to the* PROFESSOR): Are you going to close the damper before the fire's burned out?

PROFESSOR (*half-aloud, frightened*): There's a flaw in the damper that I should examine!

HORN: Are you the stove maker?

PROFESSOR: They said it smoked, and we've been very much afraid of fire since our city burned down a few years ago! [12]

HORN: Is this a fire inspection?

PROFESSOR: Oh . . . eh! So . . . I'm going to stir up the fire if you'll permit me, gentlemen . . .

GYLLENBORG: Is that fellow bright?

PROFESSOR: You see, this is my house; they have let me stay on in the attic . . . If you gentlemen will keep an eye on the fire, I'd appreciate it! (*Goes toward the right*)

HORN: People in this town look like ghosts!

GYLLENBORG: What can the King want of us?

HORN: He's inscrutable! (*They go toward the back and stop in front of the clothes tree.*)

GYLLENBORG: Look at this coat!

HORN: It's worn white under the belt, and you can see where the sword's been hanging! . . .

GYLLENBORG: There's a button missing!

HORN (*listening*): Quiet!

GYLLENBORG: Think of it, inside this door is the great man, the feared man, the one the monarchs of Europe always have had to take into consideration! Is he tall?

HORN: Hard to tell! He doesn't fit ordinary standards . . . I have seen him large as a Theseus[13] and small as a page! And his face!

GYLLENBORG: What's wrong with it?

HORN: Well, I have seen him with twenty different faces! He isn't *one* person; he is a multitude!

GYLLENBORG: You speak very strangely, but . . . many others have said something like that.

(*The door to the left is opened; they draw close to each other.*)
(FEIF *enters. They observe each other searchingly.*)

FEIF: His Majesty, the King, will be here at once! (*Silence*) I am secretary for the day! (*Silence*) My name is Feif. (*Silence*) May I tell you gentlemen one thing? . . . (*Silence*) People do not inform the King about anything, but only answer his questions, more or less completely according to His Majesty's indication of more or less interest in the answer. (*Silence*) And people do not take the opportunity to tell him anything about the state of the kingdom or express any wishes, because those are well-known matters. (*Silence*) As far as etiquette goes, you sit down when you're told to, either by word or sign. (*Silence*) Finally, may I tell you that the King, who has a sore throat, can speak aloud only with difficulty and therefore asks you gentlemen to excuse him for speaking in whispers? (*Bows and goes out the same way he entered*)

GYLLENBORG: So that was Feif! . . . Used to be apprentice to a hatmaker!

HORN: We've been schoolboys, Gyllenborg!

GYLLENBORG: That's true! (*They station themselves before the fire again.*)

HORN: I'm freezing so that my teeth are chattering!

GYLLENBORG: And it's so dark in here!

HORN: I wish I were half an hour older!

GYLLENBORG: It's as if we could feel his spirit filling this whole room. I have never been afraid before.

(*The* KING *has soundlessly come in from the left reading a paper. He is dressed in his blue-and-yellow uniform, without a sword. Now he looks up from the paper and observes the men from in back of them. He is serious, collected, dignified, and secretive, with an undecided expression on his face, which is sickly ashen gray. When he rustles the paper, they turn and fall to one knee.*)

(*The* KING *gestures for them to rise. Then he sits down in the easy chair, with* FEIF, *who has just entered, by his side.*)

(*The* KING *and* FEIF *glance through some papers. Then the* KING *gestures that the men are to sit down. They sit down in the low chairs, sinking far down, so that they seem distressed.* KING *speaks to* FEIF, *but so softly that only mumbling can be heard.*)

FEIF (*turns to the two men*): His Majesty requests Count Gyllenborg . . .

(KING *makes a restraining gesture to* FEIF *and mumbles again.*)

FEIF: Will you tell His Majesty, Count Horn, all that you know about the widely discussed . . .

(KING *mumbles to* FEIF *again.*)

FEIF: . . . the widely discussed Baron Görtz.

(HORN *rises, looks at* GYLLENBORG *in amazement.* KING *gestures to* HORN *to sit down.*)

HORN (*sits down unwillingly and seems distressed by the low, uncomfortable chair*): Your Majesty's request is certainly a command . . .

(KING *looks down at the table before him; picks up a pen and begins to draw geometric figures*)

HORN: . . . but . . .

FEIF: His Majesty requests what you might call a brief characterization of the person mentioned.

HORN: For a task like that would be needed a closer personal acquaintance with the man, and I have to admit that Baron Görtz is not among my closer . . .

(KING *looks up and fixes his eyes on* HORN *who becomes deeply alarmed.*)

HORN: Well then, according to everything I've heard, Baron Görtz . . . (*Tries to discover with his eyes what the* KING's *opinion of* GÖRTZ *is, and to compare it with the expressions on* FEIF's *face*) . . . that man is . . . an exceptionally unusual personality, and his desire to be unusual can only be measured . . . in its strength . . . by his desire for power.

(KING *draws—without looking up.*)

HORN: They say that he thinks he's the center of the world, that he looks in the papers every morning to see if the destinies of Europe have undergone any change while he has been sleeping, and the learned Swedenborg . . .

(KING *pricks up his ears.*)

HORN: . . . assures us that if Görtz died today he'd set the kingdom of the dead against the heavenly powers.

(KING *quits moving his pen, but does not look up.*)

HORN: This overwhelming desire for honor he conceals . . . tries to conceal beneath a simple exterior and a condescending manner towards his inferiors.

(GYLLENBORG *shows his uneasiness.* KING *becomes red in the face.*)

HORN: Inferiors, whom he actually despises, just as he despises all humanity.

(KING *inclines his head towards his chest.*)

HORN: These outstanding characteristics of Baron Görtz, coupled with his most exemplary insensibility to the sufferings of others, would seem incompatible with a religious spirit, but Baron Görtz is not without religion. One could say that he fears for God, without fearing God.

(FEIF, *until now inscrutable, fixes his eyes with horror on* HORN. KING *puts his fingers to his throat as if he were choking.*)

HORN (*goes on without noticing anything, completely unaware of the unconscious hints*): The learned and pious Swedenborg believes Baron Görtz uses religion as a sort of magic, through which he secures support and power for himself, even in his purely criminal activities . . . for example, in extorting funds, in getting revenge on enemies . . . because he also has the peculiarity of never being able to forgive anyone.

(KING *fixes* HORN's *glance as if he wanted to read his innermost thoughts and to see if he has any mental reservations. His mouth is open, and his upper lip quivers.*)

HORN: In a word, a great weakness . . . disguised so that it seems like a tremendous strength; a convulsive stubbornness that cannot break down his own wilfulness . . .

(KING—*there is a noise from his spurs.* HORN, *as if awakening from a dream and realizing the infernal aspect of the situation, becomes silent with horror. All look at each other with mutual embarrassment, without anyone's quite being able to break the silence. Someone knocks three times on the right door.* KING *mumbles to* FEIF, *who gets up and goes out through the door on which someone knocked.*)

KING (*in a hardly audible voice*): Gyllenborg, do you know the man who was sitting beside me just now?

GYLLENBORG: Secretary Feif! I have only heard Count Tessin[14] comment on him!

KING (*as before*): And . . .

GYLLENBORG: With your permission, and since Your Majesty commands . . . Feif is industrious, good-hearted, honest, clean in his clothes and morals, pure of heart, as well as a loyal Swede.

KING (*to* HORN): What have you heard about Feif, Horn?

(HORN *hesitates.*)

KING: Tell me!

(HORN *hesitates.*)

KING (*significantly*): I didn't believe you were afraid, Horn!

HORN: In the army offices, Feif is considered less competent but more selfish than Piper,[15] as well as coarse, vindictive, faithless, and hated by everyone who knows him!

KING: Can you tell me then, Gyllenborg, what I am to believe about Feif?

GYLLENBORG: Impossible to say, Your Majesty!

KING: Can you tell me then, Horn, what I am to believe about . . . (*significantly*) . . . Baron Görtz?

HORN (*ingeniously*): The same as Your Majesty believes about Secretary Feif!

KING (*smiles*): You may go, gentlemen!

(GYLLENBORG *and* HORN *get up and withdraw backwards.* KING *sketching again*)

ADJUTANT: Baron Görtz!

KING: Let him wait!

(GYLLENBORG *and* HORN *look at each other with embarrassment and go out.* FEIF *comes in again.*)

KING: Let Görtz wait! . . . Tell me, Feif, who is Horn nowadays?

FEIF: Count Horn is a man of honor.

KING: And Gyllenborg?

FEIF: A nobleman in the best sense of the word!

KING: You are a wise man, Feif, because it is wise always to speak

well of your neighbor! By the way . . . have you given the orders
about fatigue duty?

FEIF: Yes, Your Majesty.

KING: Then I'll put Görtz in prison, but I want to talk to him first
and look him right in the eye . . . Here in this document it says
he is the biggest rascal who has ever lived, the crudest charlatan
and so on! That he has conspired with Russia to get me deposed
is enough of a motive for me to make sure of his person! . . .
You may go, Feif!

(FEIF *dawdles.*)

KING: Why are you dawdling, Feif?

FEIF: Excuse me, Your Majesty, is it wise to be alone with such a
frightful enemy as the baron?

KING: I am not alone, Feif; I am never alone . . . Go now!

(FEIF *goes out to the left.*)

(KING *brushes his hand over his eyes as if he were collecting his
memories and his thoughts. Then he takes hold of the bell cord;
stops in the very motion and stares at the right door. Then he
rings.* ADJUTANT *enters.*)

KING: Baron Görtz may come!

(ADJUTANT *goes.* GÖRTZ *enters, slowly, uncertain, searching. He is
an attractive man with the manner of a man of the world; he has
an attractive face, but his left eye is artificial so that as he now
enters from the right his face seems dead—in profile. He falls to
one knee. Pause*)

KING (*looks amazed*): Are you Baron Görtz?

GÖRTZ: Yes, I am!

KING (*gestures*): Get up! What are you looking for?

GÖRTZ (*with emphasis*): My hero, my King . . .

KING (*furious; his voice trembles but does not become louder*):
Have you studied your Machiavelli[16] so badly, Baron, that you
think a king can be won by flattery?

GÖRTZ: Machiavelli? I have never read him!

KING: No? Then you don't know, Baron, how a prince behaves to find out if a rascal is telling the truth or not?

GÖRTZ (*tries to find the right tone to assume*): Can a person learn that sort of thing?

KING: You have associated with kings, Baron, before this?

GÖRTZ (*easily*): Everything has its time, Your Majesty, and even I have had mine. But that is past . . . (*Notices that he has missed the mark; changes his manner quickly*)

KING: The years seem to have given a measure of insight into yourself, Baron!

GÖRTZ: If I?

KING: When you know your own little weaknesses?

GÖRTZ: Little and big, I'm not ignorant about any of them, especially since all the European newspapers have written them up for nearly ten years.

KING: And you admit them all?

GÖRTZ: All of them!

KING: You are an unusual man!

GÖRTZ: Oh no!

KING: You have, for example, the weakness of writing letters?

GÖRTZ: Yes, that was my strength!

KING (*smiles unwillingly*): Preferably to princes, kings, and even emperors . . .

GÖRTZ: In so far as the czar is an emperor!

KING: Well, we've made some real progress! . . . Did you, for example, write this letter to the czar? (*Hands him a letter*)

GÖRTZ (*takes out his lorgnette, examines the letter on both sides*): With your permission . . . I have only one eye and don't see very well. May I ask what it is about?

KING: It is about . . . Baron Görtz' plans to depose the King of Sweden, to unite his nephew and the czar's daughter in marriage, and to name the nephew successor to the Swedish throne.[17]

GÖRTZ: Really! But that's really magnificent! And later on a Swedish prince heir to the throne of Russia! Why, that's brilliant! All difficulties cleared at one blow! Poltava avenged, August driven from Poland, control of the Baltic secured, and Sweden again a great power as at the death of Gustav Adolf! Why, that is colossal!

KING (*brushes his hand across his eyes as if he wanted to free himself from a net*): What was that, Baron—the czar's daughter and Charles Fredrik?

GÖRTZ: Absolutely!

KING: And . . . A-A-August in Poland!

GÖRTZ: August thrown out of Poland on his head! And his short end after that!

KING (*thoughtfully*): Do you know the czar's opinion on this question?

GÖRTZ (*warming up*): The czar's highest wish and most daring dream is to become related to the Swedish royal house and to make old, rotten Poland superfluous at the same time! Poland, which used to be a European outpost against barbaric Russia, isn't needed any more, now that Russia has been Europeanized and itself keeps watch against Asia. It is no longer a question of August or Stanislaus—nonsense! But about Poland or Russia— and consequently Sweden! (KING *sketches. Pause*)

KING (*as if to himself*): If I had a man . . .

GÖRTZ: To send to the czar, yes! . . . If I hadn't messed about as I have, if I did not have such a bad reputation, I would offer my services, because no one else knows the courts of Europe and their secrets as I do!

KING (*sketches and bites his pen*): Do you really have such a . . . bad reputation?

GÖRTZ: Yes, to the extent that no foreign ambassador may associate with me!

KING: Exaggerations, I suspect.

GÖRTZ: No, my soul, if they're exaggerations!

KING: What have you done then?

GÖRTZ: A person plays with luck a little here and a little there . . .

KING: *How* can one . . . how can one . . .

GÖRTZ: Your Majesty knows what people and the world are . . .

KING (*looks up; sternly*): What do I know? (*Pause*) If my poverty-stricken country could only raise an army . . . then I would be tempted to start reflecting . . .

GÖRTZ: Poverty-stricken? Sweden, poor! One of the richest countries in Europe! Doesn't the National Bank[18] have idle capital in quantities, aren't there crownlands to mortgage? Yes, but you have to put up with a bureau which hasn't the slightest notion about big finance!

KING: What's that you're saying?

GÖRTZ: Why, there are millions in idle cash rusting in the vaults of the National Bank; the depositors only demand interest. Well, give them their 4 per cent and throw out the capital at 6 per cent; then you'll gain 2 per cent at once! Capital in this country stands like an ox in its stall all day. Then the balance of trade comes along and says, "Out, ox, to work!"

KING (*laughs softly*): You are amusing, Baron! . . . But you do have one advantage—you see no difficulties?

GÖRTZ: Difficulties? I love difficulties, but a lazy man sees difficulties everywhere! And this blessed country is the land of difficulties because the nation is lazy! If I were a different man . . . well . . . I'd have sixty thousand men afoot within sixty days . . .

KING: Sixty?

GÖRTZ: Sixty thousand!

KING: And what would you do with them?

GÖRTZ: I'd take Norway naturally by way of compensation for Finland.[19] When I can't go east, I'd go west to the Atlantic!

KING (*amazed*): Have you been reading my thoughts?

GÖRTZ: No! But . . . Your Majesty . . . I have been following your dizzying career at a distance; I have lived your life . . . at a distance; lived through your destinies . . . Sire, I am your man, the man you are looking for!

KING (*rises, dignified, furious, and fumbles for the bell cord*):
Görtz! Do not forget who I am and who you are!
(GÖRTZ *looks as if he wants to speak but is interrupted.*)

KING: You have forgotten the point of departure of this conversation—that you are a traitor who has worked for my dethrone-
ment! Do you deny that?

GÖRTZ: Yes!

KING: Have you written that letter?

GÖRTZ: Yes! But it was only a trap which diplomats use!

KING: Write one thing and mean another?

GÖRTZ: Yes!

KING: I do not need to believe that, and for that reason I am making
sure of your person!

GÖRTZ: Then let that be done!
(KING *rings.* ADJUTANT *comes in with letters.*)

KING: What do you have there?

ADJUTANT: Dispatches of the greatest importance!

KING: Give them to me!
(ADJUTANT *hands him the letters and leaves.* KING *sits down and
opens the letters which seem to worry him.* GÖRTZ *stands motionless reading the* KING's *face.* KING *looks at* GÖRTZ *now and then
furtively.*)

GÖRTZ: Your Majesty!

KING: Silence! (*Pause.* KING *gets up and goes out through the door
to the left.* GÖRTZ *looks about uneasily.*)

ADJUTANT (*comes in with two guards*): Are you Baron Görtz?

GÖRTZ: Yes, indeed!

ADJUTANT: In the name of the King I arrest you!

GÖRTZ (*with horror*): Me? For what purpose?

ADJUTANT: To be questioned!

GÖRTZ: What does that mean? Questioned? By torture, perhaps? I
protest!

ADJUTANT: Torture or not . . . that doesn't concern me!

GÖRTZ (*his whole body trembles*): So it's torture! I don't want it!
It mustn't be; I demand a hearing. I am not a Swedish subject!
I have not done anything!

ADJUTANT: I don't know about that! . . . Guards! Do your duty!
(*The* GUARDS *put handcuffs on* GÖRTZ.)

GÖRTZ (*beside himself, but sure*): This you will regret, as sure, as
sure . . . (*He is taken out. Pause*)

KING (*comes in again with* FEIF; *exhausted, he goes over and lies
down on the army bed*): Feif!

FEIF: Your Majesty!

KING: I believe I am ill! . . . Give me the bell!
(FEIF *gives him the bell.*)

KING: Now I have six enemies!

FEIF: Six?

KING: Russia, Poland, Saxony, Prussia, Hanover, Denmark! [20]
(*Pause*) And the czar is outside Copenhagen; you can see his
ships in the sound from the window over there! (*Pause*) Where
shall I get a defense?

FEIF: In a sure peace!

KING: How stupid you are! *One* can't wage war; it takes at least
two! One can't make peace; that takes two at least! (*Pause*) Get
me an army!

FEIF: Impossible!

KING: Money then!

FEIF: Impossible!

KING: Difficulties, the land . . . and the people . . . of difficulties!

FEIF: The country is impoverished . . . and the people!

KING: And that is my fault! Did I cause the plague? Did I cause
the crop failures? Did I cause the fires? . . . Have I declared the
wars? . . . No, I have only defended myself, my country, my
royal inheritance! (*Pause*) Where did that Görtz go?

FEIF: He has been put into prison, I suspect!
(KING *rings.* ADJUTANT *enters.*)

KING: Baron Görtz is to be under detention only in his own rooms! And is to be treated respectfully!

(ADJUTANT *goes.*)

KING: Well, Feif! Tell me one thing. Why should deposits lie idle in the bank vaults instead of being in circulation earning interest?

FEIF: Because the deposits are the property of private individuals!

KING: In the Roman state there were no private individuals but only citizens of the state! And when the state was in danger, property was no longer private but became the state's!

FEIF: That's a dangerous doctrine!

KING: Everything is dangerous to a coward! (*Pause*) If there were one man in this country! (*Pause*) Feif, what do you think of Emanuel Swedenborg?

FEIF: Swedenborg is a frightfully learned man, pious in spirit, pure of morals.

KING: Is he in town?

FEIF: Yes, he's staying with Councillor Polhem,[21] to whose daughter he's engaged.

KING: Ah, is *he* engaged? . . . They do say that he is a little strange!

FEIF: They say he has a great, almost inexplicable influence on the people about him! (*Pause*)

KING: Would you go, Feif, and find Swedenborg and ask him to expect me in an hour . . . at his place!

FEIF: I will, Your Majesty! But . . . can I leave Your Majesty alone?

KING: I am never alone, I've said . . .

FEIF: But Your Majesty's rooms were to be shown to the people this hour to calm their minds from disquieting rumors!

KING: What difference does that make? They may see me, too, if they wish! . . . Now I am going to rest a little! . . . Good-bye, Feif!

FEIF: Does Your Majesty want a doctor?

KING: No, my friend, for my illness there is only one doctor!

(FEIF *goes out to the left.* KING *lies on his back and closes his eyes. Pause.* KING *opens his eyes and rings.* ADJUTANT *enters.*)

KING: Go and find Baron Görtz and tell him that he is free, but that he may not leave the city!

ADJUTANT: Your Majesty, in that case, the door will be un-guarded . . .

KING: That doesn't matter!

(ADJUTANT *leaves*)

(KING *closes his eyes again. The saraband is played on a violin outside on the street.* KING *opens his eyes but does not move.*)

(PROFESSOR *enters from the back on tiptoe without noticing the* KING. *Goes up to the stove and stirs the fire with the poker and tests the damper. Then he goes out on tiptoe through the back.* KING *has turned his head to see who it was, says nothing, but only observes what the* PROFESSOR *does. Then he draws up his arms and puts his hands under his neck.*)

(MAN, *the veteran from Siberia in the first act, comes in from the right, poorly dressed, with a cap on his head and a bludgeon in his hand. Goes slowly up to the* KING'S *cot, stops at the foot of the bed, folds his arms over his chest and stares insolently at the* KING. *The* MAN *has apparently been drinking and has lost his self-control.* KING *lies motionless and looks at the* MAN.*)

MAN: Villain!

(KING *as before*)

MAN: Villain! I said! . . .

(KING *motionless*)

MAN: Can't you talk? (*Pause*) So you're the King of Sweden who lies in bed for seven years while the country is being ruined . . . you're a king, who leaves his capital and his government, who doesn't dare to return to his home and his people up in Stockholm, because he is ashamed of his fiasco! Had sworn, of course, that he would return with an arch of triumph at North Bridge and have a conquered kingdom on every finger! . . . You're ashamed! . . .

(KING *motionless*)

MAN: Do you know where I've come from? . . . From the mines of Siberia, from the deserts of Russia! I met your friends there . . . Piper, Rehnsköld, Lewenhaupt,[22] the ones you left in the lurch when you were down in Turkey playing the fool. But I came by way of Denmark, where I saw your best man, your most faithful servant, Stenbock,[23] working in irons, because you refused to pay his ransom!

(KING *has moved slightly.*)

MAN: Villain! Do you know who I am? . . .

(KING *motionless, but stares at the* MAN)

MAN: Do you remember Krasnokutsch?[24] . . . Do you remember Taube's dragoons? Do you remember the cavalryman, who saved your life and got demoted to the infantry because in his eagerness to serve he prevented the King from saving himself as they put it?

(KING *raises himself on his elbow and stares at the* MAN.)

MAN: Yes, I was Hunger, number fifty-eight, in Taube's dragoons, and that I saved your life I now regret, because if you had gone under, there would have been no Poltava, and we would have enjoyed peace . . . six years of peace by now!

(KING *lies down again.*)

MAN: It has been marvelous to speak out for once! And now we can be just as good friends all the same . . .

(KING *rings.*)

MAN: Yes-s! No one will come, because there's no one out there! Oh yes, there is a lady, a little Polish queen without a throne . . .

(KING *rings.*)

MAN: And a king who used to be powerful protected her and her lord. And the king who used to be powerful was a dashing man who didn't squeeze his shillings . . . There, the deuce, now someone is coming! . . . Then I'm going! . . . You're welcome! Don't mention it! (*Goes*)

(KING *has raised himself and tried to call, but has not managed to get out a word. Rings again.* HULTMAN *comes in from the back.*)

KING (*rubs his eyes*): I believe I've slept! . . . Was anyone here?

HULTMAN: I didn't see anyone!

KING: Hultman! Give me the cavalry list for 1709, Taube's dragoons!

(HULTMAN *goes to a shelf and searches.*)

KING: A blue folio with a yellow back!

(HULTMAN *comes up with the desired folio.*)

KING: Open it to number fifty-eight under Taube!

HULTMAN (*looks in the list*): Number fifty-eight? . . . It says that has been vacant since 1707!

KING: Was it? . . . Look for Dragoon *Hunger!*

HULTMAN (*looks again*): Hunger? . . . An unusual name! . . . It isn't here!

KING (*rubs his eyes*): Then I have been dreaming! . . . That was horrible! . . . Have you been out in the city?

HULTMAN: Yes, Your Majesty!

KING: Tell me something pleasant!

HULTMAN: It is not pleasant in the city; the people are restless!

KING: What are they saying?

HULTMAN: Well . . . what they're saying I don't want to repeat! Not even I!

KING: They're angry with me because I am not dead!

HULTMAN: Oh, preserve us! Good heavens!

KING: And my showing up again has crushed many plans!

HULTMAN: Yes, that's one sure thing!

KING: I believe you, too, have lost your courage, Hultman.

HULTMAN (*with emotion*): Your Majesty! To tell the truth, yes!

KING: Do you believe my saga is over?

(HULTMAN *says nothing.*)

KING (*gets up and walks about on the floor*): So you do believe that! (*Pause*) Is there any more money in the box?

HULTMAN: None!

KING: How is the recruiting going?

HULTMAN: Badly! (*Pause*)

KING (*leaning on the cape of the stove; hides his face in one hand*):
Difficulties! The land of difficulties! (*Pause*) Hultman! . . . Go
out! Find Baron Görtz! And bring him here immediately!

HULTMAN (*hesitates*): Baron Görtz?

KING: Baron Görtz! Immediately!

(HULTMAN *goes.*)

CURTAIN

ACT III

*A square lined with trees, with a well in the center. At the
back ruins of burned houses. Farthest to the left at the back is
GÖRTZ' house with closed green shutters; a Swedish flag and the
national coat of arms above the entrance. This house forms a
corner of the back where an alley starts. Farthest down to the
left a smithy. To the right in the foreground a tavern with tables
and benches outside.*

The MAN (*from Act I*) *and the* DWARF *are sitting at a table
smoking their clay pipes and drinking beer. They are hidden by
several other guests and a sort of arbor.*

DWARF: You didn't let him have it anyway?

MAN: Nah! But I laid down the law to him, so he turned pale, believe me.

DWARF: Why didn't you let him have it? That's what I would
have done!

MAN: It isn't so easy to let him have it! . . . Besides, I felt sorry
for him.

DWARF: Sorry, for him?

MAN: He looked so sick and sad . . . and I suspect he hasn't had such an easy time of it; they're all after him and want money!

DWARF: Well, there'll likely be money now, now that that Görtz has been put in charge of finances!

MAN: Yes, that Görtz! . . . Can you see that the shutters are closed up there in his house?

DWARF: That's plain enough . . . but we don't know what they're up to in there!

MAN: They say that he makes gold like Paykull! [25]

DWARF: Huh! No, he doesn't!

MAN: Whatever they're making, you can be sure it's no good! Think of it, that rascal is the absolute minister of the whole kingdom of Sweden, and the villain is in there with him all day! . . . He's in there now, my friend!

DWARF: Think of it, this baron whom the whole world knows to be a cheat, an adventurer, expelled from every country in Europe, and everyone knows he has conspired to dethrone our King! And there isn't one decent Swede who can tell the King so!

MAN: Who would dare to?

DWARF: There was one, Dean Boëthius,[26] but they put him in prison first and then into the insane asylum! There is one, and that's . . . Emanuel Swedenborg.

MAN: Yes, that fellow! That fellow is a real man! And learned, too! That fellow is educated!

DWARF: You know, I have loved this king, worshipped him; once I kissed his boots . . . but now . . . If I had a barrel of powder, I'd stick it under that house! Not just because he tossed me aside on the highway . . .

(*A* MALCONTENT *comes up to the table.*)

MAN: Sit down! And talk!

MALCONTENT: The skipper of the brig *Snap-Up* has been shot because ice delayed his arrival at Stralsund, and the even more innocent crew has been whipped!

MAN: More!

MALCONTENT: His daughter's in town trying to get an audience with the villain!

MAN: More!

MALCONTENT: The university students have been driven out of their rooming houses and forced into the army!

MAN: Fine!

MALCONTENT: The hired girls and the hired men of the district are tramping the highways because the crown has taken half of their wages as a war levy.

MAN: Excellent!

MALCONTENT: The houses of the burghers are being searched, and all the table silver is being seized against receipts!

MAN: Marvelous!

MALCONTENT: The national councillor and the speakers of the four estates are still trying to get an audience with the King, who isn't receiving . . .

MAN: Tops!

MALCONTENT: . . . because he has locked himself in with that adventurer, who is busy making counterfeit money!

MAN: What'll you give me if I set fire to that house?

MALCONTENT: That's not necessary, for others are sure to do it.

MAN: Anything else?

MALCONTENT: Princess Ulrika Eleonora has arrived to meet her brother . . .

MAN: There's the succession to the throne to boot! The villain's!

DWARF (*begins to tune his violin*): You may not say villain! . . . Well, I just think it is sad to see a great man slowly come down in the world . . . It is sad! (*Plays a couple of notes of the saraband*)

MAN: Why do you always play that sad piece?

DWARF: Because I used to play it for my King, when he was sorely afflicted.

MAN: Listen to that fellow!

DWARF: And a king composed this song of sorrow—Sebastian Bach, the king of the Land of Sorrows and Pain . . . (*Plays the saraband*)

MAN (*to* MALCONTENT): Watch out! People are coming!

MALCONTENT: That's certain!

MAN: You explain, because I've been in the kingdom of the dead and no longer know the living!

(*Women of the upper classes dressed in mourning come in from the right; come up to the door of the* GÖRTZ *house, stop and confer quietly*)

MALCONTENT: The widows of the captured lords . . . I call them widows because the King refuses to ransom their captured husbands, buried alive in Russia and elsewhere . . . The widows Piper, Rehnsköld, Lewenhaupt, Stenbock . . . and others.

MAN: Why doesn't he ransom the prisoners?

MALCONTENT: Some say he doesn't want to; others, he can't! Look at them! . . . I'll bet that he won't receive those women! He's never been able to manage women! The one who is ringing is Countess Piper! But the ones who're most to be pitied are the Stenbocks! Måns Bock, who saved Scania! A wonderful man! But the King says he deserves his fate because he did not obey orders!

(COUNTESS PIPER *rings the doorbell timorously.*)

MAN: No answer from that silent house!

(*The women withdraw timidly in a group through the square to counsel.*)

MALCONTENT: New additions! . . . the widows Bjelke, Boëthius, Patkull, Paykull!

(*Four women dressed in mourning go up to the entrance; one of them rings. A little opening in the door is opened and shut. The women draw back, weeping, their handkerchiefs to their eyes.*)

MALCONTENT: Watch this! . . . Here come the exfavorites! Just look at them! Yesterday, royalists; today, rebels! Rosen, Düring, Sparre and Gyllenborg, Wellingk, Cederhielm, De la Gardie, Mörner, d'Albedyhll, Schwerin, Wrede, Horn, the great Arvid Horn . . .[27]

(*Procession of lords to the entrance.* HORN *rings three times, each time more violently.*)

MAN: See that fellow! He isn't afraid!

MALCONTENT: Because he has a nation behind him! And a future ahead of him!

(HORN *jerks off the bell rope, winds it up, and throws it on the ground. The aperture on the door is opened.*)

FEIF (*sticks out his head*): Whom are you looking for?

HORN: The King!

FEIF: Not receiving! (*Bangs the aperture to*)

(*All on the square murmur.*)

MALCONTENT: Now! . . . The national councillor and the speakers of the four estates!

(*The national* COUNCILLOR *and the* SPEAKERS *enter; go up to the entrance, but are stopped by* HORN.)

COUNCILLOR: So it has gone this far! . . .

HORN: The results of absolutism!

COUNCILLOR (*to the* SPEAKERS): Absolutism, which the little lords insisted on to crush the big lords! There you have it!

MALCONTENT: The thieves are scrapping; the farmer gets his cow back! . . . Quiet! The tramp of horses on Toll Street . . . a courier!

(*A poverty-stricken* WOMAN *with a petition in her hand goes up to the entrance. Looks for the bell rope, and, when she does not find it, knocks on the door. When no one answers, she presses on the aperture and it opens. She simply pushes her petition in and sits down on the steps to wait with her hands folded.*)

MAN: That woman knew how to do it!

COUNTESS PIPER (*comes up to the* WOMAN): What are you seeking?

WOMAN (*simply, humbly*): I'm trying to get mercy for my father!

COUNTESS PIPER: Who is he?

WOMAN: He was the skipper on the boat that was to meet the King off Stralsund. But ice delayed him . . . and though he wasn't to blame for that, he was condemned to death!

(COUNTESS PIPER *strikes her hands together and laments aloud. All who have heard the conversation express their indignation.*)

SAILOR (*comes up to the* WOMAN): Why should you be sitting here?

WOMAN: Yes-s, I should!

SAILOR: No, you shouldn't! Because your father was a rascal.

WOMAN: Should you say that about my father?

SAILOR: He wasn't my father, and since he was a rascal, I say that he was!

WOMAN: But he was my father . . .

SAILOR: But not mine! (*Takes her by the arm*) Come!

COUNTESS PIPER: What do you want of the woman?

SAILOR: That's nobody's business, because she's my wife! (*Murmuring*) And her dad, the skipper, was a traitor who raised a false flag when he saw the Danish frigate, and hadn't any ice in his way at all!

WOMAN: Just think, calling my father a traitor! (*Murmuring*)

SAILOR: When he was! And I know; I was in the crew . . . We were whipped though we were innocent . . . but I'm not complaining, because he's not much of a man who can't take a few lashes for his King. Ah, that's nothing! . . . (*Murmuring*) And sometimes you get it when you don't have it coming, and sometimes you don't get it when you have it coming! (*Murmuring*) And here are so many who should get . . . Yes!

WOMAN: What a wicked man to call my father a traitor! *My* father!

MAN (*who has pricked up his ears and observed*): What a damned unmanageable woman! . . . (*Stretches himself forward to observe something*)

MALCONTENT: What are you staring at?

MAN: Nah, it can't be! . . .

MALCONTENT: What is it? What is it?

MAN: I thought . . . well, it doesn't really matter!

MALCONTENT: What?

MAN (*sits down*): I thought it was my dead wife!

MALCONTENT: Ha, ha! . . . A courier! A courier! News!

(*Movement on the square. All look out to the right.* COURIER *hurries with a great deal of noise across the stage and disappears up the alley at the corner of the* GÖRTZ *house in order to get to the back entrance.*)

HORN (*to the national* COUNCILLOR): Big news!

COUNCILLOR: Any idea what it is?

HORN: Yes! (*They whisper.*)

(*All whisper.*)

WOMAN (*goes to the corner*): My word, I believe one can get in at the back!

MALCONTENT: That's a hell of a woman!

MAN: And so like Karoline!

HORN (*to* GYLLENBORG): What has happened? They're ringing bells and slamming doors in there!

GYLLENBORG: Haven't any idea!

HORN: Is it peace or war?

GYLLENBORG: War, of course! Always war!

(LACKEY *in red livery comes out through the entrance.*)

MALCONTENT: What the hell!

MAN: What sort of parrot is that?

MALCONTENT: Görtz's lackey!

(LACKEY *goes down the steps, turns his back to the square, and steps on the toes of the people standing near him without begging their pardon. Then he lowers the flag to half-mast.*)

HORN: What has happened?

LACKEY (*with his back to* HORN): I don't know!

HORN: Mind your manners! At least!

(WOMAN *has come back and tries to steal in through the entrance.*)

LACKEY (*presses her to the side of the entrance*): Get out of here, you!

WOMAN: I'm going to see the King!

LACKEY: Out of here, woman!

(WOMAN *steals in.*)

MAN: By my salvation, I believe it is Karoline!

MALCONTENT: But she is dead!

MAN: The devil knows!

HERALD (*preceded by drummers who are beating their drums*): Because of the death of His Majesty, the exalted king of France, Louis the Fourteenth, all it may concern are hereby commanded to assume deep mourning for fourteen days.[28]

HORN (*to* GYLLENBORG): There it is! . . . Sovereignty is dead!

GYLLENBORG: And Sweden's only friend!

COUNCILLOR: Now there will be changes in Europe!

LORD: New evil!

CLERGYMAN: And new good!

BURGHER and FARMER: Amen!

HERALD: The square is to be cleared of people since a salvo of mourning is to be fired in honor of His Majesty, the late exalted king of France, besides which the bells in the church towers of the city are to be rung as befits a king . . . without delay!

(*Drums are beaten. The groups disband and go away in various directions, speaking and murmuring.*)

MALCONTENT: Absolutism is done!

MAN: Not yet! But soon! And then?

MALCONTENT: That does not concern us!

DWARF: Then there'll be Tuesday soup . . . the same as on Sunday, but with a little more water added, without butter!

FEIF (*comes out through the entrance, leading the* WOMAN): Go now, my good woman! Your father has been condemned by the court as a traitor . . .

WOMAN: Do the judges, too, call my father a traitor?

FEIF (*angrily*): Well, when he was a rascal!

WOMAN: Think of it . . . judges like that!

FEIF (*shouts*): But your father himself confessed he was a rascal! He has confessed!

WOMAN: That is a lie!

(FEIF *goes in, slams the door shut.* WOMAN *knocks gently on the door. Now the city churches' bells begin to toll in mourning; snare drums and drums are beaten.*)

SAILOR (*comes in again, calls to his wife*): Karoline!

MAN: Now I'm really getting frightened! . . .

MALCONTENT: Is it she?

MAN (*amazed*): I don't know!

DWARF: Sovereignty is dead! . . . God save the king! . . . in any case, though he tossed me aside!

MALCONTENT: In any case! . . . Think of it; I can't get really angry with that man!

DWARF (*as he goes*): Is that really necessary?

MAN: Yes, it is absolutely necessary!

CURTAIN

ACT IV

A large garden. To the right in the foreground can be seen a couple of high open-work iron gates leading to an alley. The gates are partly concealed by trees and bushes. Immediately above is the tent-shaped veranda of the house in which the KING *is living; beyond it the* KING's *desk and chair. In front is the army cot.*

In the middle of the stage is a Tuscan column railing of stone with three pale blue glazed pots. On the middle of the railing is an old white statue of Venus.

To the left can be seen GÖRTZ's *house with its green shutters and its veranda with benches on it.*

At the back a walk along a garden wall with wooden gates decorated with the figures of Spanish knights.

(HULTMAN *arranging the desk.* PROFESSOR *fussing with the flower pots*)

HULTMAN: Aren't you a professor of medicine, sir?

PROFESSOR: Yes, that's right, I am.

HULTMAN: The King is sickly, especially since Baron Görtz left.

PROFESSOR: Ha, ha—has Baron Görtz left?

HULTMAN: Yes, he's over in Copenhagen about money matters and other things, but he's expected back at any moment.

PROFESSOR: Wha—wha—what is the matter with His Majesty?

HULTMAN: Sleeplessness, uneasiness, and irritability.

PROFESSOR: Well, well, well! And the princess is in town waiting to see him . . . his own sister!

HULTMAN: So? Sister? There are many kinds of sisters; I have one who's a shrew and a scold . . .

PROFESSOR: His own sister! . . . And newly wed, too.[29] Listen, Hultman, is it true that the King intends to get married?

HULTMAN: No, I hadn't heard that . . . we don't have time to get married! . . . But it upsets me that it's getting thick with skirts around here.

PROFESSOR: Respect for woman! Hultman! Respect!

HULTMAN: Respect for children, respect for servants, respect for me —everybody demands respect, but everybody takes care not to respect other people.

PROFESSOR: You're a woman hater, Hultman!

HULTMAN: That's right, although it's only half true, as usual . . . Look . . . there comes Doctor Swedenborg with his skirt!

PROFESSOR: The great Polhem's daughter, Emerentia!

HULTMAN: A conceited, stuck-up nitwit who has sworn she'll have the King at her feet! Because she gets students and ensigns to dance to her bidding!

PROFESSOR: Oh no, oh no! But does her sweetheart have the slightest suspicion of her ambitious plans?

HULTMAN: Swedenborg? No! He's blind and deaf like everyone who's drunk with love . . . See, there they are!

(PROFESSOR *and* HULTMAN *withdraw into the tent to the right.*)

(SWEDENBORG *and* EMERENTIA *enter from the walk to the right.*)

SWEDENBORG: My dear, I have to leave you for a while; my King and my country require my services.

EMERENTIA: But you promised that we could celebrate our engagement tomorrow . . .

SWEDENBORG: I promised on the assumption that no higher duties called me. I have to leave this evening . . .

EMERENTIA: Then you don't love me!

SWEDENBORG: What shall I say, what shall I do to show you I love you?

EMERENTIA: Stay until the day after tomorrow!

SWEDENBORG: The King will not let me.

EMERENTIA: Your King, who hates women!

SWEDENBORG: No, but he has his thoughts on other things!

EMERENTIA: May I ask him to let you stay?

SWEDENBORG: No, my dear, the troops are ready to leave, and they're waiting for me!

EMERENTIA: Let them wait!

SWEDENBORG: Let the country and the people wait . . . because of a little girl's whims!

EMERENTIA: A little girl! Watch out!

SWEDENBORG: You have threatened me so often I almost long for the blow! What should I watch out for? That you'll leave me?

EMERENTIA: But you're the one who's leaving me!

SWEDENBORG: Hm! I have to go so that I can come back and stay! But you want to go so you'll never come back! There is a difference!

EMERENTIA: Is the King in there?

SWEDENBORG: Yes, but you're to promise me not to try to get near him.

EMERENTIA: Why?

SWEDENBORG: He isn't receiving!

EMERENTIA: That will be my business!

SWEDENBORG: And mine! Because he would believe that I had sent you, and that would be to my dishonor!

EMERENTIA: That's not the reason; you have another one that you don't want to give!

SWEDENBORG: Promise me you will not try to get to the King!

EMERENTIA: You are afraid!

(SWEDENBORG *is silent.*)

EMERENTIA: I'm not afraid of dreams!

SWEDENBORG: Strange! You say that you love me; I believe you . . . often; but just the same, every word you speak is like a poisoned needle! Is that love? . . .

EMERENTIA: You call me a poisoned needle . . . You have never loved me! . . . Good-bye! (*Goes away on the walk to the right*)

SWEDENBORG (*distressed*): This is love! Earthly love! . . . Heaven above! (*Goes to the walk to the left*)

(KING *comes out of the tent; looks sick and worried.* FEIF *follows him.*)

KING (*sits down at the table*): Feif! . . . can Görtz be back soon?

FEIF: Yes, Your Majesty!

KING: That strange man! When he's present, I find him attractive, honest, faithfulness itself; when he's gone I remember him in the most bizarre forms; he acts ghostlike, repulsive, horrible. (*Pause*) Do you think his calculations are accurate?

FEIF: Your Majesty is a mathematician—I'm not!

KING: His calculations can't be solved with any known formulas . . .

FEIF: What do Polhem and Swedenborg think?

KING: They don't say anything! (*Pause*) The whole city says nothing; the whole country says nothing! A silence as of death is

beginning to close about us! (*Pause*) And besides I am sick!
(*Pause*) The streets are empty; no one comes to call! No one
protests! . . . No one says anything! (*Pause*) Say something!

FEIF: I have nothing to say, Your Majesty!

KING: Nothing? . . . Isn't it soon noon?

FEIF: Your Majesty, it is already afternoon.

KING: Heavens yes; I do remember. (*Pause*) Why don't I ever
see Müllern, Sparre, Gyllenborg any more?

FEIF: They do not dare to disturb you!

KING: Why am I left to myself? Even Hultman goes out of the
way and sulks! . . . If I send for someone, he's ill! (*Pause*) And
this silence! This silence! Once I did have Luxembourg, who
played for me, but he disappeared after Stralsund . . . Get me
a spider to play with! (*Pause*) Do you think the country can
stand ten million token coins?

FEIF: Baron Görtz felt two million would be the maximum!

KING: Oh! . . . Why doesn't the princess want to come when I've
invited her? My sister, I mean!

FEIF: Her Royal Highness made it a condition that her consort, the
landgrave of Hesse, could come along.

KING: The one who is waiting for me to die! So he'll get the throne!
. . . There are others, I suspect, who are waiting for me to die!
(*Pause*) Feif! Go up to the residency and ask the princess to
come to talk about something of importance to her . . . without
the landgrave!

(FEIF *goes out on the left path.*)

KING (*alone, in despair*): My God, my God! Let this cup be taken
from me!

(EMERENTIA *appears on the right path; she has a bouquet of
roses; primps to be attractive; and then appears before the* KING.
*But when she sees him, the expression on her face changes to one
of sympathy and respect.*)

KING (*who has had his face buried in his hands looks up, and, when
he becomes aware of* EMERENTIA, *he does not seem to know if she*

is a dream or a revelation. Then he speaks with embarrassment):
Flowers for me! Why do you give me roses?

EMERENTIA: My hero has received enough laurels . . .

KING: And thorns! The time of the cypress has probably come!

EMERENTIA: Not yet! The myrtle[30] first!

KING (*as if speaking to a child*): Little child, what are you saying?

EMERENTIA: I say? . . . This is what the most beautiful woman in
Europe to whom you turned your back once had to say:[31]

*Charles! Your steadfastness conquers every obstacle; playfully
you add heroic deed to heroic deed; I have tried the cunning of
a thousand plans in vain; but you remain what you were—in-
vincible.*

*But, young hero, when laurel wreaths cover you, when honor
walks ever by your side, happiness alone seems to conceal herself
from you. And no pleasures follow in your path.*

*Tell me why your beautiful eyes, your body which the gods
have molded, has not found a more delightful reward?*

*Forgive my boldness when I have secretly sensed that even the
hero can love.*

*If there is any beauty, who has the power to win the faith of
the greatest of mortals, she would sink at your feet. For her our
altars would burn. Merely open your arms and receive the goddess.*

KING (*has looked at her with glowing eyes*): Thank you, my child!
For awakening the memory of a happy time that's past . . . The
flattery I'll leave at its face value! . . . Tell me what your name
is!

EMERENTIA: The name of a little girl—what can that matter to a
great king?

KING: A little girl can restore self-confidence and the desire to live
to a troubled king.

EMERENTIA: Why is the great king troubled?

KING (*in a fatherly tone*): You little thing! . . . Can you play
chess?

EMERENTIA: Yes, Your Majesty! I can!

KING: Then you shall come and play with me!

EMERENTIA: But if I beat the King, he'll be angry.

KING: No, child, that he'll never be! And you can't!

EMERENTIA: Certainly! . . . I've beaten the great mathematician Polhem!

KING: My Polhem! You! . . . Do you know him?

EMERENTIA: As well as my own father.

KING: Then you know Swedenborg, too? The dreamer!

EMERENTIA: A little!

KING (*stares at her searchingly*): Do you like him?

EMERENTIA: He's boring!

KING (*his face expresses amazement*): Whom do you like then?

(EMERENTIA *casts down her eyes.*)

KING: Shall I guess?

(EMERENTIA *holds her hands over her eyes.*)

KING: Let me see your beautiful eyes . . .

(EMERENTIA *flattered*)

KING: I don't know of anything as lovely as a child's eyes!

(EMERENTIA *grimaces in disappointment.*)

KING: Yes, you are a child compared to me . . .

EMERENTIA (*takes the* KING's *hand which he withdraws*): Like me a little then!

KING: You may be my friend . . . Can you play any instrument?

EMERENTIA: I play the clavichord!

KING: You've learned that from Swedenborg.

EMERENTIA: That ugly person!

KING (*with a strange expression on his face*): Shame!

(EMERENTIA *asks with her eyes.*)

KING: Shame! I said! . . . Do you like me a little?

(EMERENTIA *conceals her face in her hands.*)

KING (*darkens*): Does that mean much?

(EMERENTIA *takes the* KING's *hand and kisses it.*)

KING: Was that the child or the woman?

EMERENTIA (*falls to her knees at the* KING's *feet*): That was the woman!

KING (*gets up, angry*): Emerentia Polhem! Get up!

(EMERENTIA *looks up.*)

KING: *Now you* are lying at the king's feet! . . . Get up, and go! You do not deserve the man who loves you, and for that reason you shall never get Emanuel Swedenborg for your husband! (*Turns his back to her*)

EMERENTIA: Mercy!

KING: Disfavor! . . .

(EMERENTIA, *ashamed, steals out on the path to the right.*)

(FEIF *enters from the left.*)

KING: Speak!

FEIF (*looking after* EMERENTIA): Her Royal Highness will be here at once!

KING: Without the landgrave?

FEIF: Nothing was said about that!

KING: Feif! . . . you have been married?

FEIF: Yes, Your Majesty!

KING: Well-l?

FEIF: Ta!

KING (*smiles*): Well-l?

FEIF (*shrugging his shoulders*): Ta!

KING: That's what you all say, but I never get to know anything!

FEIF: Neither do we!

KING: Maybe there isn't anything . . . to know! . . .

FEIF: Maybe!

(*Beating of drums and clatter of weapons*)

KING: It's the princess! . . . You may go, Feif! . . . (*Goes up to the path to the right.* FEIF *goes into the tent.*)

ADJUTANT (*comes in from the path to the right*): Her Royal Highness! (*Pause*)

(ULRIKA ELEONORA *comes in from the path to the right.*)

KING (*goes up to her, offers her his hand, and conducts her to the table*): Welcome, dear sister!

ULRIKA ELEONORA: Thank you very much, dear brother! (*They sit down.*)

KING: It is a little messy here, but we're living on a war footing. (*The conversation is carried on with pauses and with mutual embarrassment.*)

ULRIKA ELEONORA: War! Let's get a peace footing soon!

KING: Is the landgrave here?

ULRIKA ELEONORA: No, my husband is out hunting!

KING: Well-l! You're happily married, sister?

ULRIKA ELEONORA: Has Baron Görtz gone away?

KING: It has been a long time since you and I saw each other alone.

ULRIKA ELEONORA (*picks at* EMERENTIA's *roses*): Roses, I do believe!

KING: What's new in town?

ULRIKA ELEONORA: Is it true that there's going to be a campaign against Norway?

KING: Does that interest the landgrave? (*Pause*)

(ULRIKA ELEONORA *gives the* KING *a sharp look by way of answer.*)

KING: There have been many changes these past years!

(ULRIKA ELEONORA *says nothing, but plays with her fan.*)

KING: An unusually beautiful fan!

ULRIKA ELEONORA: Have you heard about the latest lampoon, printed in Holland?

KING: Do I have to?

ULRIKA ELEONORA: It is the most vulgar thing I've ever read!

KING: Please don't tell me!

ULRIKA ELEONORA: King David went out on his roof and saw Uriah's wife, Bathsheba; and then he sent Uriah to war!

KING: *Was denn?*

ULRIKA ELEONORA: These are beautiful roses! Lovely fragrance!

KING: Please take them!

ULRIKA ELEONORA: I? Used flowers? No, thank you.

KING (*tosses the roses aside*): Speak plainly, sister, but don't come with gossip, because I won't answer then!

ULRIKA ELEONORA: I had thought . . . that is . . . I had hoped that my dear brother had so much confidence in his sister that he would not conceal his plans when they concern others'—his closest relative's . . . most sacred interests!

KING: Is it the succession to the throne?

ULRIKA ELEONORA: Don't be brutal even if you are a king!

KING (*gets up*): Without circumlocution! Otherwise, I'll be off!

ULRIKA ELEONORA: Yes, you always go when it concerns . . .

KING: Sister! . . . They say you are unhappily married!

ULRIKA ELEONORA: I? Oh no, I am very happy, very!

KING: They say your husband is a pig! And we don't want a pig on the throne of Sweden.

ULRIKA ELEONORA: But fools! As if your favorite Charles Fredrik isn't a fool! But you like fools—for example, that Baron Görtz!

KING: Stick to the subject!

ULRIKA ELEONORA: Charles Fredrik of Holstein, whom you want to put on the throne, is a good-for-nothing, who's controlled by his valet Ropstock.[32] So it will be a valet who will rule Sweden after you die!

KING: Woman!

ULRIKA ELEONORA: Yes, that's how you are! You are very great, but you are stupid! Yes, you are, but why you're great I don't know! For the past eighteen years you've done nothing but what's stupid, and I don't know the name of a single battlefield but that of Poltava, where you ran away. Only defeats and without honor! . . . *That* you got for "woman," you woman-hater!

KING: Careful!

ULRIKA ELEONORA: Of what?

KING: That my sympathies aren't transferred to your husband, who must have a hot hell . . . as all married men do, so far as that goes!

ULRIKA ELEONORA: There! You came out with it! So your sympathies
go out to that beast the landgrave. That I can believe . . . that
dishonorable beast, who treats his wife . . . Yes . . . what . . .
haven't . . . I, had, to suffer . . .

KING: But you were so happy just now!

ULRIKA ELEONORA: Just now? . . . Ha, ha! Just now! he says . . .

KING: Remember I am not married to you!

ULRIKA ELEONORA: How so?

KING: So that you treat me as your brother and your king, and
don't give me bedroom lessons as if I were your husband!

ULRIKA ELEONORA: You, married? . . . Well, why aren't you married? Yes, because you're afraid of women! The hero is afraid!

KING: When I listen to you, I really become afraid! And in these
brief moments I have gained the very greatest sympathy for the
landgrave! I love him . . . almost!

ULRIKA ELEONORA (*weeping in her handkerchief*): Yes, yes, yes . . .

KING: For heaven's sake, don't cry—scold me instead! Tears are the
worst I know!

ULRIKA ELEONORA (*changes her manner*): Since you love the landgrave, make him successor to the throne!

KING: Let me die first! Time enough to choose my successor then!
. . . Sister, perhaps my career will soon have run its course . . .
This is probably the last time we shall see each other!

ULRIKA ELEONORA (*seriously, gently*): Brother, dear, darling, how
you do talk!

KING: Yes, to you, my mother's child, I want to confess that the
position of the kingdom is hopelessly desperate.

ULRIKA ELEONORA: Why, they've been whispering that for a long
time, but they thought that that Görtz . . .

KING: I thought so, too, but . . . he has miscalculated or he doesn't
understand finances . . . I knew all his vices, of course, but I
depended on his superior intellect and knowledge . . . but even
they turned out to be . . . hollow . . .

ULRIKA ELEONORA: Is it that desperate, dear?

KING: Absolutely hopeless! . . . I wish I were dead!

ULRIKA ELEONORA: Can I do anything for you? . . . Is there something . . .

KING: No, my friend! And as for who is to succeed to the throne, leave that in God's hands! . . . Excuse me; I am ill . . . and have to lie down! (*Lies down on the cot*)

ULRIKA ELEONORA (*on her knees beside the bed*): What is it, what is the matter, my dear?

KING: "The moments of life are over, smiling I want to die!" Do you remember what that is? . . . Ragnar Lodbrok in the snake-pit! [33] (*Pause*) They thought I was impenetrable because I did not talk; and I did not talk because I did not drink; because I alone protected my senses among drunkards, they thought I was a fool. (*Pause*) Ulla! Put your hand on my forehead! Now you are like my mother! The only woman I have ever loved, because she was my mother, and so . . . was not a woman to me! (*Pause*) There isn't an act that I cannot defend, but I do not take care of myself! (*Pause*) The apprentice calls the journeyman a tyrant, and the journeyman calls the master a despot. All people in power seem to be despots. They would all like to have power, all of them, if they might, if they could! (*Pause*) Yes, you women! I have stood outside windows and looked into homes; that's why I saw more than others, because the ones who are inside see only their own . . . The most delightful, the most bitter! . . . Love is almost identical with hate! (*Pause*) Now I shall go to sleep! Sleep, the best there is! The next best! (*He falls asleep. The saraband is played in the distance.*)

(ULRIKA ELEONORA *gets up, goes towards the back, and signals to a chamberlain.* CHAMBERLAIN *enters.*)

ULRIKA ELEONORA: Taube, I have the greatest confidence in you for reasons that you alone know! Am I right?

(CHAMBERLAIN *bows.*)

ULRIKA ELEONORA: Find the landgrave at once! Tell him that the situation is favorable for us, and that he is to be ready to go to Norway!

(CHAMBERLAIN *bows and goes.*)

ULRIKA ELEONORA (*goes, a few steps behind him, and then comes in again with the deposed Polish king Stanislaus Leczinski's wife,* KATARINA LECZINSKA): Katarina Leczinska! . . . The meeting that was never granted you, I grant to you now!

KATARINA: So I'll get to see the man who has been playing with my destiny and that of my people . . .

ULRIKA ELEONORA: Hush! He's sleeping, but you're to wait . . .

KATARINA (*steals silently up and looks at the* KING): Is this he?

ULRIKA ELEONORA: My poor brother is ill—he probably won't live long!

KATARINA: Is this he? So far down! . . . As far down as we!

(KING *moves and breathes heavily.*)

ULRIKA ELEONORA (*goes to the right*): He's waking up! Let me expect you at the residency! (*Goes out*)

(KATARINA *places herself with her arms akimbo as if she were waiting for the* KING's *awakening to lay down the law to him.*)

KING (*awakens; raises himself calmly and with dignity and stands up*): Katarina Leczinska! I dreamt about you, perhaps because I was expecting you! . . . Please sit down!

KATARINA: Sire, you were not expecting me!

KING (*angry*): Do you want to say that I am lying? . . . What do you have to say?

KATARINA: I want to ask you, sire, where my husband and my children are!

KING: Be so good as to lower your voice when you speak with a monarch.

KATARINA: Be so good as to use another tone when you speak with a woman!

KING: A woman? Bah! . . . That sovereignty I have never acknowledged! . . . However, to help you with the audience that I want to make brief, I will deliver your message so that it doesn't get entangled with talk! . . . Please sit down!

KATARINA (*raging*): And this I'm to listen to!

KING: You will listen, and the King will talk! . . . So where your husband and your children happen to be does not concern me! . . . But, when I chose Stanislaus, your husband, as king of Poland, I believed he was born to rule . . . I was mistaken, because he lacked the courage to use the power the nation had given him. He was born to obey . . . so he had to go! . . . He did that with pleasure, incidentally; yes, he ran! Since then I have assigned subsidies to him and his family . . . about one hundred thousand dalers a year . . . without having any obligation to do so! That these means have not been regularly forthcoming is not my fault, nor anyone else's, because there were no means, and, where there isn't any, there isn't any! Now there is! So go to the treasury and take it!

KATARINA: King Stanislaus . . .

KING: Stanislaus could not govern any more than King August who let himself be ruled by women . . . The audience is over! (*Rings*)

   (ADJUTANT *enters.*)

KING: Let Doctor Swedenborg come in!

KATARINA: That is a man!

KING (*to the* ADJUTANT): Doctor Swedenborg! . . . Escort the woman out!

   (KATARINA *goes.* KING *puts a hand to his forehead as if he had a headache.*)

   (SWEDENBORG *comes in; looks worried*)

KING: Emanuel! . . . Are you ready to go to Norway with the engineer's corps?

SWEDENBORG: Your Majesty!

KING: Tonight, this very evening? . . . I know that your engagement was to be announced tomorrow . . .

SWEDENBORG: It's my happiness that's involved . . .

KING: Happiness? . . . A woman! Always a woman comes and takes away my best man! Emanuel! Your country is calling you; your King begs you; follow us!

SWEDENBORG: The duties of my heart are sacred . . .

KING: Doesn't your heart beat for king and country, first of all?

SWEDENBORG: Your Majesty!

KING (*with one knee on an armchair*): It's Emerentia! Listen to me, who is Emerentia?

SWEDENBORG: She is an angel!

KING (*rocks the chair*): This is the most inexplicable of all the ailments of the mind! Love! Is she an angel?

SWEDENBORG: Yes!

KING: Emanuel! Even if it should cost me your friendship, you are going to hear it! . . . Emerentia was here a little while ago!

SWEDENBORG: Here? In spite of my pleadings?

KING: She is not the woman you are going to marry! . . . Gossip had prepared me . . . She had sworn she would have me at her feet. Well, her attempts were rather simple . . . and I'll say nothing about them . . . but she lowered herself to speaking ill of you, ridiculing you!

(SWEDENBORG *weeps*.)

KING: There! Now he's weeping! . . . You know, boys, now I've had enough of your skirt stories . . . Does it hurt so much? (*Pats him on his back*) Emanuel, pull yourself together and be a man! . . . You, a soothsayer, born for great deeds and great dreams, what do you have to do with either women or wine? Are you going to put your head in a lap and let her clip the hair of your strength?

SWEDENBORG: I have promised her to be faithful . . .

KING: But she broke her promise when she was faithless . . . faithless as a lady's man like King August . . . Up! Emanuel! Honor and duty call you!

FEIF (*comes in from the tent*): Excuse me, Your Majesty!

KING: What is it?

FEIF: Görtz has returned!

KING: Bring him here! . . . Emanuel, go in there and wait!

(SWEDENBORG *is going into the tent.*)

KING (*to* SWEDENBORG): If they don't get them, they weep, and if they get them, they cry, too! . . . A strange game, that! The game of tears or the game of fools! . . . No, wait! . . . Stay here and listen! . . . The one who's coming now is for you, Emanuel . . . Emanuel, that means God be with us!

(SWEDENBORG *stays.* GÖRTZ *comes in hastily from the left.*)

(*At the iron-grill gate people now gather; among them are the* MAN *from Act I, the* MALCONTENT, *and the* WOMAN *from Act III. They are all silent, but horrible to look upon.*)

KING: Speak! But quickly!

GÖRTZ: Everything is lost!

KING: In what respect?

GÖRTZ: Ruin, bankruptcy! The country is aflame! . . . They were about to kill me!

KING: Is it the token coins?

GÖRTZ: The token coins and their consequences! But who has put out twenty million instead of two?

KING: Twenty? Good God! I thought it was only ten! I have seven on my conscience that I'm certain of! But who has put out the other ten?

GÖRTZ: Who? No one knows, but now the river of green copper is spreading out and coloring and poisoning the whole country!

KING: Great God! We have become counterfeiters against our will!

GÖRTZ: They're already threatening me with the scaffold!

KING: Not as long as I'm alive!

GÖRTZ: But, what's worse . . . the most popular man in the country for the moment is the landgrave of Hesse!

KING: The landgrave? My brother-in-law! How has he become that?

GÖRTZ: Hate always ends by loving . . . somebody else! And he is promising . . . freedom! [34]

KING: What a word!

(*Shabby-looking men and boys begin to gather by the wall at the back. They appear silently, unnoticeably, and sit there one, two, three, but are not noticed yet by the people on the stage.*)

GÖRTZ (*uneasy*): Something is happening that makes me uneasy but that I don't understand . . . There's a smell like that of poor people's clothes . . .

KING: Do you see anything? I see nothing, but I hear this terrible silence! . . . Wait a moment, so I can think! (*Pause*)

KING (*sits down—in despair*): Does he promise freedom?

GÖRTZ: Your Majesty! Don't desert me! I am not to blame!

KING: We're all a little to blame, no doubt, but the intention was good . . . fairly good this time! . . . What are you afraid of?

(GÖRTZ *looks about without seeing anything definite. Pause.* KING *pulls himself together and rings.* ADJUTANT *enters.*)

KING: My sword! My cape! And my hat!

(ADJUTANT *goes after them.*)

KING (*gets up*): Görtz! Now I'm going to the residency to find the landgrave of Hesse whom I have named general of the army.[35]

GÖRTZ: When did that happen?

KING: Now! Just now! . . . Then I'll be off already this evening for the field . . .

GÖRTZ: And I?

KING: You'll go along!

GÖRTZ: Against Norway?

KING: Against . . . the enemy . . . whoever wants to be . . . toward a victory . . . or certain defeat! (*To* SWEDENBORG) Now you'll certainly come along?

SWEDENBORG: Now I'll accompany Your Majesty!

KING (*points at the statue of Venus*): And not that goddess! . . . Görtz, conduct us out, your way!

(ADJUTANT *enters with sword, hat and cape.*)

KING (*puts on these; seems to be trying in vain to find words. Pulls on his gloves*): I should have said something to Hultman . . .

but, it doesn't matter . . . So, we'll go then! (*Goes through*
GÖRTZ' *house followed by* GÖRTZ *and* SWEDENBORG)

(*Now the iron-grill gate is opened, and shabby figures steal in,
silent, ghostlike, curious, and fingering everything; the figures by
the wall silently join them.*)

CURTAIN

ACT V

Before Fredriksten Fortress[36] *in Norway. Towards the top of
the background can be seen a part of the fortress. The roof resembles a large, black sarcophagus. Below on the terracelike terrain
trenches and breastworks. To the left to the front of the foreground a simple table with two field chairs; next to them, the*
KING's *army bed in blue and yellow silk under a tent roof. To the
right of the bed a campfire. Next to the bed are lighted torches.*

*To the left in the background there is another campfire with
chairs near it.*

*To the right in the background there is a third campfire with
chairs near it.*

To the right in the foreground is Secretary FEIF's *table lighted
by a large lantern.*

*It is evening; there are moonlight and rapidly moving clouds,
and it is chilly.*

GÖRTZ *is sitting on a cannon not far from the* KING.

Wearing his cape, the KING *is lying on his bed staring into the
fire.*

HULTMAN *is tending a kettle over the fire with the help of boy
cook's assistants.*

FEIF and SWEDENBORG *are sitting at* FEIF's *table.*
In the background officers of various ranks are walking.
People can be seen passing the campfires; among these are wagon-train people.
Farthest down to the right on some military hampers in a hollow sit the MAN, MALCONTENT, *and the* DWARF.

SWEDENBORG (*to* FEIF): Isn't it as if everyone were waiting for something?

FEIF: Yes, I think they're planning to storm the fortress towards morning.

SWEDENBORG: That isn't what I meant! . . . Have you noticed what the roof of the fortress looks like, Feif?

FEIF: This country definitely can't be conquered.

SWEDENBORG: I suppose someone protects it, too!

FEIF: Even if we get the fortress, what good will that do us? You can't bombard mountains, and besides half the people live on the sea! . . .

SWEDENBORG: The King seems to wage this war as if he were trying to keep busy while he's waiting for something . . .

FEIF: And Görtz seems to be waiting to be blown sky high! See how he's sitting—on the cannon. A lot of people would like to light the powder! . . . And at headquarters the landgrave and the duke are waiting for the throne; Arvid Horn is waiting for the landgrave and freedom; Gyllenborg is waiting for the duke and absolutism . . . What is the king waiting for?

SWEDENBORG: Who knows! . . . See how he's lying staring into the fire! A great rich life is passing in review . . .

FEIF: Has passed by . . . a great man!

SWEDENBORG: Great, not great! Can we give the measure of a man with a few small words? . . . Are you tired, Feif?

FEIF: We all are!

SWEDENBORG: Yes, perhaps!

FEIF: It's the first Sunday in Advent today! Soon it will be Christmas!

SWEDENBORG: And New Year's! . . . Poor Görtz!

FEIF: He sits there with his one eye as if he were sighting with a gun . . . It certainly is strange that the King has surrounded himself with one-eyed people these last few years!

SWEDENBORG: Oh no!

FEIF: Yes, indeed! Frölich, Müllern, Grothusen, and Görtz[37] see only with one eye!

SWEDENBORG: It would be amusing if there weren't a hidden meaning in it!

FEIF: Bah! Pure chance!

SWEDENBORG: No, Feif . . . but that you'll never understand . . .

FEIF: Dreams, Swedenborg, I don't understand!

SWEDENBORG: Sh-h, here come great lords! . . .

FEIF (*looks about*): Horn and Gyllenborg!

(HORN *and* GYLLENBORG *enter the foreground from the right.*)

HORN (*looks towards the* KING): Is he asleep?

GYLLENBORG: No, his eyes are open—he's looking into the fire!

HORN: Gyllenborg! We are not friends, but for the sake of our country we must agree!

GYLLENBORG: An armistice, Horn! Gladly!

HORN: It's not a secret that our King is physically and spiritually worn out—in a word, what they call . . . done for! And it is strange that we don't notice his presence any more or bother about him! If there are any rumors going about the camp I don't know, but there seems to be a silent agreement by everyone that something has to happen here . . . that we have gone this far, but shall go no farther. We're expecting a flash of lightning from heaven, an omen, an earthquake—yes, there are even those who have dreamed about . . . a shot! . . . And all this has become so clear to everyone, for no good reason, that at headquarters horses stand saddled and couriers are ready to mount so that they can be on their way.

GYLLENBORG: Where?

HORN: To Stockholm, of course! (*Notices that he has blundered and gives* GYLLENBORG *a sharp look*) Gyllenborg, don't abuse my confidence!

GYLLENBORG: Not at all! My hand, my heart! . . . Go on!

HORN (*carried away by his eloquence*): That man, who is lying there waiting for his journey to the grave—for he is dead—was once the man of destiny . . . and success upon success attended him as long as he walked the paths of justice. But after that, when he wanted to walk his own paths eighteen years ago and to control the destinies of people and nations . . . then destiny took him by the ear and played blindman's buff with him! And now he stands . . . or lies divided against himself! He has wasted eighteen years to keep one vow—that Peter of Russia and August of Poland be exterminated from the earth! His whole life has revolved about these two poles! And now . . . now he's negotiating to get related by marriage to the Russians . . . one day, and for friendship with Poland, the next . . . all this while he has lain down in Norway! In Norway! . . . And this paradox that looks like a colossal hoax. He wanted to raise a strong Poland against Russia, but then he broke up Poland and did the work of Russia! Wanted one thing and did another! That is how destiny plays with those who want to play the part of destiny!

GYLLENBORG: You who are so eloquent, Horn, can't you try to explain that to the King?

HORN (*fixes* GYLLENBORG's *glance and continues*): No! I do not want to speak with him; he has insulted me, and I do not find him sympathetic!

GYLLENBORG: To what do you attribute all these misfortunes of the King and of the country?

HORN: Absolutism, of course!

GYLLENBORG: Absolutism isn't so bad, if it only gets into the right hands! Eh?

HORN: I don't understand at . . .

GYLLENBORG (*disingenuously*): No?

HORN: I don't understand at all!

GYLLENBORG: Try! Why, you do have such a good head!

HORN: Someone told me—no one shall have Gyllenborg for an enemy, but the devil himself must be his friend!

GYLLENBORG: You're swearing, Horn?

HORN: Yes, in your company!

GYLLENBORG: In good company a person can show his colors!

HORN: I don't play cards!

GYLLENBORG: We'll meet in Stockholm then?

HORN: That I promise! . . . If only . . . this comedy were over! . . . What a King!

GYLLENBORG: Sh-h!

HORN: He's ashamed of Görtz; doesn't want to talk with him! But doesn't dare to let him go!

(*Now the scene begins to be lighted occasionally by flares sent up from the fortress.*)

GYLLENBORG: Now they'll soon start shooting again!

HORN: Too good to be true! . . . Now he's moving! (HORN *and* GYLLENBORG *go slowly towards the back of the stage.*)

(*The* KING *gets up from the bed; gestures that he does not want* HULTMAN's *help. Comes upstage and looks at the fortress. Then goes up to* FEIF's *table, where he sits down.*)

KING (*tired, indifferent*): The mail!

(FEIF *gives him letters.*)

KING (*opens letters and glances at them; stops with one*): It is miserable! . . . That raving woman whose father was shot as a confessed traitor because he had betrayed his ship has succeeded in convincing the French ambassador . . . Isn't it as if lies had a guardian angel? (*Pause*) And this! Katarina Leczinska says I've laid hands on her! (*Pause*) And the princess . . . only women the whole way! . . . And they were the ones who hated me because I did not want to acknowledge their power . . . It is too much! (*Pause*) Here is a life saver! It will interest Emanuel! Just think of it, every day I get letters from unknown soldiers, who demand money for having saved my life . . . When I die

I suppose there'll be a host of them who'll boast that they took
my life! (*He reads on.*) No, it is *too* much! . . . The story of
David and Uriah, who was sent to war . . . Emanuel is supposed to be Uriah . . . Hu! (*He rolls the letters into a ball.*)
The whole of life is like this ball, a web of lies, mistakes, mis-
understandings! To hell with it! . . . Forgive me for swearing!
(*Throws the ball into the closest fire. Pause*) I cannot fight with
lies and the father of lies . . . My own sister . . . Certainly I
haven't been any angel, but so devilishly black I wasn't, either!
Let the people amuse themselves! The Sabbath ended at six
o'clock! (*The saraband is played.*) Who is playing my saraband?
. . . There is someone behind the hamper over there! . . .
Come forward, musician!

    (DWARF *comes forward.*)

KING: Luxembourg! No! Where have you been? Eh? You ran away
from me after Stralsund!

DWARF (*on his knees*): Your Majesty, I did not leave, but I was
dismissed . . .

KING: Never by me! I have asked for you several times, but there
was always such a hurry! . . . Have you believed I threw you
out?

DWARF: Yes, Your Majesty . . .

KING: There you see! In the meanwhile you've gone about spreading slander about me, I suppose . . . and perhaps . . . perhaps
organized the mischief at my house down in Lund?

DWARF: Mercy!

KING: That is ugly! . . . Go to the wagon train and play now, you
little fool! . . . *Syllogismus perversicus:* I have *not* thrown out
my dwarf musician, *ergo* he goes about slandering me! March!

    (DWARF *wants to speak.*)

KING: No, you may not speak! March!

    (DWARF *goes toward the back.*)

KING (*to* SWEDENBORG): Life is like that; what can death be like?

SWEDENBORG: Nature is consistent!

KING (*looks about himself*): Are they shooting from the fortress, or what is it that's singing about my ears?

SWEDENBORG: The night wind, I suspect . . .

KING: The glass in the lantern just broke . . . They must be shooting . . .

SWEDENBORG: We ought to be able to hear it!

KING (*gets up in anguish*): I do not know . . . but I would like a glass of wine! . . . Hultman! . . . You see, now he's gone! When I need him! . . . No, no, don't go . . . Feif! . . . Let it be! . . .

(ADJUTANT *comes in with a dispatch.* KING *reads it and is on the verge of collapse; goes up to* GÖRTZ *and shows him the dispatch and then gives it to him.* GÖRTZ *makes gestures of despair. Pause*)

KING (*to* SWEDENBORG): Good night, Emanuel! Now I shall start the assault!

SWEDENBORG: Your Majesty, for heaven's sake . . .

KING: Good night! (*Gestures to him with his hand and goes up towards the back and then out to the right*)

SWEDENBORG (*over to* GÖRTZ): What was it?

GÖRTZ: I cannot say it! (*He is overwhelmed with questions.*)

SWEDENBORG (*goes to* FEIF): What do you think, Feif?

FEIF: Something's gone wrong again!

SWEDENBORG: But what?

FEIF: See, if he only turns his back, everything will break up . . . Just look! Transportation men and vagabonds! Royal councillors and generals!

SPARRE (*enters, goes up to the* ADJUTANT): Where is the King?

ADJUTANT: He went up into the first trench!

SPARRE: Good lord! (*Goes out to the right*)

DE LA GARDIE (*enters, goes up to the* ADJUTANT): Has the King gone?

ADJUTANT: The King went to the first trench to . . .

DE LA GARDIE: But they're shooting from the fortress! (*Goes out to the right*)

MÖRNER (*enters*): Where in Christ's name is the King?

ADJUTANT: He's in the first trench. (*A flare from the fortress lights up the stage at the back. The* KING *can be seen up in the trench signaling downwards with his yellow glove.*) There's the King!

MÖRNER: Heaven preserve us! (*Goes out*)

FEIF: Do you see him?

SWEDENBORG: Yes! He's on his knees as if he were praying!

FEIF: Praying? What is he looking for up there?

SWEDENBORG: What he's looking for! . . . That strange man!

FEIF: Have you ever understood his destiny?

SWEDENBORG: No, and we'll probably never understand it! I have never understood *one* human destiny, not even my own insignificant one.

FEIF: Are you aware that we are talking as if he were dead?

SWEDENBORG: He *is* dead!

(*A flare lights up the stage and expires with a report. Everyone on stage is silent as if in death, and all look up towards the fortress. The* MAN *and* MALCONTENT *stand watching* GÖRTZ.)

FEIF: I feel as if we, too, were standing waiting for something.

SWEDENBORG: Not the assault, though?

FEIF: No!

SWEDENBORG: The will of God be done!

(*Pause*)

CRY (*from above*): The king is shot!

CRY (*from below*): The king is shot!

SAILOR: The greatest of all Sweden's kings is dead! God save us!

MAN: Is the villain dead?

MALCONTENT: He is dead! And now I forgive him!

MAN: Think of it, I couldn't get really angry with that fellow! A devil of a fellow all the same!

SWEDENBORG: God be merciful to his soul! . . . But where did the bullet come from? [38]

FEIF (*points to the fortress*): From up *there!*

SWEDENBORG (*points to heaven*): From up *there!*

FEIF: Let us believe that!

SWEDENBORG: And if it didn't, it should have come from there!

(*Everything breaks up. The* MAN *and* MALCONTENT *throw themselves upon* GÖRTZ *and drag him out. All rush out in confusion; the campfires go out; the torches and the lanterns are carried out. The stage becomes dark. Finally a large lantern can be seen up in the trench.*)

CURTAIN

Notes on
'Charles XII'

WHEN CHARLES XII came to the throne in 1697, Sweden was one of the great powers; when he was killed at Fredrikshald in 1718, Sweden had lost most of its territorial gains of the preceding century and a half and was at the mercy of its enemies. How much of the disasters that struck Sweden during his reign can be attributed to Charles himself no one knows; at least, there are no two historians who agree on the matter. Certain it is that not all the harm was done by the king, who has been Sweden's hero king to his admirers and a villain and a destroyer to those who have not admired him.

The Estates' declaration of the fifteen-year-old Charles of age and consequently absolute ruler of Sweden was one mistake. His training which had emphasized that he was responsible for his acts to no earthly power was another. When his three neighbors—Fredrik IV of Denmark, August II of Poland, and Peter I of Russia—attacked his country and its ally Holstein without provocation in 1700, Charles behaved like a military genius; within short order, he forced Denmark to make peace, and with a force of 10,000 men defeated Peter's army of 40,000 at the Battle of Narva in 1700, and, within a few months, had defeated August at Riga. Charles could have had peace with his neighbors then, but he refused to consider peace with August. He spent three years in his Polish war, winning victory after victory, deposing August and having the Poles place Stanislaus Leczinski on their throne; and then had to spend three years more to secure Stanislaus' position. Then in 1708, Charles turned against Russia only to find Peter's classically Russian method of defense—the scorched earth policy —highly effective; in the summer of 1709 came Charles's first major defeat—the Battle of Poltava. Charles fled with some two thousand of his men to the Turkish-controlled Bender near the Black Sea; the major portion of the Swedish army surrendered to the Russians; most of the Swedish soldiers were taken as prisoners to the interior of Russia or Siberia. Not until peace was concluded in 1721 did most of the survivors see Sweden again.

The Danes and August seized the opportunity for revenge; the Danes overran Skåne, but General Magnus Stenbock, its governor, freed Skåne of Danes in short order. Russian forces, however, occupied all of the Swedish possessions on the eastern shore of the Baltic. Unfortunately for Sweden, Stenbock's army was ordered to attack Poland; Stenbock did bring the army across the Baltic, but without having secured Charles's approval turned against the Danish army and pursued it into Holstein-Gottorp, where, because of lack of supplies and widespread illness among his men, he was forced to surrender to the Danes in 1713.

In the meanwhile, Sweden proper was reduced to extreme want and distress because of unusually bad and unfavorable weather year after year, resultant famines, the plague which raged violently in the years about 1710, labor shortages, and economic chaos.

Why Charles stayed in Turkey until 1715 in spite of his country's need is debatable. Perhaps he had hoped to overcome the Russians at the head of a victorious Turkish army. Why he did not make serious efforts to secure peace is also debatable. Charles felt responsible to himself alone; he did not confide even in his advisers.

In the period of Charles XII's life that Strindberg has telescoped in his play—from his return to Sweden at the end of 1715 to his death at Fredrikssten in 1718, Charles was not inclined to peace which would involve the surrender of any part of the Swedish territory he had inherited. Instead, with the ingenious help of Baron Görtz of Holstein, he set out to raise the means to bring a Swedish army into existence— Strindberg refers to the main methods—and, that having been done, to invade Norway in the fall of 1718 as the first step in making up for the defeats and losses of the preceding years. How practically everyone in the Swedish forces and throughout the country felt about the situation and about his death, Strindberg has conveyed in the play. The results of his career were tragic for both Charles and for the Swedish people.

See "The House of Vasa" on page 82. When Charles XII died, his younger sister, Ulrika Eleonora, was *elected* queen by the Estates after they had eliminated absolutism and set up a government that was party-controlled and in which the ruler was little more than a figurehead. Queen Ulrika Eleonora tried to have her husband, Fredrik of Hesse, accepted as king and "coruler," but instead, the Estates made Fredrik king and sole "ruler" in 1720. A good-natured, far from brilliant man who liked women and hunting, Fredrik I was both the first and last of his line. Having no legitimate children, he was succeeded in 1751 by Adolf Fredrik, the father of Gustav III. See page 269.

THE CHARACTERS

Charles XII (1682-1718) came to the throne when he was fifteen years old and was declared of age almost immediately by the Estates. By nature intelligent and courageous, Charles had been reared to love justice and moral principle as well as to regard himself as the sole ruler of his people responsible in no way to the Estates. The attack of the northern alliance—Russia, Poland, and Denmark—on Sweden demonstrated to the whole world that Charles was a military genius that would have to be reckoned with; not until his death did his enemies feel secure.

The simplicity of his mode of life—avoiding pointless amusements and sharing the hardships of war equally with his men—his courage, his firmness of purpose, and his fundamental patriotism have endeared him to many Swedes from his own day to ours. His stubbornness, his willingness to gamble without consideration of the loss of human lives, and the tragic results—for Sweden—of his whole reign have made many Swedes willing to accept his foreign nickname, Madman of the North.

His relationship with women has puzzled many. He never married, and apparently never seriously considered doing so. For accounts of Charles and his time, see Verner von Heidenstam's *The Charles Men* or Voltaire's biography (1731).

Princess Ulrika Eleonora (1688-1741), the youngest and least favored

child of Charles XI, was neglected in her childhood and developed
into a shy woman who lacked self-confidence and the ability to establish
close relations with other people. Her parents died when she was very
young, and her paternal grandmother concentrated her affections on
young King Charles and the older sister Hedvig Sofia, and, after the
latter's death, on Hedvig Sofia's son, Charles Fredrik of Holstein, who
rarely if ever treated Ulrika Eleonora with respect. Throughout her life
she hated her nephew and did everything she could to prevent his succession. Her marriage to the handsome Fredrik of Hesse in 1716 was
unhappy; they had no children; and Fredrik was an extremely faithless
husband. Yet after her accession as queen, she tried to have him declared king and coruler, and in 1720 acquiesced in his election as king
and in having what little power she had had taken over by him. She
was generally admired for her moral life, her sense of justice, and her
observation of the conventions of social conduct.

Baron George Henrik von Görtz (1688-1719), a Holsteiner, was a
handsome, brilliant, resourceful and calculating man of the world who
had the gift of talking and writing persuasively; he rarely if ever suffered from pangs of conscience. After Charles's return from Turkey,
Görtz became the king's major adviser and leading minister. As SB
(VII, 384-385) says: "Actually Görtz was more than anyone else created
to be Charles XII's minister. Courage for great undertakings, perseverance in executing them, a defiant play with all difficulties and all opposition, and openhandedness approaching wastefulness—all these were
parts of the nature of both." It was Görtz' resourcefulness and schemes
that permitted Charles XII to raise his last army and to conduct his
last military campaign. After the death of the king, Görtz was arrested
and executed after a trial that was anything but just. While a young
man, Görtz had lost one eye.

Count Arvid Horn (1664-1742), one of Sweden's greatest statesmen,
saved the life of Charles XII's grandmother, Dowager Queen Hedvig
in 1696, was favored by Charles XI as a result, became one of Charles
XII's best military men until 1706 when he entered the government
service in Stockholm. There, without incurring the king's active dis-
pleasure, Horn became the leader of the men in the Estates who wished
to abolish absolutism. From 1720 to 1738, Arvid Horn was for all practical purposes the ruler of Sweden. These eighteen years were, without

question, happy years for Sweden and the Swedes for they were years of peaceful efforts to restore Sweden to order and a measure of strength.

Count Karl Gyllenborg (1679-1746) was sent by Charles XII to London first as a secretary in the Swedish legation (1703-1710); upon the death of Leijoncrona, the Swedish minister, Gyllenborg was made resident and then in 1715 minister. Married to a rich British widow, Gyllenborg became involved in the plot to restore the Stuarts, was arrested in 1717, was released in 1718, and was allowed to return to Sweden. Politically, Gyllenborg was Horn's opponent; Gyllenborg favored absolutism and the succession of Charles Fredrik, Horn a limited monarchy under Ulrika Eleonora. In 1738, he succeeded Horn as the real ruler of Sweden but soon demonstrated his lack of statesmanship. He was, incidentally, a poet and a dramatist. The best Swedish play of the first half of the eighteenth century was Gyllenborg's *The Swedish Fop* (*Den svenske sprätthöken*). He was at the time Strindberg presents him a tall, handsome man of the world with exceptional social and literary gifts.

Baron Casten Feif (1661-1739), one of Charles XII's most loyal subjects, came of humble origins, was as a child apprenticed to a hatmaker, but managed through his general ability and knowledge of Finnish to gain government employment. He served for a time, as Strindberg says, as the king's secretary.

Queen Katarina Leczinska (1677-1766) was the wife of Stanislaus Leczinski, the Polish nobleman who with the help of Charles XII was elected king of Poland as Stanislaus I in 1704. The young king had many excellent qualities, but will power and perseverance were not among them. He was deposed in 1709. He and his family were, as Strindberg suggests, supported financially by Charles XII; they lived in Sweden for many years.

Emanuel Swedenborg (1688-1772), the natural scientist, philosopher, founder of Swedenborgianism, and mystic, was the son of Bishop Jesper Svedberg of Skara. A genius, he had plans for submarines, steam engines, airplanes, a new kind of cannon, and other inventions that have since been realized. He was an assistant of Christopher Polhem, to whose daughter Emerentia he was for some time engaged. After Charles XII's return to Sweden, the king employed him in various practical projects, including the transportation of eight vessels across hills and valleys from Strömstad to Idefjord for the siege of Fredrikshald. For an introduction to the gentle and brilliant Swedenborg, see Signe Toksvig's biography, *Emanuel Swedenborg: Scientist and Mystic* (Yale University Press, 1948).

ACT I

1. Charles XII returned to Sweden in December, 1715, after an absence of fifteen years. The country he returned to was impoverished and almost half depopulated because of his wars, famine, and the plague.

2. Stavstorp was one of the Scanian coastal villages destroyed by the invading Danes in 1709.

3. The Battle of Poltava in the Ukraine ended in the disastrous defeat of the Swedish army in the summer of 1709. Thousands of the Swedish soldiers were imprisoned in both Russia proper and Siberia, and most of the survivors were not released until the peace treaty was signed in 1721.

4. Stralsund in Swedish Pomerania fell late in 1715.

5. The allusion is apparently to the beautiful and intelligent Aurora von Königsmarck, the mistress of August II of Poland, who in 1702 sent her to Charles XII's winter quarters at Würgen to secure peace between Poland and Sweden. Charles XII, as literary men such as Voltaire and Tegnér have pointed out, refused to see the seductive noblewoman. Strindberg suggests that fear of women may have been the king's real reason.

6. One of Strindberg's major sources, Fryxell's *Berättelser ur svenska historien,* Part 26, pp. 67-69, says that when Charles had to flee from Stralsund, he gave orders that the two ships *Snapp-Opp* and *Snare-Sven* await him at Hiddensee. A sloop took him through a channel that had to be cut through the ice out to the appointed meeting place; neither of the ships had arrived; fortunately a small Swedish freight boat, *Hvalfisken,* was there. Only after that ship had carried the king far out into the open Baltic did the brigantine *Snapp-Opp* appear; it carried Charles to Sweden. Fryxell says that the captain received corporal punishment in spite of his plea that he had been delayed by ice, and that the

captain of the *Snare-Sven,* which had not shown up, was later executed and his crew whipped.

7. Karlskrona was the city in the province of Blekinge which was the headquarters of the Swedish navy.

8. See note 3. Several of the Swedish prisoners served as teachers.

9. By November, 1713, conditions at home in Sweden had become so acutely bad that the national council—without the approval of the absolute monarch who was then still in Turkey—added his younger sister, Princess Ulrika Eleonora, to the council and summoned the Estates to assemble in December to consider the distressing state of the nation and ways and means for bringing order out of chaos in the absence of Charles. Without the legal right even to be in session, the Estates could only address a communication to the king calling his attention to conditions at home and pleading humbly that he secure peace with the enemy. At this assembly, there was much talk, however, of making the princess regent and even the ruling queen, the limitation of the royal power, and the like. Charles was almost always kept carefully informed by loyal supporters as to what was happening at home even while he was in Turkey.

10. Johan Kristofer von Düring and Gustaf Fredrik Rosen were Charles XII's adjutants who accompanied him on his return to Sweden from Stralsund. Rosen and a brother of Düring had been his companions on the long ride from Turkey to Stralsund.

ACT II

11. From 1716 on, Charles's headquarters were in Lund, the university city in southwestern Sweden. As a result, the housing of students became almost completely impossible; even some of the professors' homes were taken over to house military and other personnel.

12. Lund was partly destroyed by fire in 1711.

13. Theseus was the Greek hero, who, according to legend, cleared Attica of evildoers, slew the Minotaur, conquered the Amazons, married their queen, etc.

14. Count Nicodemus Tessin (1654-1728) was not only Sweden's leading architect of his time but served Charles XII as royal councillor, lord high marshal, and, in 1718, head of the Swedish police.

15. Count Carl Piper (1647-1716) was a statesman who influenced Charles XII very much until he was captured by the Russians at Poltava in 1709. He died in captivity. He was both highly competent in his governmental duties and able to look after his own financial interests.

16. Nicolo di Machiavelli (1469-1527), an Italian statesman and writer, who in his book, *The Prince,* and elsewhere preached his political ideal of the Renaissance ruler who without moral compunction advances the interests of the state by any means.

17. One of Görtz's schemes was to arrange a marriage between Charles Fredrik of Holstein—Charles XII's nephew and closest male relative—and Anne, the daughter of Peter I of Russia. The nephew did marry Anne, but never succeeded to the Swedish throne.

18. Görtz raised money for Charles XII's military campaigns by lending money on the security of the private property of Swedish citizens and by issuing token money. Various officials managed to protect the National Bank from ruin, however. Charles XII, who did not understand high finance, issued—in Görtz's absence—more token money than was bearable by the national economy, as Strindberg suggests. The National Bank had been founded in 1668.

19. The Russians had conquered all of Finland by 1713; most of it was, contrary to the fears of many leading Swedes, restored to Sweden in the peace treaty of 1721.

20. These were Sweden's major enemies. One of the most unfortunate facts for Charles XII and his successors throughout the eighteenth century was that Denmark-Norway, closely related to Sweden racially and culturally, was allied with Russia.

21. Christofer Polhem (1661-1751) was an engineering and universal genius whose inventions and ideas served both the king and the Swedish people well.

22. These were among the Swedish leaders who were captured at or shortly after the Battle of Poltava. For Piper, see note 15. Count Carl Gustav Rehnsköld (1651-1722) and Count Adam Ludvig Lewenhaupt (1659-1719) were two of the captured generals; during his imprisonment, Rehnsköld conducted a sort of military school for young Swedish officers in Moscow; he was released by the czar in 1718. Lewenhaupt died in captivity, having spent it partly in writing his autobiography.

23. Field Marshal Magnus Stenbock (1664-1717), the most famous of Charles XII's generals, surrendered to the Danes in 1713. Never enthusiastic about ransoming his captured officers, Charles was particularly unwilling to ransom Stenbock because of the latter's independence of action in undertaking his last campaign.

24. On February 11, 1709, at Krasnokutsch in the Ukraine, according to SB (VII, 154), Charles XII found himself and a small group of Swedish dragoons surrounded by an overwhelming number of Russians. The dragoons formed a circle about the king and fought with unbelievable courage. Through the efforts of the Taube regiment, most of the dragoons and the king were saved. In the original *Hunger* is *Svält*.

ACT III

25. Otto Arnold Paykull (*ca.* 1662-1707), condemned unjustly to death on the king's insistence, tried in vain to save his life by claiming that he could convert lead to gold.

26. Jakob Boëthius, a prominent clergyman, in 1697 protested in print and in speech against absolutism. Arrested, tried, and condemned to death, Boëthius had his sentence reduced to life imprisonment by the king. Later on he refused the king's pardon, was sent to Danviken —the insane asylum, and finally died in 1718. Boëthius is remembered for his frank public criticism of Charles.

27. Most of these men were supposed to be interested in bringing an end to absolutism.

28. From the early seventeenth century to the time of the French Revolution, France and Sweden were, except on rare occasions, allied or on friendly terms. Louis XIV died on September 1, 1715!

ACT IV

29. Ulrika Eleonora, Charles XII's younger sister and successor, was married in the spring of 1716 to Fredrik, the landgrave of Hesse (Hessen-Kassel). He was notorious for his extramarital love affairs. Next to women, he loved hunting.

30. The myrtle has traditionally been used for Swedish bridal crowns.

31. See note 5.

32. According to SB (VII, 359), Charles Fredrik was controlled by his valet and other favorites.

33. According to the Old Scandinavian saga, Ragnar Lodbrok was a Danish hero whom King Ella of England cast into a den of serpents. See Munch's *Norse Mythology* for detailed information about him.

34. Freedom from absolutism.

35. The landgrave of Hesse was an experienced and even courageous soldier. The real power Charles XII kept in his own hands.

ACT V

36. The Norwegian city of Fredrikshald (now Halden) lies about eight miles west of the Swedish border. The Danes, who then controlled Norway, had in 1716 strengthened the fortress of Fredrikssten which defended the city.

37. General Carl Gustav Frölich (d. 1714) was a member of the council; Baron Christian Albrecht Grothusen (1680-1715) was Charles XII's favorite and his companion in Turkey; Baron Henrik Gustav von Müllern (1664-1719) was another close companion of the king during his stay in Turkey.

38. It has never been definitely determined whether Charles XII was killed by a bullet fired from an enemy gun or was assassinated by a fellow countryman.

Introduction to 'Gustav III'

No OTHER Swedish rulers have been as much and as directly interested in the theater as Queen Christina (1632-1654) and King Gustav III (1771-1792), and no reigning monarch has been so thoroughly affected by drama in so many of its phases as Gustav. He was, after all, not only an actor but also a playwright who wrote either alone or in collaboration with others some of the most noteworthy Swedish plays of his century; he was a manager and producer of plays in his theaters at Drottningholm and Gripsholm as well as of colorful open-air spectacles at Drottningholm and elsewhere. There was no phase of theatrical activity that escaped his interest and attention: casting, costuming, stage diction, theories and practices of acting, stage design, dramatic composition, dramatic theory, rehearsals, and production, and even the setting up and printing of programs for performances fascinated him. Gustav III "lived" the theater as no other royal person—including Christina—ever did.

Yet Strindberg knew that Gustav was not only interested in his own theaters in Stockholm and at Drottningholm and Gripsholm but in a much larger theater. Note what Strindberg says in his *Open Letters to the Intimate Theater:*

> *Gustav III.* The enlightened despot, who carries through the French Revolution at home in Sweden—that is to say, crushes the aristocrats with the help of the third estate. That is a paradox that is hard to deal with. And as a character, he is full of contradictions, a tragedian who plays comedy in life, a hero and a dancing master,

an absolute monarch who is a friend of liberty, a man who strives
for humanitarian [reforms], a disciple of Fredrik the Great, Joseph
II, and Voltaire. Almost sympathetic, he, the Revolutionist, falls at
the hand of the Revolutionists. Anckarström [the assassin of Gustav III] was, namely, a man of the Revolution who has had his
story written by the Swedish court of appeals (*Svea Hovrätt*).

As Strindberg understood Gustav, the king was a consummate
actor for whom "the whole world was a stage" and for whom life
itself was a play and living synonymous with acting on the stage of
world history. The king's concept of his role, as Strindberg saw it,
was a heroic one; he wanted to be like his two great predecessors
on the throne—Gustav I Vasa, who had set Sweden free in the
1520's and who had unified and developed it, and Gustav II Adolf,
who in the seventeenth century had made Sweden one of the great
powers politically and who had secured religious freedom for
Protestants. From Gustav III's point of view, both of the earlier
Gustavs had played their parts in the drama of Swedish and European history well, and he, too, intended to play his role brilliantly.

Strindberg's Gustav III has the overwhelming ambition to domi-
nate the action. To do so, he must by direct action and by intrigue
curb the power of the aristocrats, his dangerous competitors for
power and consequently for attention, in order to carry through a
program that will stamp him in the eyes of his audience—not only
the people of Sweden but of the whole world and particularly of its
leading "critics" (Voltaire and Rousseau, for example) as a HERO
who has accomplished great things and who as a result will go
down in history as one of the great heroes of all time.

Gustav's goal is then both domestic and foreign recognition as the
man of freedom of his time and as the ruler who would extend his
people's liberties and raise his country's status by humanitarian
reforms at home such as increasing the privileges and rights of the
common people at the cost of the powerful aristocrats; by the
achievement of a greater role in Europe for his country through
military victories over its two principal enemies—Russia and Den-

mark; and by raising it to the cultural level of France, the country he thought had reached the highest level of civilization in the world.

Strindberg emphasizes and illustrates a fundamental contradiction in Gustav again and again: the man who wants to accomplish great things, wants consciously or unconsciously to accomplish them *as* an actor who will secure the applause of an audience, who will be the center of attention and the dominant actor while on the stage and the director of the action when he is not. For Gustav, Strindberg felt, the major facts became the effect he was making, the applause he was getting, and the pleasure he personally received from intriguing to achieve his ends. The goals themselves became subordinate, for their attainment too frequently involved planning and detail work that could not be accomplished on the lighted stage either of an actual theater or of the greater one of the world.

Strindberg's interpretation of Gustav III then is first of all that of the actor on the throne, an actor who shares with many of his fellow actors a superficiality that does not involve much more than the mastery of the lines, the development of a technique of improvisation when necessary, the delivery of the lines in a fashion that will impress the audience—both seen and unseen, an attention to the details that concern effects, and, briefly put, the performance of a role rather than the performance of deeds and the realization of a program. Included in this interpretation is the charm of manner, the elegance of dress, and the emphasis on appropriate gesture, walk and speech. That sort of thing has become the important factor; *playing* Gustav III as a hero in worthy succession to the earlier heroic Gustavs has become, for the most part unconsciously, far more important to the king than *being* Gustav III the hero.

To present Gustav the actor on the throne who not only charmed and fascinated Strindberg as actors and particularly actresses did (two of his wives were actresses) but also irritated and annoyed him because of their superficiality and chameleonlike qualities, Strindberg has selected a form that is not a little like that of the

Scribean historical comedy with its emphasis on intrigues and conspiracies, fencing—literal and figurative, its neatly arranged scenes,
and its superficiality that is decidedly theatrical. Strindberg did this
deliberately, I suspect, to convey his interpretation of a crowned
actor for whom life was a stage, for whom living was usually acting, and for whom adapting his acting to the situation had become
a habit.

Strindberg felt that no other period in Swedish history had been
so charming or so superficial in its social behavior as the Gustavian.
Court and social life had never attained a higher level of elegance
and charm or of pomp and ceremony in Sweden than it did in the
Gustavian period; Swedish culture became like that of Versailles,
but it should be added that it never became merely imitative;
instead, it borrowed, adapted, and made what it wanted its own.
Gustavian manners, arts from literature to furniture, and behavior
in general at least on the upper social levels took on attractive
aspects that Strindberg has exploited in presenting the historical
environment and atmosphere of the time, a presentation that is one
of the very real merits of *Gustav III*. Note not only the behavior of
the king and the secondary characters but also the incidental appearance of such literary figures as Bellman, Thorild, Kellgren,
Hallman, and Kexell; the use of Holmberg's book store as the setting of Act I; the settings of Act II at Gustav's own Haga and of
Act IV at the eighteenth-century China Castle at Drottningholm;
and the appearance of Megaera and the graces. These are all in
keeping with the essence of the Gustavian period in all its rococo
charm, emphasis on the esthetic, superficiality, and frequently intellectual awareness, all of them essential background for Strindberg's
charmer-king.

Swedish life on its upper levels was, moreover, during this period,
one might say, not a little Scribean in its intrigues and conspiracies.
Not only Gustav III but people like Baron Pechlin and Lady
Schröderheim enjoyed intensely—according to Strindberg's sources
—indulging in what was for them the pleasure of intrigue and

counterintrigue; it tested their wits and satisfied their need for stimulation in an artificial environment. The Gustavian courtiers were fencers and card players; many of their ladies, like Anne-Charlotte Schröderheim, were not only masters of the techniques of *trisette* and the many other popular card games but also masters of fencing —figuratively—with their tongues and other resources of coquetry. Even politics were to an emphasized degree a game played for high stakes by means of intrigues and counterintrigues. Strindberg could hardly have hit upon a happier idea to convey the background of his major character than to emphasize such an important basic fact about the king's environment. Superficially considered, the play may strike one as Scribean; the parallels are there; for Strindberg has used several of the elements of the Scribean historical comedy most effectively in presenting the king and the people surrounding him. But Gustav III struck Strindberg as a character out of a Scribean historical comedy; he presents him as such and then proceeds to do much more with his characterization.

The events before Gustav's coup d'état of 1789 when, with the help of the three lower estates—the clergy, the burghers, and the farmers, he seized greater personal power and then extended the privileges of the commoners were among the most dramatic and even most melodramatic in Gustav's reign, as Strindberg realized. The struggle for power between the lords and Gustav was more intense than ever before; Strindberg's primary sources—Starbäck and Bäckström's *Berättelser ur svenska historien* and Crusenstolpe's *Morianen*—emphasized the antagonisms as revealed in intrigues and counterintrigues. It is into the very midst of such an environment that Strindberg plunges us when the curtain first goes up. The dissatisfied lords represented by idealists who had once admired Gustav (Horn, Ribbing), selfish opportunists (Munck, Pechlin, Taube), proud aristocrats who remember the previous reigns when the lords had had almost unrestricted political power (von Fersen, De Geer), the king's primarily personal enemy and later assassin (Anckarström), the king's loyal supporters (Nordström, Olsson,

Badin), the commoners who have become disaffected because the
king has taken back part of what he has given (Halldin, Holmberg), the intellectual leaders (Kellgren, Thorild)—all help to
make clear the unhappy situation in which the crowned actor finds
himself. The actor is no longer playing to a universally enthusiastic
audience; in fact, those who applaud have gradually decreased in
number as the actor has found it necessary to depart from the lines
of his role as he had conceived them at an earlier date. From being
the defender of freedom of the press, he has felt it necessary to im-
pose censorship because of unfavorable public reaction to the unfortunate results of his hastily improvised and poorly executed plans for
curbing liquor consumption and for improving the national finances.
His carelessness in financial expenditures has made him improvise unfortunately by starting a war with Russia which he had no constitutional right to do and in which he needed badly the help of the
antagonistic lords. The royal actor has been turned upon by part
of his audience; he is in danger of losing not only his throne but
his life as well; now if ever he must overcome his opponents and
gain the center of the stage as the object of the applauding millions.

In Act II, Gustav appears for the first time—against the background of political, international, personal, and family problems
which have either been explained or hinted at only to be taken up
again and developed. The slight, delicate, handsome king—elegantly
and colorfully dressed, and appreciably effeminate in his manner,
walk and speech—that makes his appearance is, except for rare
moments, an actor through and through. Note his looking into the
mirror to check on his appearance and his expressions just before
Olsson enters, his behavior during Pechlin's audience, his preparation of Schröderheim for the divorce, his exchanges with Lady
Schröderheim, and his conversation with Armfelt at the end of the
act. The last illustrates the point:

> ARMFELT: That's not badly put together! Considered as a play!
> (*Touches the Dalecarlian folk costume with his cane*)
> KING: Who knows? Perhaps the whole thing is a play?

ARMFELT: But the last act! Do you have that?
KING: It will come of itself!
ARMFELT: It will come of itself!

Yet it is not only Gustav the actor and as such the great artist that
Strindberg manages to present to us in this act. There is also the
Gustav that the acting is intended to conceal.

Note by way of illustration, his relaxation in the company of
Armfelt, his favorite; his brusqueness with Taube; his reactions to
mentions of Anckarström; and his momentary inability to appear
unaffected by Pechlin's moves; and his obvious disturbance at Lady
Schröderheim's presence. Behind Gustav the actor is a very human
being deliberately concealed when possible and very much troubled
by a very human sense of insecurity and inadequacy.

Nor is Strindberg's characterization limited to such obvious matters as those just mentioned. Strindberg recognized in Gustav a
gifted idealist and intellectual:

> KING: Why, I am the radical, the democrat, the one who hates
> the nobility, the first citizen in a free country! The man of the
> people and the defender of the oppressed! I am the disciple of
> Rousseau . . . and of Voltaire! . . . The social contract, *Le Con-
> trat Social,* is my gospel; I have it on my table next to my bed!
> George Washington is my friend! Franklin, my ideal! There you
> have me!

Sincere in believing this, Gustav is also sincere in his self-
appraisal:

> KING: No, the time is past when the Russian ambassador and the
> English chose the members of our parliament, appointed the
> secret committee, and named our national council; yes, it was
> Russia that gave my father, the prince-bishop of Lübeck, the
> throne of Sweden and me a consort. Those times are past, and
> that is my modest achievement, which people have forgotten, and
> to the degree that they haven't understood my last war against
> Russia which they call treason. Recently a court poet compared

me with Gustav Vasa, the liberator from foreign oppression; I
smiled when I read it, but there may be a grain of truth in the
flattery . . .

Even his analysis of his actions which have contradicted his ideals
is not superficial:

> KING: Do not forget to see to the parliamentary elections! The royal
> sheriffs and pastors—in your parishes—are to employ all means!
> All! I won't leave anything to chance these days! . . . Yes, I
> have ceased to believe in honesty and truth and the like! During
> the last session of parliament I scorned pressure and bribery; now
> I command them! That is what I have learned from experience
> and from Anjala!

The cynicism, as Strindberg sees it, does not mean, however, that
Gustav has given up his dream of becoming a hero who would be
recognized down through the ages; it does mean a shift from his
naive faith in his ability to move men by appealing to their essential
goodness to a cynical faith in his ability to move them by appealing
to their selfish interests.

Another important episode in Act II that shows that Strindberg's
Gustav is not merely superficial and artificial is the episode with
his wife, Queen Sofia Magdalena. The Gustav who is acting and the
Gustav who is not are easily distinguishable. (See pages 230-233.)
Note particularly such realistic frank speeches as this:

> KING: I suppose you, no doubt, know as well as I that our marriage
> was arranged by the secret committee in its day and by the em-
> press of Russia at the time of the peace treaty; in other words,
> the government at that time was forced to select a bride for me
> without the slightest regard for our personal feelings. That time
> when we both yielded to the powerful interests of two nations,
> we made a sacrifice that has cost us our personal happiness . . .
> The concept *sacrifice* implies giving up happiness . . . Can't
> then the knowledge that we have suffered together for others, for

many others, keep up our courage until the cup has been drained? Aren't there other reasons than the political for our bearing the burden all the way? Hasn't our son the first right to be reared by parents, by his father and his mother . . .

Strindberg here goes far beyond Scribe.

It is a highly complex human being that Strindberg gives us—a man who is the product of a rich heredity and an artificial environment which have made him what he is: an idealistic, enlightened monarch who unfortunately cannot usually distinguish between what is real and what is unreal, between life as a very serious matter indeed and life as a play in which he must always be aware of how he is seen, how he is heard, and how he is received by his audience.

Act III presents the leading conspirators, each of them fully enough individualized in their roles as enemies of the king—the gentle idealistic poet Horn, the personally aggrieved and frankly forthright assassin-to-be Anckarström, the realistic and class-conscious Ribbing, and the conniving Pechlin. As Strindberg presents them and their conspiracy, there is only one among them that can match the king in idealistic goals—young Baron Horn, who wishes to deprive Gustav of power in order to make it possible to realize a more ideal form of government. The others are all selfish men interested either in personal revenge (Anckarström) or in strengthening the position of their class—the aristocrats—by giving it the real power in Sweden. Strindberg does not, however, present these men as evil through and through; even Pechlin, the worst of them, is given human qualities that are understandable. Note, by way of illustration, Anckarström's love for his family and Pechlin's unwillingness to approve the plan to assassinate the king.

In Act III, too, Strindberg develops his characterization of the king in the conspirators' discussion of the king and by having the king appear alone at Huvudsta where the conspirators are meeting. Such comments as:

PECHLIN: But the king is a pretty good player . . . that is to say!
. . . Yes, yes! Just because he never follows the rules, he's very
difficult . . . and besides he learns so easily . . .

and

ANCKARSTRÖM: He has one good quality; he isn't a coward.
PECHLIN: Yes, he is; he lacks courage, but he relies on bravado! . . .

are only a few of the bits of information about the king's character
that come out of the conspirators' discussion of the king, their objections to him, and their plans to do something about him and his
program. The sudden theatrical appearance of the king in their
midst—prepared for by Pechlin (p. 240) illustrates his bravado, his
gift for a battle of words, and the pointing of the antagonisms between him and his opponents. In the characterization of a crowned
actor, Pechlin's lines, "The exit was not quite as happy as the entrance! But that happens to even the best of actors!" are highly
appropriate.

Technically, Act IV is the most Scribean. The presence of the
conspirators at the fete at Drottningholm heightens the tension
between the king and his opponents in the Scribe fashion. Such
episodes as the attempt of Fersen and De Geer to arrest the king,
their discussion of fencing, Badin's success in saving him, and
above all, the queen's inadvertent walking between the king and
the man who intends to assassinate him are in the Scribe tradition.

But there is much more to Act IV than these Scribean elements.
Most important for the characterization of the king is the information about the king's early environment and unhappy marriage,
both of which have been touched upon earlier in the play but which
need the further development that they get in this act. Note such
exchanges as these:

QUEEN: How did you ever get started embroidering, sire?
KING: My mother taught me, and afterwards I got pleasure out of
it! I think very clearly when I embroider, and then I feel that

I have the strings in my hand. (*Pause*) You despise handiwork, don't you?

QUEEN: Pretty much!

KING: And *I* learned it primarily to lend respect to woman's work! Making sacrifices is rewarding!

and

FERSEN: And the King! He was taught to lie as a child—especially during the unsuccessful coups d'état . . . I was along then! And since then he has lied so much he doesn't know who he is himself, and as he jokes about everything he can't tell the difference between a joke and what's serious.

Note in this final act Strindberg's careful presentation of information about the king's background that has made him what he is: a gifted artist that has more and more placed the major emphasis on appearing as the heroic Gustav III and only secondary emphasis on being the heroic and worthy successor of the two earlier Gustavs; a crowned actor for whom outward forms have come to mean more than inner meanings; an unfortunate human being who has meant well but who because of his environment has never been quite able to realize his potentialities for greatness. How very human he is comes out again and again. For example:

PECHLIN: They intend to murder you!

KING: Intend! Haven't they been up to that as long as I can remember? Haven't they murdered my honor and my wife's? Didn't they murder my child in his mother's womb? What's left for them?

His marriage for state reasons, the incompatibility of temperaments (the scintillating, imaginative, intellectually alive husband vs. the stiff, dull, conventional wife), and the biggest scandal of the period—the queen mother's and others' assertion that the crown prince was not the son of Gustav III but of the queen's favorite

Baron Munck—have helped make Gustav increasingly cynical about people. But the good actor that he is, he feels that he must carry on, and never wholly pessimistic about his abilities nor about ultimately attaining his goals, he feels he may yet go down in history as having played his royal role well:

> ARMFELT: Now you are cynical, Gustav!
>
> KING: Yes, now I am cynical! Just as cynical as . . . the others!
>
> ARMFELT: The Bastille has fallen . . . and Gustav III becomes an absolute monarch!
>
> KING: Yes! That he does! But I have made the revolution myself!
>
> ARMFELT: What a paradox! What a trick!
>
> KING: Now we shall go to look at the people!
>
> ARMFELT: And then?
>
> KING: We shall dance!
>
> ARMFELT: You are divine at any rate!
>
> KING: Nonsense!
>
> ARMFELT: Yes, people admire you, though they despise you!
>
> KING: And they hate me, though they love me! That makes sense!
>
> ARMFELT: They have to take you as you are!
>
> KING: And I am what I have become! I have not made myself! . . .

Strindberg's characterization of Gustav III does this: presents the king as he is at one specific period in his life, and explains why he has become what he is. There is no doubt either that Strindberg both admired and despised Gustav III.

In addition to his characterization of the king, Strindberg presents a gallery of interesting characters ranging from the Schröderheims to Badin, the Negro presented to Gustav's mother when he was a boy and brought up with Gustav and his brothers. In keeping with his usual practice in the historical plays, Strindberg characterizes most of these supporting and incidental characters only in so far as they throw light on Gustav himself. Armfelt and Munck appear as royal favorites; Pechlin, Horn, Ribbing, and Anckarström as conspirators; Fersen and De Geer as political opponents; Olsson, Taube, Liljensparre, Nordström, and Papillon in their official roles;

Holmberg and Halldin as people who have suffered because of Gustav's contradictory actions; the literary men as literary men of a period when writers were encouraged by the king; and Queen Sofia Magdalena as the unhappy victim of a state marriage.

The Schröderheims alone are given especially detailed attention. In most of their appearances, Strindberg presents them in a manner that is decidedly reminiscent of his technique in *Creditors*. Note particularly pages 254-258 for a searching analysis of them and their marriage. Both Elis Schröderheim, the state secretary, and his wife are highly individualized; the account of their marriage offers both an effective contrast and an effective parallel to the royal marriage, but, as a close examination will show, it is a parallel that is carefully distinguished from the royal marriage in terms of the individual characters of the two husbands and the two wives.

Strindberg did not live long enough to see his *Gustav III* become one of the great successes on the Swedish stage. If he had, his conviction that he had produced great theater in this play would have been confirmed. He would have known, too, that this play would gain recognition for his happy presentation of the historical Gustavian environment in its manifold phases and that in his characterization of Gustav he had caught very nicely the spirit of the charmer-king who still has a role to play in Swedish life. Gustav's monuments are still there—the Swedish Academy, the Royal Opera, the theaters at Drottningholm and Gripsholm, and Haga, to mention only a few, and they still play a vital role.

Gustav III · A Play in Four Acts

Characters

GUSTAV III

ARMFELT

ELIS SCHRÖDERHEIM

GENERAL PECHLIN

HORN

RIBBING

ANCKARSTRÖM

FERSEN

DE GEER

MUNCK

TAUBE

LILJENSPARRE

CAPTAIN NORDSTRÖM *(butcher by profession)*

OLOF OLSSON, *speaker in the Farmers' Estate*

KELLGREN

THORILD

BELLMAN

HALLMAN

KEXELL

HOLMBERG, *book store proprietor*

HALLDIN

BADIN, *the Dowager Queen's Negro*

PAPILLON, *valet*

QUEEN SOFIA MAGDALENA

LADY SCHRÖDERHEIM

MINOR CHARACTERS

Settings

ACT I: *Holmberg's Book Store*
ACT II: *The King's reception room at Haga Palace*
ACT III: *A room at Huvudsta Manor House*
ACT IV: *In China Castle at Drottningholm*

ACT I

The Holmberg Book Store[1] in Stockholm. Counter and shelves
to the right. HOLMBERG *is standing by a green pulpit examining*
a record book, with his glasses resting on his forehead. HALLDIN
is standing back of the counter.

At the back are windows and open glass doors facing the har-
bor; masts and sails can be seen.

To the right in the corner is a tile stove with a bust of Rousseau
in its recess. Close to the stove ANCKARSTRÖM *is standing reading*
a French journal; KLAS HORN *is reading the same periodical over*
ANCKARSTRÖM's *shoulder.*

In the middle of the floor is a table on which are writing mate-
rials, papers, and books.

PAPILLON (*the* KING's *valet enters hastily*): Has the paper come?

HALLDIN (*giving him a paper*): Here you are!

HOLMBERG: Mr. Papillon! Already out papilloning! Anything new
in town?

PAPILLON: Her Majesty is breakfasting at the Clas-on-the-Corner[2]
with Lady Manderström at eleven!

HOLMBERG: That's the Queen! But where's the King?

PAPILLON: In Finland, of course.

HOLMBERG: In the Russian War,[3] of course, but where? Where?

PAPILLON: I don't know!

HOLMBERG: Look at the paper . . . and you'll find out!

(PAPILLON *glances at the paper. Becomes frightened*)

(ANCKARSTRÖM *looks up.* HORN *looks up.*)

PAPILLON: Is that true?

HOLMBERG: I don't know! Maybe you do, Halldin?

HALLDIN (*frightened*): I never know anything!

PAPILLON: Not even how bread and water taste? You probably won't forget that very soon!

HALLDIN: I've tasted the bitterness of death, Mr. Papillon, but Mr. Holmberg has tasted bread and water . . .

PAPILLON: All because of that blessed liquor.

HALLDIN: The liquor law,[4] Mr. Papillon . . .

HORN (*with a dull voice*): Do you have a copy of the law governing the freedom of the press, Mr. Holmberg?

HOLMBERG: Do you mean the old one of 1766,[5] Major Horn?

HORN: Yes, that's it!

HOLMBERG (*pointing to the rear wall*): There it is, framed in glass with the King's commentary!

PAPILLON (*leaves hastily*): Good-bye, Mr. Holmberg!

HOLMBERG: Good-bye, Mr. Papillon!

HORN (*reading the freedom of the press law*): Those are proud words, worthy of a great king. "Freedom of the press informs the general public about its true welfare and does not permit the ruler to be ignorant of what the people think."

HOLMBERG: And this . . . I know it by heart: "If freedom of the press had been permitted in the last century, King Charles XI[6] would perhaps not have taken such measures at the cost of public security as to make the royal power detestable."

HORN: Or this: "Through freedom of the press a king learns the truth, which people frequently with much effort and unfortunately often enough with much success conceal from him."

HOLMBERG: Our gracious King wrote that himself, and at the time he was so proud of his generosity that he sent a French copy to Voltaire, who graciously approved and complimented the author, which didn't prevent His Majesty from having Halldin there condemned to death, because he wrote against the liquor law. And he had me in jail for fourteen days on bread and water because I printed the article. As you know, Halldin was pardoned, but I wasn't!

HORN (*evasively*): Is it true what today's paper says?

HOLMBERG: Hard to tell, but most likely there's something to it. The King was at Kymendegård, with the Russians to the east and his army in full rebellion to the west. One hundred and eight of his officers threw down their weapons at the King's feet and renounced their fealty and obedience . . . There was talk about His Majesty's arrest by the Anjala men[7] . . . Then the King fled in despair by way of Helsingfors, Åbo, and the Åland Sea! All those bits of information are accurate! It's absolutely certain that Denmark has declared war, and that a ship with some of the rebellious officers aboard has already passed the toll station . . . It will be on the stream at any moment!

HORN: The war was illegal, directly contrary to the constitution, and stupid, besides!

HOLMBERG: You can say that! . . . Armfelt, his favorite, most likely suggested the war as a last resource to cover up the King's disastrous private affairs . . .[8] Yes, that's how it is! . . . (*Looks out at the street*) Munck is coming!

(ANCKARSTRÖM *turns toward the stove.*)

HORN: That horrible person!

MUNCK (*enters, cross and vain*): I want to pay for the last books . . . although I don't know why I . . . cut copies with lice specks on every fifth page . . . It's a hell of a print shop you have . . .

HOLMBERG: If you feel you've been unfairly treated, sir . . .

MUNCK: Shut up! And if you send a statement before six months are up, I'll kick your man out next time . . . There you are! (*Throws a bill on the counter*)

HOLMBERG: Excuse me, Baron, but we don't accept Russian bills![9]

MUNCK: What the hell? . . . Is there anything wrong with it?

HOLMBERG: Yes, there is a slight flaw; the bill is counterfeit!

MUNCK: When you're an exconvict, you should have enough sense to choose your words . . .

HORN (*comes forward*): Baron, simple humanity demands that you not berate a person who has served his sentence for an old crime —least of all in this case, when the victim was innocent!

MUNCK: Horn, the defender of innocence . . . Do you mean the court sentenced Holmkvist unjustly?

HORN: Yes, I do . . . and, besides, his name is Holmberg!

MUNCK: Holmgren or Holmström . . . it's all the same to me . . . The lords of the realm have other things to do than to memorize the directory . . . and lists of prisoners . . . However, if you don't want to accept this money, you won't . . .

PECHLIN (*has entered and overheard the last part of the conversation*): Excuse me, gentlemen, for interrupting such a lively conversation, but when the fatherland is in danger . . .

MUNCK: What did you say, Baron Pechlin?

PECHLIN: Gentlemen, the King has fled from the army, and they say he's imprisoned in Borgå!

MUNCK (*collapses into a chair*): Imprisoned?

PECHLIN: That's what they say! . . . The sun has set, and some people will lose their places in the sun!

MUNCK: Deposed, perhaps?

PECHLIN: Most likely!

(ANCKARSTRÖM *turns*.)

HORN: It's his own fault!

MUNCK (*gets up, takes the bill from the counter*): Send me your statement, and I'll pay it in current coin. Good-bye, Mr. Holmberg! Farewell, gentlemen! (*Leaves*)

HOLMBERG (*to* PECHLIN): The comedy is over!

PECHLIN: Not yet!

HOLMBERG: Wasn't what you said true, my lord?

PECHLIN: It's true that they've said it, but Munck doesn't need to know they've spread a false rumor! Now I have to write a letter!

(*Nods to* ANCKARSTRÖM; *sits down at the table and writes; with his hand conceals what he's writing*)

HORN (*to* HOLMBERG): What sort of note was it?

HOLMBERG: A counterfeit ruble—one of those the King and Munck had printed at Drottningholm and are circulating in Finland.

HORN: Don't they have any shame?

HOLMBERG: No, they have no shame when they follow the example of Fredrik the Great who discovered how to wage war with counterfeit money!

PECHLIN (*continues writing*): They're not ashamed to make Lieutenant Taube court chaplain to save him from financial ruin; they're not ashamed to sell pastorates; Schröderheim just sold the fattest one in Värmland so he could supply the regimental band with gold braid; they pay the ambassadors' gambling debts out of the national treasury; and they use the liquor tax receipts for the courtiers' mistresses . . . Have you gentlemen heard that the French Estates have been called into session in Paris?

ALL: No!

PECHLIN: And that Washington has been elected president of the American Republic?

ALL: No!

PECHLIN: A lot of things are happening all over the world these days! . . .

HORN: The Estates summoned to Paris . . .

PECHLIN: And Marquis de Mirabeau[10] elected . . . to the supreme council!

HOLMBERG: Is something new going to happen in this world of ours?

HORN: That is our hope!

HOLMBERG: Halldin! There are people who hope!

HALLDIN: Not I!

(BELLMAN, HALLMAN, *and* KEXELL *enter. They look weary and despondent.* KEXELL *goes up to* HOLMBERG. *The other two stay by the door.*)

KEXELL (*speaks privately to* HOLMBERG): Have any been sold?

HOLMBERG: No! The public seems to have things to think about other than your comic songs . . .

KEXELL: Well, well! Politics perhaps? But we're not interested in that; it isn't our field, not our world!

HOLMBERG: I know, and I can't object to that!

KEXELL (*embarrassed*): Times are bad when there's a war on; the poets don't sing then . . . Nice weather today . . .

HOLMBERG: I don't have any money!

KEXELL (*wiping the sweat from his forehead*): Money? A trifle isn't money . . .

HOLMBERG: But can become! . . . Are you going out to Djurgårn? [11]

KEXELL: Yes, we have something to do out there . . .

HOLMBERG: Order drinks maybe?

KEXELL: That's it!

HOLMBERG: I can never say no to anything like that! (*Gives him a bill*)

KEXELL (*touched*): Holmberg! Do you know me?

HOLMBERG: Thoroughly!

KEXELL: Do you despise me?

HOLMBERG: The very opposite!

KEXELL: Don't despise me!

HOLMBERG: Go out and have your drinks, and don't talk nonsense!

KEXELL: May I shake your hand?

HOLMBERG: Not for a trifle like that! Go on! Go! . . . Big shots are coming!

(KEXELL, BELLMAN, *and* HALLMAN *leave.* FREDRIK AXEL VON FERSEN *and* CARL DE GEER *enter.*)

FERSEN (*to* HOLMBERG): They say Baron Pechlin is here!

PECHLIN: That's right!

DE GEER: And, there he is!

PECHLIN: Are they going to arrest me?

FERSEN: Why?

PECHLIN: In this country there can't be any disturbance without my being arrested.

FERSEN: In this country nothing important happens without your knowing about it first!

PECHLIN: How can I?

FERSEN: Need you ask? . . . However, Baron De Geer and I now ask you—where is the King?

PECHLIN: At the front, of course!

DE GEER: But you've spread the rumor that His Majesty is . . .

PECHLIN: Mere talk! I know absolutely nothing about it, and if I did I'd keep still. I'm always to be involved . . .

FERSEN (*to* HOLMBERG): Have you heard anything, Mr. Holmberg?

HOLMBERG: Nah! I've heard nothing.

(FERSEN *sits down at the table and writes; conceals with his hand when he sees* PECHLIN *is doing so.* DE GEER *picks up a book; reads*)

OLOF OLSSON (*enters; goes up to the counter*): Can a person buy the constitution?

PECHLIN: Yes, it's no doubt for sale.

OLSSON (*naively*): Isn't it for sale?

PECHLIN: Everything's for sale! The constitution and the provisions for the royal succession, the bishops' hats, and national marshal's staffs . . .

(FERSEN *looks up; smiles.* DE GEER *turns toward* PECHLIN.)

OLSSON (*to* PECHLIN): Are you the assistant?

DE GEER: Yes, he assists at every proposal of the opposition, all cabals, all intrigues . . .

OLSSON: Oh no!

FERSEN: Is that you, Olsson? Up here in Stockholm?

OLSSON: Yes, Count!

FERSEN: Is this how you take care of your tenancy and my estate? . . . Take off your cap . . .

PECHLIN: There aren't any caps[12] any more . . . just hats . . .

FERSEN: What do you want with the constitution? Stay at home in the stable! That's where you have your say!

OLSSON: Yes, I suppose one may look at it like that . . . and it may be enough to practice on the cattle . . .

FERSEN: You're getting pretty big in the mouth, Olle. Did you have liquor for breakfast?

OLSSON: We didn't get any liquor, but there certainly was plenty of wine . . .

PECHLIN (*to* FERSEN): I'll wager that he ate with the government secretary, the one who looks after the parliamentary elections . . .

FERSEN: That fellow . . . a member of parliament? Is he going to become a member of parliament?

PECHLIN: No, he isn't going to become . . .

FERSEN: You know that, too, do you?

PECHLIN: He isn't going to become, because he already is!

FERSEN: Olle Olsson? My tenant?

OLSSON: Yes! Once upon a time there was a farmer whose name was Olof Håkansson.[13] He became a member of parliament and the speaker of his estate. When he died, he was buried in Riddarholm Church, and because of his close relations with the national marshal, Axel von Fersen, he was buried in the Fersen chapel!

FERSEN: That was then!

OLSSON: And he had a son who was made a baron, and right now he's a member of the temporary regency!

FERSEN: And you're thinking of making the same sort of career?

OLSSON: Oh no, not at all . . . Listen, Mr. Bookseller, do you have a copy of the statutes on the privileges of the nobility?

HOLMBERG: Yes, I do!

FERSEN: What have you got to do with the statutes of the nobility?

OLSSON: Well, you see, we were thinking of making a few changes . . .

DE GEER: Come on, Fersen! Come along!

OLSSON: Can you tell me, gentlemen, why a farmer may not buy land from a nobleman's estate? Isn't it the same soil, the same

manure, and the same money? Maybe it's true of people as it's
true of manure—that they're the same manure, the whole bunch!

FERSEN (*leaps up and puts his hand on his sword*): *Sacrebleu!*

DE GEER (*who has been looking out through the window*): Come
on, Fersen! . . . The Finnish ship with the officers has just
anchored!

FERSEN: Then I'll go and spit in their faces!

(FERSEN *and* DE GEER *leave; they meet* LIEUTENANT TAUBE *in his
uniform.*)

TAUBE (*to* HOLMBERG): Do you have any theological literature?

HOLMBERG: No, I don't!

PECHLIN: Lieutenant Taube! Studying for the ministry! Is it true
you're to be court chaplain?

TAUBE: What in hell is a person to do?

HORN (*to* ANCKARSTRÖM): Let's meet the officers who've come
home . . .

(ANCKARSTRÖM *signals that he wants to stay.*)

TAUBE (*sits down at a table*): You're always writing letters, aren't
you, Baron Pechlin?

PECHLIN: Almost always!

TAUBE: To whom can you write that much?

PECHLIN: To my friends, naturally, and to my enemies, too. What
I've just been writing—may I read it to you? . . . I who never
have any secrets?

TAUBE: No thanks! That's unnecessary, I suspect . . .

PECHLIN: Maybe so! Especially since the person I've written to will
come in here in a moment . . . Oh, I'm no spiritualist; I see
him through the window!

TAUBE: Who is it?

PECHLIN: Nordström, the butcher and the captain in the burghers'
cavalry.

TAUBE: Who's in command of the guards during the absence of the
royal guards? Wonderful!

PECHLIN: The King's *royal* lifeguard then!

(NORDSTRÖM *enters. He is a stately man, dressed as a captain with golden loops on his hat and with a white armband.* TAUBE *turns his back and pretends to read.*)

NORDSTRÖM (*to* OLSSON, *who has been standing at the counter reading*): Good morning, sir! Are you here?

OLSSON: Yes! Why, this Holmberg is the source and fountain of wisdom . . . and here we all meet as we do at the furrier's!

NORDSTRÖM: Yes, after we've lost our hides!

PECHLIN (*still writing*): You can still joke, eh, captain?

NORDSTRÖM (*putting his hand on* TAUBE's *shoulder*): Good morning, comrade!

TAUBE: Don't touch me! I'm not my butcher's comrade!

NORDSTRÖM (*angry*): No, but a lieutenant is outranked by a captain! And is to salute his superior in military fashion!

TAUBE (*remains seated*): The military fashion would be to run the sword through your middle! But now I have other thoughts and other duties . . .

PECHLIN (*to* NORDSTRÖM): General Pechlin commands Captain Nordström to dispense with official formalities today!

NORDSTRÖM: The man who insults the royal uniform insults the King!

ANCKARSTRÖM: Well, would that matter? (*General horror*)

NORDSTRÖM (*who did not hear what* ANCKARSTRÖM *said*): What did you say, my lord?

PECHLIN (*to* NORDSTRÖM): Listen, this isn't a police hearing, is it? Go out and keep the people under control when the officers land!

NORDSTRÖM: They have already landed, the traitors, and got the reception they deserved!

(ANCKARSTRÖM *takes* HORN *by the arm and they go out.*)

PECHLIN: Listen, Captain, I'm arranging a little dinner at the club to honor the King on his return. May I put your name on the list?

NORDSTRÖM: That depends on who are going to be there!

PECHLIN: Here's the list! Go ahead; look at it!

NORDSTRÖM (*takes the list*[14] *and reads aloud*): Baron Karl Fredrik Ehrensvärd! . . . a good name! Kristoffer Aegidius von Hartmansdorff! Will do! Count Ture Johan Bjelke. He's O.K.! Jakob von Engeström! Good enough! . . . Adolf Ludvig Ribbing. Fine! Carl Fredrik Horn, the son of King Gustav's friend! Splendid! Carl Pontus Liljehorn, lieutenant colonel! Hm! . . . And then we have Jacob Johan Anckarström. Don't know him . . . Yes, I can be on that list!

PECHLIN (*gives him a goose pen*): Please sign your name!

NORDSTRÖM: Here?

PECHLIN: There!

NORDSTRÖM (*writes*): There you are!

PECHLIN (*to* OLSSON, *who has been listening to the conversation with varying facial expressions*): Maybe you'd like to come?

OLSSON: Yes, it would really be fun to see King Gustav's true friends together in one room . . . a lot of fun!

PECHLIN (*reaching him the pen*): Go ahead!

OLSSON: Am *I* to sign that paper? I?

PECHLIN: Yes, of course!

OLSSON: But I can't write! Won't you do it for me, general?

PECHLIN: I never sign other people's names.

OLSSON: I still less!

PECHLIN: If I hold on to your hand?

OLSSON: No, that would look pretty bad . . . Go ahead, general, write it; I'll be responsible for my signature, and I'll certainly come. That's sure!

PECHLIN (*writes*): Fine! I'm signing for you!

OLSSON (*examining the paper*): But your own name is missing, general!

PECHLIN: Why, I'm the host!

OLSSON: That's right! Of course!

    (*Commotion outside*)

NORDSTRÖM: Good-bye, gentlemen! Duty calls! . . .

PECHLIN: Is it a riot? Then you'll be arresting me, I suspect!

NORDSTRÖM: Not yet! Good-bye!

PECHLIN (*gets up*): Now I'll say good-bye to you, Olsson! And welcome to our dinner!

OLSSON: Oh, I'm leaving, too! Perhaps we can go together!

PECHLIN (*embarrassed*): But I'm only going upstairs! . . . Goodbye, Olsson! (*Embraces him*)

OLSSON: Good-bye then, general!

PECHLIN (*embraces* OLSSON *and sticks his tongue out at him behind his back*): You soul of honor!

OLSSON (*sticks his tongue out at* PECHLIN *behind his back*): Goodness! Nice to have run into you! *Very* nice! (*Releases himself from the embrace and leaves*)

PECHLIN (*puts the paper in his pocket*): There! That's that!

(KELLGREN *and* THORILD *come in in heated discussion; they greet the people present.*)

THORILD: I have never said that, Kellgren!

KELLGREN: Thorild, in the name of truth, explain yourself!

THORILD: This I have said, this I have meant! But you are a scoffer, a Voltaire, a royal ape: "Does not the whole world consist of weakness? Are you not, am I not little, poverty-stricken, feeble, in need of protection? For that reason, I consider the one who tramples frivolously on weakness the worst criminal in the world!"

KELLGREN: Wait a minute!

THORILD: No, I can not wait! "Kings who become insolent on their thrones; ministers who break the law and disregard the rights of man; priests who betray God and the people; the learned and the wise who sacrifice truth—all these must be warned! If they do not obey, judgment will follow! *Frappez!* That is to say, strike them down! Strike! Strike!"

KELLGREN (*to* HOLMBERG): He's crazy!

THORILD: "Those fools and rascals who are too powerful to be judged according to ordinary human laws shall be treated as monsters, as monsters in the heroic age or as villains in the age of chivalry!"

KELLGREN: Come on; have done!

THORILD: "Free communities of individual households, considered dead, which from rank misery and the Babel of oppression have reverted to nature are gradually restored to life. Actually, however, a new religion, no plebeian gods, no eternalized human fool on the throne of heaven, but, quite simply, God, the God who exists! New laws . . . natural rights! New morals, a new way of life . . . the way of liberty and joy!"

KELLGREN: *Parbleu!* Let me breathe! Come into the street again!

THORILD: "A scoundrel, a rascal, is one who insolently and openly prevents the happiness of humanity; who protects, promotes fools and scoundrels; shows in open clear acts that nothing is right and sacred to him!"

KELLGREN (*leaves*): No, I'm going! Good-bye, Mr. Holmberg. I'll be back later!

THORILD (*continues without dismay*): "To them belong all confirmed toadies and flatterers; all the weak fathers of all slavery; those who would rather not leave their occupations than to be the slaves of habit, formality, and comfortable treason!"

TAUBE: What a horrible person!

THORILD: "Is it not time that the oppressors are struck down? . . . It is necessary! Humanity can no longer be trampled upon! The fury of mankind is too great! The earth can no longer be governed by them!"

TAUBE: Amen!

(THORILD *stops before Rousseau's bust.*)

BADIN (*runs in*): Camphio, Camphio, Camphio! [15]

HOLMBERG: Who is to have them?

BADIN: Madame Skroderhem!

TAUBE: Behave yourself, nigger!

THORILD (*to* TAUBE): Why insult your black brother, man? Isn't he born of woman, with human rights, even as you and I?

TAUBE: Do you know who I am?

THORILD: You're a human being who happens to have been born with a white face . . . Even the great Gustav Adolf's daughter was black when she was born, covered with hair from her head to her knees, according to what she herself says! [16] (*To* BADIN) Therefore, child of nature, be proud of your origin, but do not be vain; rejoice that you were born in a time when, on the other side of the globe at least, your brothers have received the rights of citizenship in the great republic! To be sure, you serve a king, because you have been dragged into a rotten civilization that now is descending into its grave.

BADIN: Massa talk a lot, quite a lot! But Madame Skroderhem talk quite a lot more. She talk poem against King, she now in disfavor!

TAUBE (*to the Negro*): Where is the King, Negro?

BADIN: Majesty King land Grisslehamn! [17] and come to Haga in a few minutes!

TAUBE (*gets up and leaves*): Thank you for the information, Badin!

HORN (*enters hastily; goes up to* HOLMBERG): Holmberg!

HOLMBERG: Count!

HORN: Anckarström is charged with treason . . .

HOLMBERG: Good lord, why?

HORN: He cheered the returned officers right on the dock . . . There was a riot! The people were spitting at the traitors . . .

HOLMBERG: That Anckarström! He never can restrain himself . . .

HORN: Watch out . . . Badin is listening—he's spying for Liljensparre.

HOLMBERG (*giving the cards to* BADIN): Here are the cards, Badin! See to it that you play well . . .

BADIN (*dances with the deck of cards and sings Bellman's "Epistle No. 42"*): "Ren calad jag spår och tror . . ." [18]

HORN (*to* HOLMBERG): They say Baron De Geer offered the Anjala rebels his protection . . . but was attacked and beaten by the mob . . .

HOLMBERG: And Fersen?

HORN: He's keeping his distance . . .

HOLMBERG: Hästesko and Jägerhorn will lose their lives, I suppose . . .

HORN: That's what they say!

HOLMBERG: What don't we have to live through? Quiet! Liljensparre himself!

LILJENSPARRE (*in the doorway*): Close your store! (*General amazement*) All the stores are to be closed because of the riot!

HOLMBERG: At once . . . chief of police!

LILJENSPARRE: And Mr. Thorild is to keep his mouth shut; otherwise, he'll be exiled!

THORILD: Go, lictor, and tell your master that you have seen Thomas Thorild before the bust of Jean Jacques . . . Your master who has as much genius as you have lack of sense will then know what the world may expect! I could happily go to my death if I didn't think it worth being alive just now! The old world did not see and our children shall not see what divine truth now is letting us see. (*Beating of drums outside*)

LILJENSPARRE: Close your store right now!

(*General uneasiness and confusion.* THORILD *stands alone, calm, and unmoved.*)

CURTAIN

ACT II

The KING's *reception room at Haga Palace.*[19]
Tile stove with a mirror to the right. On the top of the stove is a bust of Voltaire. The whole back wall consists of open glass

doors through which can be seen a part of the park and Brunns-viken. Down on the stage to the right are a desk and a chair.

ARMFELT *is sitting nonchalantly at ease in a chair down on the stage to the right. He is cleaning his fingernails with a knife.* MUNCK *enters from the left, serious, depressed.*

ARMFELT: Now you're afraid, Munck!

MUNCK: No, but I don't feel like joking . . .

ARMFELT: That's what Struensee[20] said when they were going to cut off his head!

MUNCK: That's vulgar!

ARMFELT: You're very refined—at times! But then you've just been regent, too! How was it?

MUNCK: Regent?

ARMFELT: Why, you've been a member of the temporary regency!

MUNCK: Yes, of course! . . . Is it really true, Armfelt? . . .

ARMFELT (*interrupts*): Here at court people are always asking if it's true; I suppose because they're always lying so damnably!

MUNCK: I suppose you never lie, Armfelt?

ARMFELT: Never? That's saying too much!

MUNCK: Are there people waiting for an audience?

ARMFELT: Packed!

MUNCK: Will the King get out of this?

ARMFELT: He'll manage if he only finds out what the situation is! Where the land lies, where the enemy is! Perhaps you know the situation, Munck?

MUNCK: It's the strangest setup I've ever had anything to do with! The burghers and the farmers are aristocrats, and the highest nobility are the democratic opposition!

ARMFELT: Absolutely false! The lower estates are democrats like the king for whom they vote, and the nobility are as always aristocrats!

MUNCK: What are you then, Armfelt?

ARMFELT: And what are you, Munck? (*Pause*) What I am? The devil knows . . .

MUNCK: What is the King doing?

ARMFELT: He's changing his suit! . . . to meet the Queen . . . and the others!

MUNCK: This war with Denmark certainly has unpleasant consequences for their majesties!

ARMFELT (*coughs*): Hm! . . . Well, Fredrik V's daughter, our gracious Queen, can't very easily be neutral when her fatherland has declared war on our King! That's a difficult problem that I'll let you solve!

MUNCK (*after some consideration*): The friendship with which Her Majesty has honored me implies no guarantee for a successful mediation in this difficult case . . .

ARMFELT (*looking at the floor*): It has always been difficult to go between husband and wife . . . and, putting it bluntly, you'd better not depend on the Queen's friendship . . . If they make up, you'll be the sacrificial goat . . .

MUNCK: Oh no!

ARMFELT: Think of Struensee and Karolina Mathilda, our Queen's sister-in-law . . . Well, I'll not say anything, but now that the old rumor of the King's getting a divorce is afloat again . . .

MUNCK: Divorce?

ARMFELT: Of course! As you know, the King started divorce proceedings once.[21] This time maybe the Queen will insist on one! And then our King won't have any claim to the Danish crown. Be careful, Munck, so you don't compromise your queen of hearts! (*Makes a gesture with his penknife*) The audience is over!

MUNCK: *Comment? Diable,* which one of us was granting an audience?

ARMFELT (*insolently*): I was! . . . *Allez!*

MUNCK: I will have the honor of sending my seconds to Great Orchard Street . . .

ARMFELT: No, send them to Stockholm Palace where I'm living!

MUNCK: Stockholm Palace?

ARMFELT: Yes, in the Queen's apartment! . . .

(MUNCK *beaten; searches for words, which he can't find.* BADIN *enters from the back.*)

ARMFELT (*to* BADIN): Well, Massa, have you seen your pappy today?

MUNCK (*to* ARMFELT): Gösta Mauritz Armfelt . . .

ARMFELT (*to* BADIN *without paying any attention to* MUNCK): Did you catch any fish?

BADIN: No-o, the hooks weren't quite as crooked as they might have been . . .

ARMFELT: Hooks usually aren't as crooked as they should be . . .

PAPILLON (*enters at rear, speaks to* ARMFELT): I beg your pardon, Baron, there are people in the park.

ARMFELT: Kick 'em out!

MUNCK (*to* ARMFELT): Baron Armfelt!

ARMFELT (*to* PAPILLON): Can you see His Majesty?

PAPILLON: His Majesty will be here in a minute!

ARMFELT: Get out then; off with you; disappear!

MUNCK: *I* am expecting His Majesty.

ARMFELT: Perhaps! But the King expects me! (*To* PAPILLON) Show Mr. Struensee the way . . .

MUNCK: Which way?

ARMFELT: To Varberg's citadel! [22]

MUNCK: Citadel?

ARMFELT: Yes! You see you're accused . . . in a newspaper, to be sure . . . of having tried rather stupidly to pass off counterfeit money at Holmberg's Book Store!

MUNCK: That's a lie!

ARMFELT: Is it?

MUNCK (*spits towards* ARMFELT): Damn you! (*Goes out at back*)

ARMFELT: There! Now we're rid of him! . . . Badin! Report!

BADIN (*completely lays aside his foolish manner and broken speech*): Baron!

ARMFELT (*to* PAPILLON): Go!

(PAPILLON *leaves.*)

ARMFELT: So the Holmberg Book Store is the place where it's happening?

BADIN: Yes, Baron! But I don't quite get what's happening!

ARMFELT: Was General Pechlin there?

BADIN: Yes, the general was arranging a dinner, a subscription dinner, to celebrate the King's return!

ARMFELT: Pechlin? Let me see what that can mean . . . (*Thinks*) Who are in on it? Do you know?

BADIN: I saw only Captain Nordström and Olof Olsson, the farmer, sign the list.

ARMFELT: Strange! . . . However, there is a list! Get it!

BADIN: That's easily said! And if it were in any pocket but General Pechlin's, I'd get it.

ARMFELT: So you can't manage Pechlin!

BADIN: No, I can't manage that fellow!

ARMFELT: Try! . . . He's a damnable fellow, that Pechlin! . . . Listen . . . can't you recall any other name?

BADIN: Let's see! Yes, one more, but I might have misheard!

ARMFELT: Just say it. It might be one end of the skein!

BADIN (*looks about*): Captain Anckarström!

ARMFELT: Already arrested, so he's out! Not quite, though! . . . Badin, you were brought up in the royal family . . . can you tell me, confidentially and honestly, why the King and Anckarström hate each other?

BADIN: No! I can't say!

ARMFELT: But you know?

BADIN: No, but I can guess, and I might be wrong.

(*Pause*)

ARMFELT: Do you remember the time when Anckarström was the King's page?

BADIN: I remember the time but nothing else! But I do recall that the late dowager queen Lovisa Ulrika suddenly got a grudge against Anckarström and tried to have him dismissed from court!

ARMFELT: Why?

BADIN: Don't know!

(*Pause*)

ARMFELT: One thing you are sure of, though! That there is a conspiracy, with the object of limiting the royal power or something
still worse!

BADIN: That I am sure of!

ARMFELT: Are you just as sure that Lady Schröderheim is on intimate terms with the Queen and is trying to arouse her against
the King?

BADIN: Just as sure!

(*Pause*)

ARMFELT: Butcher Nordström of the House of Burghers and Olof
Olsson of the Farmers' Estate . . . with Pechlin! The King's best
friends *with* his worst enemy . . . Be on your way, Badin, and
keep your eyes open!

BADIN: Yes, Baron, but release me from one thing—just one!

ARMFELT: What?

BADIN: Don't make me have anything to do with Liljensparre! I'll
be ears and eyes for the King, but to spy for the chief of police—
that's ugly!

ARMFELT (*thoughtfully*): All right . . . on one condition!

BADIN: And that is?

ARMFELT: That you keep an eye on Liljensparre!

BADIN: Yes, that . . . (*Falls to his knees*) God bless you, Baron!

ARMFELT: The times are evil, and you can't depend on anyone!

BADIN (*gets up, happy*): I'll spy on the chief of police! Ha ha!
(*Leaves*)

(ARMFELT *alone; winds his watch, which strikes a few times.*
CHAMBERLAIN *enters from the left; opens the door wide*)

ARMFELT (*remains seated, almost as nonchalantly, self-confidently as
before*): Is it the King?

CHAMBERLAIN: His Majesty!

ARMFELT (*as before*): Is he alone?

CHAMBERLAIN: His Majesty is coming . . . alone!

(*Pause*)

KING (*enters from the left with a red-and-gold morocco briefcase, dressed in pale violet*): This looks bad, my dear Gösta, but I will straighten it out, I will . . . (*Stops*) If I can only get to a desk . . . (*Goes up to the desk where he sits down and opens the briefcase*) . . . and with a pen in my hand; I'm soaring now!

ARMFELT: The pen or an embroidery needle, not the sword.

KING: The audience list then! . . . Don't sit like that if someone should come!

ARMFELT: No one will come!

KING (*hands* ARMFELT *some gilded goose pens*): There, you can sharpen these while I'm talking . . .

(ARMFELT *sharpens pens during the following conversation.*)

KING (*now and then looks into the wall mirror directly opposite his place*): Where shall I begin?

ARMFELT: At the beginning!

KING: What's that—a catchword, Armfelt?

ARMFELT: The Anjala men!

KING: Absolutely right; and if one only begins, the rest will continue of itself, just as in a play. The Anjala men, then! A dozen with Hästesko at their head condemned by court-martial to be beheaded! That would do! But fifty-seven other officers condemned to be shot!

ARMFELT: Shoot them!

KING: I can't spare fifty-seven officers when the Danes are at the gates of Gothenburg!

ARMFELT: Promote lower officers from the commoners' rank instead, and you'll have the middle class on your side, and you'll have solved the blessed question about noncommissioned officers!

KING: Fine! . . . But that is contrary to law!

ARMFELT: Change the law!

KING: It was recently changed!

ARMFELT: Then you have a precedent!

KING: Don't be cynical, Armfelt!

ARMFELT: But I am serious! You committed a *faute* when you began the war against Russia contrary to the constitution. Now when everybody is pointing at that *faute,* which is really an error in form only, try to get the constitution changed and slip in the word aggression, and this whole pyramid of talk will fall.

KING: Change? How?

ARMFELT: Try it legally first, that is, with the three lower estates! Schröderheim will line up the clergy, Anders Liidberg[23] the burghers, and Ahlman[24] the farmers.

KING: Ahlman?

ARMFELT: Yes, just he! He's a regular rascal who threatens them with the police if they don't sign!

KING: A free people . . .

ARMFELT: Yes, yes, yes! If it can't be done legally, it'll have to be done illegally!

KING: Not again!

ARMFELT: *Ein mal ist kein mal, aber zwei mal, das ist was!*

KING: Never!

ARMFELT: If you're forced to?

KING: Who could force me?

ARMFELT: Various things! For example—a conspiracy!

KING: At that again?

ARMFELT: We are! But you don't believe in conspiracies even though you have just seen Anjala!

KING: Who is conspiring?

ARMFELT: Hard to tell! . . . It's disturbing, though, that two of your friends, Olof Olsson and Butcher Nordström, are more than suspected.

KING: What do you mean?

ARMFELT: That you can't trust anyone!

KING: But I made Olsson a member of parliament myself to block Fersen! What does this mean?

ARMFELT: That we're on thin ice that can break at any time!
(*Pause*)

KING: Let's drop the conspirators, and take up the Danish War!

ARMFELT: That's almost over!

KING: What's that?

ARMFELT: The English and Prussian ambassadors are threatening
Denmark . . . so that war will be settled diplomatically!

KING: Then I am lost! . . . As you know, I needed that war . . .
Who has done this to me?

ARMFELT: Circumstances . . .

KING: I am lost!

ARMFELT: How were you going to wage a war without an army,
and with your officers rebellious?

KING: I had a plan . . .

ARMFELT: For a play?

KING: Shame on you!

ARMFELT: The one with the Dalesmen!

KING: Yes!

ARMFELT: That's a play, if it's anything! Do you believe the Dalesmen would lift a finger for their king after what happened to
them on Norrmalm's Square? [25]

KING: I *know* that they will! The army's treason has stirred them
up, and if I go to them personally . . .

ARMFELT: In costume? Eh? As Gustav Vasa? . . .[26] That's a masquerade, and the Dalesmen don't understand that!

KING: Let's go to the next point!

ARMFELT: That is the Queen!

KING: No! We do not talk about the Queen!

ARMFELT: About Lady Skroderhjelm then!

KING: Lady Schröderheim, yes! She has spread another infamous
pasquille about me, and now she has to fall!

ARMFELT: She has a tendency toward falling, but now she should be
ruined!

KING: Exile from court to begin with! . . .

ARMFELT: How will that be managed?

KING: It will be managed like this! Public opinion . . . do you know it? . . . Public opinion will not permit the state secretary to live in shame with a *galant dame,* who interferes in the government and conspires with the enemies of the nation . . . so Elis will have to get a divorce!

ARMFELT: Poor devil! Then he'll collapse!

KING: He may, but my state secretary may not be ridiculous!

ARMFELT: Ridiculous? In these days, when . . . besides . . . You were talking about public opinion . . . apropos . . . that Munck was just here . . .

KING (*shortly*): What did he want?

ARMFELT: He was afraid because of the Russian bills he's trying to pass out in Stockholm.

KING: In Stockholm? The Russian rubles were intended for the Russian War . . . Munck is a fool!

ARMFELT: I hinted at something like that . . .

KING: I am tired of that fellow . . . Can you get rid of him?

ARMFELT: That's already done! I frightened him away! (*Pause*)

ARMFELT: What has Anckarström been up to that warrants arresting him?

KING (*nervously*): Anckarström? Why did you mention him now? Just now?

ARMFELT: Because I happen to have been talking about him earlier today! What has he done?

KING (*irritated*): He has demonstrated for the rebels in public. That is what he has done! . . . His father-in-law[27] is in the Russian service, and the whole fellow is suspect! (*Rings*)

(CHAMBERLAIN *enters.*)

KING: Bring me the audience list!

(CHAMBERLAIN *goes.*)

ARMFELT (*takes up his watch*): While we're talking, time passes; events take place; people think and act; opinions are formed and create deeds! The one who is ready first wins the game! (*The watch strikes.*)

KING: I am soon ready! Do you want to go out in the park for a while? But wait for my orders! Yes, I need to assemble my thoughts!

(ARMFELT *gets up; darkens.* CHAMBERLAIN *enters; gives the* KING *the audience list.* KING *studies the list.* ARMFELT *tries to read it, but the* KING *conceals it.*)

KING (*to* ARMFELT, *impatiently*): Leave me!

ARMFELT: I will leave you! . . . to your fate! (*Goes out at the back*)

KING (*to* CHAMBERLAIN): Baron Taube may come!

(CHAMBERLAIN *goes out.* KING *alone; examines himself in the mirror.* TAUBE *enters—in clerical garb.*)

KING: There! Already done! . . . Have you been consecrated, too? Ordained, I mean?

TAUBE: Yes, Your Majesty!

KING: Be prepared to accompany me to Dalarna! . . . Adieu!

(TAUBE *lingers.*)

KING: I have much to do! Out!

(TAUBE *exits at back.* KING *rings.* CHAMBERLAIN *enters.*)

KING: State Secretary Schröderheim!

(CHAMBERLAIN *goes out.* KING *alone; tests a pen on his fingernail.* SCHRÖDERHEIM *enters.*)

KING: Come closer so no one will hear us!

(SCHRÖDERHEIM *approaches the table.*)

KING: Everyone in this house listens! . . . Did you see Armfelt?

SCHRÖDERHEIM: He went upstairs a little while ago!

KING (*pointing upwards*): Up there? And I asked him to go into the park! There you see! *Bellum omnium inter omnes!* . . . Listen! . . . First you're to go to the English and Prussian ambassadors and beg or threaten them, whichever is necessary; try to persuade them not to influence Denmark before I have assembled troops! Have you understood?

SCHRÖDERHEIM: Perfectly!

KING: Number two: there is no time to waste, you see! . . . Have you heard anything about a new conspiracy?

SCHRÖDERHEIM: Yes, Your Majesty!

KING: Do you believe it?

SCHRÖDERHEIM: Liljensparre *knows* about it!

KING: He isn't gullible! . . . And it concerns limiting the King's powers, of course?

SCHRÖDERHEIM: Naturally!

KING: Well, then I'll go to Dalarna and get troops against Denmark —do you hear that?—against the enemy at the gates of Gothenburg. Beyond that you may guess as you please, but say nothing! (SCHRÖDERHEIM *bows*.)

KING: Number three! . . . Listen carefully, and understand my half-uttered hint . . . Elis! Do you believe a high-ranking person can or should live in a marriage that brings him dishonor and ridicule? Do you believe he has the right to, no matter how unprejudiced our times and morals may be?

SCHRÖDERHEIM (*who believes that the* KING *is talking about his own marriage answers easily*): No, Your Majesty! He does not have the right to compromise his high position!

KING: Not even if he has to suffer the agony of death through the painful operation which is called divorce!

SCHRÖDERHEIM (*nonchalantly*): It cannot be painful to free oneself from dishonor! The very opposite . . .

KING: That is then your profoundest conviction . . .

SCHRÖDERHEIM: My absolute conviction, all the more since such an act would be applauded by all right-thinking people!

KING: *Bien!* Then you'll put in your application for divorce today! My court chaplain Taube will look after the details in the consistory!

SCHRÖDERHEIM (*struck*): No! . . . Am I?

KING: Yes, you! . . . Have you understood?

SCHRÖDERHEIM: I have understood!

KING: Go quickly then and release yourself from dishonor and ridicule—as you say, that can't be painful! (*Rings*)

(SCHRÖDERHEIM *goes out slowly.* KING *writes.*)

KING (*to* SCHRÖDERHEIM): Do not forget to see to the parliamentary elections! The royal sheriffs and pastors . . . in your parishes . . . are to employ all means! All! I won't leave anything to chance these days! . . . Yes, I have ceased to believe in honesty and truth and the like! During the last session of parliament, I scorned pressure and bribes; now I command them! That is what I have learned from experience and from Anjala!

(SCHRÖDERHEIM *exits.* CHAMBERLAIN *enters.*)

KING: Olsson, member of parliament!

(CHAMBERLAIN *exits.* KING *gets up; assumes a new, genial expression before the mirror.* OLSSON *enters.*)

KING (*goes up to* OLSSON; *pretends to be amazed*): No! Well! . . . my friend Olsson! You are welcome company! Welcome to my house. (*Embraces him and pats him on the shoulder*) Listen, Olof, I have something to ask of you! A service, a favor if you wish, and then a bit of information!

OLSSON: Your Majesty, may I start with the information? Then I may be in favor!

KING: What can it be? Is it a conspiracy? Are you party to it?

OLSSON: Good heavens, no!

KING: Then we'll start with the favor! Olsson, you are a very able man, and you know better than I how influential you are! Will you be the speaker in your estate, if I ask you humbly?

OLSSON: Hm! The others will be so envious that . . .

KING: Which others? Fersen, your squire? But that's the intention, isn't it? Why, I am the radical, the democrat, the one who hates the nobility, the first citizen in a free country! The man of the people and the defender of the oppressed! I am the disciple of Rousseau . . . and of Voltaire! . . . The social contract, *Le Contrat Social,* is my gospel; I have it on the table next to my bed!

George Washington is my friend! Franklin my ideal! There you have me!

OLSSON (*thoughtfully*): These ideas expressed by Your Majesty amaze me somewhat, especially since I heard them taught by one Master Thorild, who is not known for his royal sympathies!

KING: Master Thorild and I are the only people in the country who logically respect the modern ways of thinking, and you certainly cannot accuse me of being a royalist? Can you?

OLSSON: Well, you see, I can't straighten this out in a flash, but, what we are looking for at the moment—when the idea of power vested in the majority is beginning to come back—is to have a king . . . who is very much a king!

KING (*turns on his heel*): There you are! Now I know Olof Olsson! . . . Take my hand! . . . You know, there was a person a little while ago who wanted to make me suspicious of you, who wanted to insinuate not only that you were indifferent but also that you had joined the party of malcontents.

OLSSON: I?

KING: Yes, he even tossed out an accusation . . .

OLSSON: It is that Pechlin list that I wanted to tell about!

KING: Pechlin? Is he at it again?

OLSSON: Forgive me, Your Majesty, but this is going a little too fast for me . . . I'm used to the plow, and you don't turn in the middle of the furrow with that!

KING: But we are always in a hurry! So, what sort of list is it?

OLSSON: Briefly then! . . . Under the pretext of arranging a subscription banquet to receive the King, General Pechlin has been circulating a list . . . So as not to reveal my suspicions of the real meaning of the list, I let him write my name next to Captain Nordström's. But my conviction is that these names belong to the people who are conspiring against the king and the government.

KING: That is the fox's track! That is Pechlin! . . . Can you remember some of these "loyal" subjects' names?

OLSSON: Some I remember!—Liljehorn, von Engeström, Ribbing, Horn . . .

KING: Impossible!

OLSSON: Anckarström . . .

KING (*unpleasantly affected*): Always that one! . . . Wait a moment! (*Rings*)

(CHAMBERLAIN *enters.*)

KING: Send a messenger to Liljensparre and command him to arrest General Pechlin!

CHAMBERLAIN: Your Majesty, Chief Liljensparre is in the audience room!

KING: *Tiens!* Ask him to come in the next time I ring!

(CHAMBERLAIN *goes.*)

KING (*sits down at the desk and looks tired*): Let's return to our point of departure . . . Remember, if you are the speaker always to come back to the point of departure; otherwise, they'll talk you into confusion! . . . So then, do you want to be speaker in the Farmers' Estate?

OLSSON: Yes, but . . .

KING: And you promise to serve the cause of freedom and the people?

OLSSON: Preferably the King's!

KING: That is the same cause! (*They stare into each other's eyes for a moment.*)

OLSSON: Your Majesty, words change their values in the course of time; words become ambiguous, finally meaningless. I can't straighten out this maze of words, but the cause I have promised to serve I will be faithful to, the class into which I was born I will not desert, but illegal means I detest!

KING: Well said! *You* can talk, when you want to! . . . Go into the park and stay for the evening's entertainment as my guest!

OLSSON (*bows*): Your Majesty! . . .

KING: Olsson, never put your faith in any human being!

OLSSON: No, Your Majesty, I don't, either! (*Goes out*)

(KING *stares at him hastily. Then he rings. Pause.* CHAMBERLAIN *opens the door.*)

(LILJENSPARRE *enters.*)

KING: What's new in town? Is everything quiet?

LILJENSPARRE (*worried*): No, Your Majesty, it isn't!

KING: What is up . . . Pechlin?

LILJENSPARRE: If he were the only one! But there is something else!

KING: Speak out!

LILJENSPARRE: How shall I put it? . . . You don't see it; you don't hear it, but you feel it. You can't take hold of it—new ideas, new doctrines—I think they call it the spirit of the times . . .

KING: I do not believe in spirits . . . Is it Thorild's doctrines? A talker and a half-fool!—rather entertaining at that!

LILJENSPARRE: The events in Paris! . . .

KING: Those I know . . . just froth on the surface! . . . Let's talk about our concerns! . . . I want you to have General Pechlin arrested at once and his house searched!

LILJENSPARRE: Will be done, Your Majesty!

KING: I especially command you to obtain a list with certain names on it!

LILJENSPARRE: General Pechlin never keeps dangerous papers in his possession!

KING: Then I am better informed! . . . I believe you are tired, Liljensparre, and need a rest!

LILJENSPARRE: No, Your Majesty!

KING: Are you watching Nordin and Walquist? [28]

LILJENSPARRE: They appear very little!

KING: Because they are working in silence! Now I command you to leave them undisturbed! Never mention their names, and if you hear them mentioned, pretend that they don't exist! . . . Now go and arrest Pechlin!

(LILJENSPARRE *tarries as if he wanted to say something.* CHAMBERLAIN *in*)

KING: What do you want?

CHAMBERLAIN: Your Majesty, Baron Pechlin requests an audience on a highly important matter!

KING: Pechlin! (*To* LILJENSPARRE) Have you ever heard the like? (*To the* CHAMBERLAIN) He may come when I ring!

(CHAMBERLAIN *goes.*)

KING: This is the most shameless insolence I have ever witnessed in my life!

LILJENSPARRE: Those are the Pechlin tactics!

KING: Just wait, old man, and I'll soon have learned your tactics! (*Writes on a piece of paper*) We will have a memorandum so that we don't speak beside the point! . . . And now go and stand behind the pillar so that you'll hear every word . . . because it will be a war of words; Pechlin does not use other weapons! . . . What do you think he wants? From what side will he attack?

LILJENSPARRE: Most likely he'll offer some dangerous secrets which aren't at all dangerous. (*At the door*)

KING: His errand is to try to avert danger . . . to protect himself behind others' backs . . . even if the backs belong to his best friends . . . To your place, Liljensparre! (*Takes hold of the bell*) So! . . . Why I believe my hand is trembling! He is a devil of a man! (*Rubs his forehead*) I have to take the lead; otherwise, he'll talk me down! . . . Tableau! (*Rings*)

(LILJENSPARRE *stands just outside the doors at the back.*)

(CHAMBERLAIN *opens the door.* PECHLIN *enters.*)

KING: Good day, old friend! (*To the* CHAMBERLAIN) Offer the baron a chair! There! . . . It is just as welcome as unexpected for me to see you, General! Please sit down! . . . And the baroness is well? I had the honor of greeting her when I came in! . . . Well, what has given me the pleasure of seeing you at Haga, Baron?

PECHLIN (*who has been standing beside the chair*): Your Majesty, I come as a supplicant . . .

KING: Oh! That's unusual! It isn't every day you supplicate, Baron . . .

PECHLIN: Consequently there must be urgent reasons . . .

KING: Governmental reasons are urgent, and, Baron, you do interest yourself in the nation, the government, and the general welfare! . . . Go on!

PECHLIN: A certain opinion, resulting from the recently ended Russian war, hm . . .

KING: Produce the paper . . . Don't be embarrassed . . .

PECHLIN (*startled*): A certain uneasiness in people's minds needs to be allayed . . .

KING: Speak plainly, Baron!

PECHLIN: . . . calmed, and for that reason we, a number of Your Majesty's faithful subjects, have decided to express our faithful feelings by means of a public banquet.

KING: Very good! Where is it to be held?

PECHLIN: At the Exchange! . . . But a banquet without the guest of honor . . .

KING: Am I to be there, too? That is . . .

PECHLIN: That is the whole of my supplication! (*Pause*)

KING (*controls himself and turns*): Good! Give me the list!
    (PECHLIN *pretends to search in his pockets.*)

KING: Don't you have it with you?

PECHLIN: Yes, of course! . . . My word, no, I must have forgotten it!

KING (*looks toward the back*): It doesn't matter; we'll find it. I have such competent finders of lost things; we have a whole section in the police department that does nothing else! (*They look at each other for a moment with hate-filled eyes.*) I need only say a word to Liljensparre, and he'll find it at once!

PECHLIN: I don't believe that will be necessary, Your Majesty . . .

KING: I don't believe so either! (*Pause*)

PECHLIN: Why not, Your Majesty?

KING: Because we can write a new one! (*Pause*)

PECHLIN: We can do that, too!

KING (*gets up*): Sit down here at the desk!

PECHLIN: No, thank you! That wouldn't do!

KING (*sharply*): Sit down!

(PECHLIN *sits down; reads the* KING's *memorandum and smiles without being noticed by the* KING.)

KING (*looks toward the back*): Write!

PECHLIN (*takes the pen, writes and dictates*): Liljehorn!

KING: The younger, yes! Klas Horn!

PECHLIN (*without amazement*): Klas Horn!

KING (*with increasing amazement*): Von Engeström!

PECHLIN (*with unshaken calmness*): No, Anckarström first!

KING (*becomes pale and looks at himself in the mirror*): It pleases me particularly to see Anckarström's name; he is my special friend, and his father-in-law, who is in the Russian service, can do me great service.

(PECHLIN *gets up and goes hastily to the left door.*)

KING (*signals toward the back*): Where are you going?

(LILJENSPARRE *appears but quickly withdraws.*)

PECHLIN: Heavens, why, I forgot that I have the list in my hat! (*He takes the list from his hat, which is lying on a chair by the door.*)

KING: Give it to me!

(PECHLIN *gives him the list, which the* KING *glances through.*)

KING (*mocking*): Yes, yes, this is a fine collection! . . . Tell your friends that I am coming! . . . Shall I add my name, perhaps? (*Sits down and writes*) "Gustav" *m.p.,* by his own hand! . . . Perhaps I may copy it?

PECHLIN: With the greatest pleasure, Your Majesty!

KING: Perhaps you yourself? . . .

PECHLIN: I am in somewhat of a hurry . . .

KING: We will ask Liljensparre . . .

PECHLIN: He is a secretary who will do!

KING (*calls toward the back*): Liljensparre!

LILJENSPARRE (*enters*): Your Majesty!

PECHLIN (*unforced to* LILJENSPARRE): Well, good day to you! Are you here?

KING (*to* LILJENSPARRE): Copy this list!

PECHLIN: Perhaps you'd like to come to the banquet, Liljensparre?

KING: He certainly would! He goes to all your celebrations, Pechlin! And he can take a few friends with him, I suspect?

PECHLIN: As many as he wants to!

KING (*laughing*): And as strong ones as he can get in the event you'd want to arrest me?

PECHLIN (*laughing*): Not that! It is only General Pechlin that gets arrested!

KING: But he is always released!

PECHLIN: Because he's found innocent . . .

KING: Innocent because of lack of proof!

PECHLIN: Yes, proof, Your Majesty, that is the heart of the matter! They think they have their hands full of material evidence, obvious proof, and all the same they lose in every court . . . I know one scoundrel . . .

KING (*smiling bitterly*): I know a fox, who for thirty long years believed he had pulled justice by the nose, but who was finally caught when his own tail got caught in the fence . . .

PECHLIN: I know a goose . . .

KING (*rings and raises his voice*): You will wait out there until the copy has been made, Baron Pechlin! . . . Farewell, Baron, yet another time; tell your friends that I will come. (*Shakes* PECHLIN's *hand rather hard and with irony*)

PECHLIN: I shall forward . . .

KING (*interrupts*): And I will come *as* is befitting a guest of honor and a king!

PECHLIN: Royally, in a word! (*Goes*)

KING: Yes, royally, you damned fox! . . . (*To* LILJENSPARRE) That was the most insolent thing I have seen in my life! (*Violently*) Shall I have him arrested?

LILJENSPARRE: No, Your Majesty, that will only increase his popularity and make him still more dangerous!

KING (*goes hastily to the desk*): And look here! He has read my papers and my memorandum for his audience! (*Strikes his fore-*

head) Now the cup is overflowing! . . . Listen, there are people
who consider regicide justified . . . Can't a king have a bandit
murdered then? . . . He has read my memorandum . . . I had
written "the fox"; with my own pen he has added "and the goose
—a fable!" (*Breaks his pen into pieces and tramples them under
his feet*) At my own desk! (*Collapses in a chair*) And I may
not have him arrested! Because . . . then I'd be the butt of ridicule! (*Pause*) Liljensparre, go to all the restaurant keepers in
town and order them to find excuses . . . No, the Danish War
shall save me, even from this banquet! (*Pause*) Do you believe
these are the names of the conspirators?

LILJENSPARRE: Now I do!

KING: Why did he give me the names?

LILJENSPARRE: To show how numerous they are and to frighten you!

KING: Only blameless men—Klas Horn, the son of my friend
Fredrik Horn, who commanded the guards during the revolution
in 1772! That hurts me most. A young man, a young fellow with
the most idealistic way of thinking, idealistically inclined, a poet,
highly educated . . . What do they want of me? What have I
done to them? (*Pause*) Go now, Liljensparre!

LILJENSPARRE: What is to be done to the people on the list?

KING: I don't know! . . . Nothing! . . . I can't do anything!

LILJENSPARRE (*looks out uneasily*): Your Majesty, someone is coming!

KING (*jumps up*): Who is it?

LILJENSPARRE: Her Majesty, the Queen!

KING: God in heaven! . . . What shall I do . . . one, two, three!
I'll go in and rest for a few minutes! . . . Tell the chamberlain
to ask the Queen to wait . . . a few minutes! (*Goes out to the
right*)

(LILJENSPARRE *goes to the left.*)

(CHAMBERLAIN *enters, goes to the back.* QUEEN *and* LADY SCHRÖ-
DERHEIM *enter from the park.*)

CHAMBERLAIN: His Majesty said that he will be here immediately! (*Goes to the left*)

QUEEN (*looks about the room*): There seems to be room enough here!

LADY SCHRÖDERHEIM: His Majesty has so many friends, of course . . .

QUEEN: There are many of them, but what kind?

LADY SCHRÖDERHEIM: Elis, my husband, is the best of them, though . . .

QUEEN: That's why he is in disfavor, too . . . while Armfelt, who doesn't have a conscience, has risen so high that he has taken over my apartment in Stockholm Palace.

LADY SCHRÖDERHEIM: There are situations when one can say "the worse, the better!" Don't complain, Your Majesty!

QUEEN: You mean, Anne Charlotte, that one doesn't need to look for the reason . . .

LADY SCHRÖDERHEIM: Not when it's obvious, no! Besides, the Danish War is sufficient excuse for Your Majesty's return to her family!

QUEEN: You have put it into words, and . . . well, I shall return . . .

LADY SCHRÖDERHEIM: Accompanied by the sympathy of all right-thinking women, because if an example is set here, it will have even greater effect in the lower classes!

QUEEN: When I listen to you, Anne Charlotte, I am strong, but as soon as I am alone . . . Don't desert me . . . stay by my side when he comes, because I am afraid of him. He is still trying to get the Danish crown to which I have hereditary claims!

LADY SCHRÖDERHEIM: But he is afraid of me! Be easy, Your Majesty, I have fought with him before . . . and not without success!

QUEEN: If I get out of this, it will be your accomplishment and the honor will be yours!

LADY SCHRÖDERHEIM: The honor will be slight, but the pleasure greater . . .

QUEEN: Pleasure? . . . I lose my son . . .

LADY SCHRÖDERHEIM: Take him with you!

QUEEN: Away from his father? That would break his young
heart . . .

LADY SCHRÖDERHEIM: It will heal quickly . . .

QUEEN: You're terrible . . . Don't you have a heart? . . .

LADY SCHRÖDERHEIM: Not at all! And that's why I always win in
affairs of the heart . . . Always!

(KING *enters from the right, goes, calm and friendly towards
the* QUEEN, *but stops, startled, when he sees* LADY SCHRÖDERHEIM.)

KING: Good day, my consort! That I am still alive and have the
pleasure of seeing you, I attribute only to a lucky chance! (*He
takes the* QUEEN's *hand and conducts her to a sofa, and sits down
on a chair directly opposite her.*) You look radiant, so I conclude
you did not miss me as much as I missed you! How is my son?

(QUEEN *indicates with a gesture that* LADY SCHRÖDERHEIM *is
present.*)

KING (*gets up*): Ah! Dear Lady Schröderheim, forgive me for not
seeing you! Why, I believe you have grown since I last saw you
. . . made new conquests . . .

LADY SCHRÖDERHEIM: Not over the Russians at least . . .

KING: As witty and quick as ever . . . A shame that I didn't take
you along to the war . . .

LADY SCHRÖDERHEIM: I wouldn't have thrown down my weapons like
the other officers . . .

KING: At the feet of your King, you mean! No, I would have relied
on you as my best friend . . . you, faithful Elis' gracious wife
. . . Apropos, have you seen Elis?

LADY SCHRÖDERHEIM: No, not today; besides . . .

KING: Oh! He is sitting out there waiting for you! . . .

LADY SCHRÖDERHEIM: For me?

KING: Because of a highly important matter!

LADY SCHRÖDERHEIM: What can that be?

KING: I shall tell the tale out of school! He has written a new play
with the leading role for you!

LADY SCHRÖDERHEIM (*happy*): No! Is it . . .

KING: Yes, it's cut very low—come. (*He takes her hand politely and conducts her to the left door.*)

QUEEN: Lady Schröderheim is staying with me . . .

KING: She is going, it seems to me . . . going to her husband, where her place is . . . and I assume you, my dear, do not want to separate husband and wife! Or do you? (*Conducts* LADY SCHRÖDERHEIM *politely out, locks the door. Then he goes and sits down opposite the* QUEEN.)

KING: Alone at last! (*Pause*) Have you any request to make?

QUEEN: Only one!

KING: Name it!

QUEEN: I want my freedom again!

KING: Which freedom?

(QUEEN *remains silent.*)

KING: Have you lacked freedom here? . . .

(QUEEN *looks at the floor.*)

KING: Have I demanded an accounting for your actions, including those that have transgressed the limits of convention?

QUEEN: When Your Majesty began to seek the dissolution of our marriage last time, your friends persuaded you not to, mostly out of fear of war with Denmark . . . Now, when this war has already broken out, it seems to me that the main objections have disappeared . . .

KING: I suppose you, no doubt, know as well as I that our marriage was arranged by the secret committee[29] in its day and by the empress of Russia at the time of the peace treaty; in other words, the government at that time was forced to select a bride for me without the slightest regard for our personal feelings. That time when we both yielded to the powerful interests of two nations, we made a sacrifice that has cost us our personal happiness . . . The concept *sacrifice* implies giving up happiness . . . Can't then the knowledge that we have suffered together for others, for many others, keep up our courage until the cup has been drained? Aren't there other reasons than the political for our bearing the

burden all the way? Hasn't our son the first right to be reared by
parents, by his father and his mother . . .

QUEEN (*gets up*): No, I cannot answer so many questions at the
same time! I demand my freedom . . .

KING: Which freedom? I ask that again. Both of us are bound by
family bonds, and I, like you, have given up my freedom to
found another family!

QUEEN: You do not understand me, sire!

KING: We have never understood each other; and I have never insisted on knowing your secrets. When I asked for this meeting,
it was only to hear your wishes! Madame!

QUEEN: You have heard my only wish, sire.

KING: You know that I once nourished the same wish, but then
you did not want to. Now I do not want to!

QUEEN: All because of Russia!

KING: No, the time is past when the Russian ambassador and the
English chose the members of our parliament, appointed the
secret committee, and named our national council; yes, it was
Russia that gave my father, the prince-bishop of Lübeck, the
throne of Sweden and me a consort. Those times are past, and
that is my modest achievement, which people have forgotten, and
to the degree that they haven't understood my last war against
Russia which they call treason. Recently a court poet compared
me with Gustav Vasa, the liberator from foreign oppression; I
smiled when I read it, but there may be a grain of truth in the
flattery . . .

QUEEN: If my memory doesn't play me false, it was the Danes who
were driven out by Gustav Vasa . . .

KING: Yes, and now they are going to be driven out by Gustav III!

QUEEN (*goes toward the back*): Then I will have the honor of
being the first one Your Majesty drives out!

KING: First or last, but, madame, you are a Swedish subject . . .

QUEEN: Subject? Yes, Your Majesty's subject . . .

KING: Enjoying all the rights that I secured the people in the revolution of 1772, even the liberty to breakfast at the Clas-on-the-Corner, among other things! Shall we consider the subject closed?

QUEEN: For all time, I hope!

KING: We have said that so many times, madame, but a little quarrel now and then seems to fulfill the purpose of reconciling us!

QUEEN: Or to separate us still more . . .

KING: Still more! Bravo! . . . Tell me, though, before we separate still more, why do you hate me?

(QUEEN *remains silent*.)

KING: I remember that you wept when I sent my chamberlain to Ekolsund to tell you that my revolution had succeeded . . . when I played Brutus and destroyed the Caesars in homespun . . .[30] In a tender moment you admitted that they were tears of miscalculation as you had not believed me capable of a manly act . . . From that moment you hated me, because it was my feminine qualities you loved, and I had become feminine because I had been reared too long among skirts and at the embroidery hoop—that was not my fault! You loved, but despised me; because you received my tactfulness as a sign of respect, which you nevertheless despised, and when I acted as I should . . . as a man . . . you called it coarseness and hated me! . . . So I had to choose between your contempt and your hatred, and I finally chose your hatred!

QUEEN (*after some consideration*): You forget, sire, that there are some details of our life together . . .

KING: That have to be forgotten . . . I have forgotten them!

QUEEN: But I haven't!

KING: That is too bad, for, if you have forgotten yourself once, the only thing to do is to keep on forgetting!

(QUEEN *turns away*.)

KING: Now we have surely drained every subject dry . . . I can already feel it . . . I have more important matters to attend to . . . and I'm very tired . . . I have not slept for eight nights . . .

QUEEN: You have just come from Finland, sire?

KING: Yes, madame! Fleeing from my own countrymen across the Åland Sea . . . I assure you I am not happy . . . War and death sentences lie ahead . . . and then I have another conspiracy at my throat . . .

QUEEN: And you can take that so lightly? . . .

KING: Who knows? . . . Permit me to ring for the state secretary!

QUEEN: Farewell, sire!

KING (*takes her hand*): Farewell, my Queen! . . . May I ask one favor?

QUEEN: Certainly!

KING: Out of consideration for our son, have a little respect for my name and my reputation! . . . I do not ask much, because I don't deserve it!

QUEEN: Sire, I do not know . . .

KING: Do not say anything . . . do only as I ask . . .

QUEEN (*appeased*): For the prince's sake, yes!

KING (*kisses her hand*): Thank you for that!

QUEEN (*moved*): Thank you . . . for that! (*Leaves at the back*)

    (KING *rings.* CHAMBERLAIN *enters.*)

KING: Bring me my suit, my Dalecarlian costume . . . and the writing case!

    (CHAMBERLAIN *goes out; comes in again immediately with a Dalecarlian folk costume and a writing case, which he places on a table*)

KING: Fine! . . . Call Baron Armfelt!

    (CHAMBERLAIN *goes.* KING *sits down at the desk.* ARMFELT *appears at the back.*)

KING (*gets up*): There you are! . . . I want to say good-bye to you, because now I am going, first to Dalarna, afterwards to Gothenburg! . . . When I return . . . we will change the form of government!

ARMFELT: Bravo!

KING: Wait until I'm done!

ARMFELT: For what?

KING: Your instructions! . . . First, give the Queen her rooms again!

ARMFELT: Hm! . . . That I understand!

KING: Then recall the complaint against Anckarström . . .

ARMFELT: That I do not understand!

KING: You don't need to! . . . Further, you probably don't remember that after the death of Charles XII, the Swedish government sued the Görtz heirs for money that was due it. Strangely enough, the commission finally came to the conclusion that the Swedish government owed Görtz's heirs seventy thousand dalers.[31]

ARMFELT: That was comic!

KING: Tragic rather, I feel, for, as we know, Görtz had to suffer because of supposed thefts . . . Well, the estates have never wanted to acknowledge this debt . . . for the sake of Charles XII, of course . . . Now I command that it be paid at once!

ARMFELT: That I understand!

KING: *Tant mieux!* . . .

ARMFELT: And then the women who kill their children, I suppose?

KING: Exactly! Have my views about a milder punishment for infanticide[32] and the whole argument printed!

ARMFELT: What will the clergymen say to that?

KING: Nordin and Wallqvist will take care of that matter!

ARMFELT: The invisible ones!

KING: Whom you will be so good as to give a free hand; don't be stingy with the food money for the club! [33]

ARMFELT: But the hired hurrah boys and the servant girls?

KING: Papillon is chairman of the gang, and Badin will look after the girls, which will go all the more easily since I am already supporting the milder servant law.[32]

ARMFELT: Who is to spread the false rumors then?

KING: Liljensparre, naturally! . . .

ARMFELT: That's not badly put together! Considered as a play!

(*Touches the Dalecarlian folk costume with his cane*)

KING: Who knows? Perhaps the whole thing is a play?
ARMFELT: But the last act! Do you have that?
KING: It will come of itself!
ARMFELT: It will come of itself!
   (*They look at each other for a moment; then the* KING *goes hastily to the right.*)

CURTAIN

ACT III

At Huvudsta, KLAS HORN's *manor, near Stockholm. A large room, with open French doors to a large wooden veranda facing the garden. In the middle of the room is a round dining table with a tablecloth on it; on the table is a laurel tree in a green pot; the tree has been cut into the shape of a small pyramid and strung with ribbons in the French tricolor. Doors to the right and left.* RIBBING, HORN, *and* ANCKARSTRÖM *are sitting at the table.*

HORN: This is how far we have come . . . The King went to Dalarna, and after he had prayed on his knees at the altar in every church, he spoke . . . dressed as a Dalesman . . . to the people! And succeeded! He was offered twenty thousand men, but took only six thousand, and they are at Drottningholm now under Armfelt's command. Then he went to Gothenburg with the intention of waging the alleged Danish War, which was called off, however, by the English and Prussian ambassadors. Upon his return to Stockholm he summoned parliament, the parliament which is to decide the fate of the country and of liberty! Because he *has* decided on a coup d'état,[34] and on an absolute monarchy! Your turn, Anckarström!

ANCKARSTRÖM: I still think you talk too much!

HORN: But we have to straighten out this matter so that no injustice will be done!

ANCKARSTRÖM: It can't be straightened out; that's why it has to be cut!

HORN: Wait a minute!

ANCKARSTRÖM: No! Don't as much as touch his tangled skein. If you do, you'll be caught in it! All his schemes are as if the devil himself had put them together! He passes himself off as the man of the people and of liberty, crushes the lords, and makes himself absolute master of the four estates! Don't you see that he's acting Mirabeau and blinding us? Why, he *seems* to carry through the French Revolution—he, the King! Why, that's as perverse as he is, through and through!

RIBBING: Anckarström is right!

HORN: No, he's going to have to explain!

ANCKARSTRÖM (*gets up*): Go ahead and talk. I'll wait until my time comes! (*He goes and fills a pipe; sits down in the open doorway at the back and looks out into the garden*)

HORN: Now we'll let Ribbing in on the secret . . . since he has expressed his approval of Anckarström's views.

ANCKARSTRÖM: Anckarström has only one point of view—*frappez, strike!*

HORN: Then I don't have to say it, and I don't need to admit that I share his opinion, that is, if the other plan can't be carried through! . . . The other plan is Pechlin's, you see, and consists only of arresting and deposing him and setting up a new form of government under the duke and the queen!

RIBBING: One question—does Pechlin know your plan?

HORN: No! And he'll not be told! Pechlin believes we're hunting for his sake, while he retrieves for us!

RIBBING: One more question—do any of you have a personal interest in this, or, in other words . . . do you intend to become part of the new government?

HORN: No! We're working only for the cause!

RIBBING (*gets up*): Then I am your man! And by this sacred tree of liberty, I swear . . .

ANCKARSTRÖM: Don't swear!

RIBBING: You hate the King, Anckarström! That is my only misgiving!

ANCKARSTRÖM: If I loved him, I wouldn't be sitting here! . . . Besides, would you like it better if I had any sympathy for a faithless, infamous comedian, the enemy of his kingdom? Yes, the kingdom's enemy, because that is what his own constitution labels the person who injures it. He is the national enemy, and that's why . . . Strike!

RIBBING: You're concealing personal motives, Anckarström . . .

ANCKARSTRÖM: If I *also* have personal motives, they strengthen my duty to act on behalf of the general public, and since I am no dreamer I don't let myself be led astray by abstract theories or hazy dreams, as Master Thorild, who philosophizes about freedom, and leaves the country when it's time for action! . . . Have you talked enough?

HORN: Gentlemen, I want to call your attention to the fact that all the doors at Huvudsta are standing open . . . to avoid suspicion. We have to be ready for visits, which won't be announced!

ANCKARSTRÖM (*gets up; speaks to* RIBBING): You haven't seen Huvudsta before?

RIBBING: No!

ANCKARSTRÖM: It's a place with a past! They say Göran Persson[35] lived here!

RIBBING: Our family had a past like that, too! Christian the Tyrant[36] had the heads of three Ribbings cut off and Charles IX took a couple, I believe!

HORN: But Peder Ribbing was the judge at the Blood Bath at Linköping . . .

ANCKARSTRÖM: Where Göran Persson's son,[36] the King's favorite, served as the prosecutor . . .

HORN: And sentenced Christer Horn to death; he was pardoned, however, on the place of execution! . . . Sh-h, someone's on the stairs!

ANCKARSTRÖM: Then it's Pechlin!

RIBBING: Is that old man fit to work with us?

ANCKARSTRÖM: He's very much fit for the King!

HORN: What no one else wants to touch, Pechlin will!

ANCKARSTRÖM: I saw a caricature yesterday of the King and Pechlin carrying something on a rod; but as they had their backs to each other, I couldn't tell where they were going! . . . Now he's here! . . . We won't tell him about our great goal because his little mind wouldn't grasp it.

HORN: If circumstances don't force us to! . . . Look at that beautiful sunset! If we could row out on the lake to listen to the last songs of the thrush before the present king withdraws into his star chamber . . .

ANCKARSTRÖM: Do you know what the star chamber is?

HORN: What it is? What do you mean?

ANCKARSTRÖM: It was an English law court that judged on hearsay and had men tortured . . .

PECHLIN: Good day, young gentlemen! What's new?

HORN: Not a thing! . . . What do you know, General?

PECHLIN: What the whole world knows! There aren't any secrets here, and that's why we need not be embarrassed. I was at a supper yesterday with both national councillors and generals. They talked openly about the King's revolution and about the counterrevolution, just as if they were talking about the next play.

RIBBING: What frivolity, when it's a question of the nation's weal or woe!

PECHLIN: The times are like that, young man, and the less seriousness, the better! Isn't that right, Anckarström?

ANCKARSTRÖM: I don't understand . . .

PECHLIN (*sitting down by the table*): By the way, as you know, I gave the King the list of the so-called conspirators myself, which had the result of releasing Anckarström among other things. But the King is a pretty good player . . . that is to say! . . . Yes, yes! Just because he never follows the rules, he's very difficult . . . and besides he learns so easily . . . Can you imagine what happened to me out on the highway just now? . . . I was about to pass Karlberg[37] when a team with outriders drove past me! . . . It was the King! "Where are you going, old joker?" he called. "I'm going to Huvudsta!" I answered! . . . "Greet the conspirators!" he called . . . and disappeared.

HORN: You're acting, you two!

PECHLIN: We kid each other a little, König and I . . .

ANCKARSTRÖM: He has one good quality; he isn't a coward.

PECHLIN: Yes, he is; he lacks courage, but he relies on bravado! You know I have a crazy idea . . . I believe he's capable of coming over here!

ANCKARSTRÖM: Here?

PECHLIN: Yes, I only think so! . . . Have you heard that he's planning to make Schröderheim archbishop?

ANCKARSTRÖM: That little swine!

PECHLIN: To succeed Mennander! [38] And for that reason he is separating Elis from his wife! Lady Schröderheim wouldn't do as the wife of an archbishop, of course . . .

HORN: Why, that's a farce . . .

RIBBING: Nothing is respected, nothing! . . . Do you know, General, how far they've gone in Paris?

PECHLIN: They've given up the Estates and set up a national assembly; that you know! They've had a meeting at the Tennis Hall where they have taken an oath not to disband before they've changed the constitution . . .

ANCKARSTRÖM: That is the revolution . . .

HORN: Why isn't there anything about this in our papers?

PECHLIN: Because König does not like revolutions—oh yes, when he makes them himself!

RIBBING: Is freedom of the press gone then?

PECHLIN: Yes, that freedom, and all the others . . . Be calm, Ribbing young man, and we'll see what can be done . . .

RIBBING: No, I can't! I cannot when I see arbitrary force and injustice; I choke when I feel the best in my soul rise up against . . .

(SERVANT *enters with a letter for* ANCKARSTRÖM. *Goes out again*)

PECHLIN: So! So! So!

HORN: General Pechlin, if you would want to understand us, could understand us, I believe that we could more easily attain our *great* goal! If I may read the beginning of an essay called "The Rights of Man," you will get a fair idea of the direction of our thinking.

PECHLIN (*gets up and lights a pipe*): Go ahead, but not too long . . .

HORN (*picks up a printed sheet and reads*): "All mankind seems to be awakening out of its errors as from a deep sleep to ask itself: What are your rights? And then the thinker answers: Man shed his blood at birth to be free . . ."

ANCKARSTRÖM and RIBBING: Bravo!

A VOICE OUTSIDE: Bravo!

ALL IN THE ROOM: Who was that?

PECHLIN: That was Liljehorn! Wasn't it?

HORN: No, he uses a Swedish *r*! [39]

ANCKARSTRÖM: I believe I recognize that voice!

RIBBING: It was *he!*

PECHLIN: The King!

(*General silence.* ANCKARSTRÖM *goes out on the veranda.*)

PECHLIN: Watch your tongues, boys! And don't forget that Hästesko is being executed today . . . perhaps this very moment down on Packer Square! . . . Hush!

KING (*enters from the left*): Well! All old friends—young friends, I mean, for the general gets younger all the time! . . .

PECHLIN: Here are the conspirators, Your Majesty!

KING: Dancing around the Maypole or whatever that tree is!

PECHLIN: It's a so-called liberty tree, Your Majesty!

KING: Well, is that what it looks like? . . . Does it bear fruit, too?

PECHLIN: Fruit, Your Majesty! . . . Red fruit!

KING: Apropos liberty, what Klas Horn said just now was beauti-
fully said! Who wrote it? It sounded as if I had said it myself!

HORN: Twenty years ago, yes!

KING: What is it you're plotting now?

PECHLIN: Well, we're plotting against the present form of government . . .

KING: Just as I am! So . . . "Soyons amis, Cinna, c'est moi qui t'en
convie."

PECHLIN: "Pour être plus qu'un roi, tu te crois quelque chose!"

KING: "Prends un siège, Cinna . . . ," and we can talk a little! But
first I want to fulfill my errand. As you remember, I was honored by an invitation just before I went into the Danish War;
reasons of state—hm!—prevented me from receiving this tribute
. . . Now . . . to show you I have a good memory, I invite you
to a fête champêtre, at Drottningholm, the day after tomorrow!
(*General silence*) Do you want to come?

PECHLIN: The honor is too great, Your Majesty . . .

KING: For you or for me?

PECHLIN: For us, of course! Of course!

KING: Your modesty never denies itself, Baron . . . What do you
young gentlemen say?

RIBBING and HORN: Your Majesty . . .

KING: That means consent! Welcome then . . . the day after tomorrow! . . . Well, give me some news before I go! Haven't you
heard any rumors, General?

PECHLIN: Yes, they say that Hästesko is to be executed today, and
that the burghers don't feel particularly honored by having to
keep watch at the place of execution!

KING (*unpleasantly touched*): That was a nasty rumor! . . . Well,
what else?

PECHLIN: Well, they say that Duke Charles[40] has taken the fleet back to Karlskrona, and that the King intends to put him in prison for doing so!

KING (*controls his anger*): Who is spreading such false rumors?

PECHLIN: Liljensparre, of course!

KING: Now it is my turn! Have you heard that Anckarström has lost his youngest child?

ALL: No!

KING: And that Baroness Pechlin has run away with her lover? . . . Well, they're only rumors!

PECHLIN: Has she run away? Then I say as Sulla[41] . . . I am saved!

KING (*bites his lip*): Have you heard that Schröderheim is getting a divorce?

PECHLIN: No, but that his wife . . .

KING (*uneasy*): Is there a cat in the room? It feels strange!

PECHLIN: Here at Huvudsta there are no cats, but they say the ghost of Göran Persson does walk again . . .

KING: Not in the daytime . . .

PECHLIN: He was an unusual man . . .

KING: And a poor councillor . . .

PECHLIN: For a poor king . . .

KING: Now we'll stop! . . . Farewell, gentlemen! And welcome the day after tomorrow! To Drottningholm! (*Goes out at the left*)

PECHLIN: The exit was not quite as happy as the entrance! But that happens to even the best of actors!

(HORN *puts a finger to his mouth.*)

PECHLIN: Is he listening? I believe that of him!

(ANCKARSTRÖM *enters from the veranda, pale and disturbed.*)

PECHLIN: Have you really lost a child, Captain? Or was that just a cruel joke?

ANCKARSTRÖM: It was no joke, but it was cruel to make a joke of it . . . May we talk about the matter now? . . . General Pechlin, you're going to Drottningholm the day after tomorrow?

PECHLIN: Yes, naturally! Are you going?

ANCKARSTRÖM: If I'm going? . . . As certainly as I'm alive and as surely the king shall die!

PECHLIN (*jumps up*): What's that? Is it a question of . . . murder?

ANCKARSTRÖM: Of course!

PECHLIN: And you dare say that to me? I am no murderer! Let me withdraw from this right now!

ANCKARSTRÖM: It's too late!

PECHLIN: Then I'll expose you!

ANCKARSTRÖM: You already have, so that is also too late!

PECHLIN (*beside himself*): To think I could let myself be fooled so completely!

ANCKARSTRÖM: General Pechlin, with your age and your great experience in affairs of state, organize your work for the day after tomorrow, because the King will have his plan of destruction ready by that time . . . and I mine!

PECHLIN: Good God! . . . to get mixed up . . . get involved in murder, I who have never had anything but loyal aims for the good of the country!

ANCKARSTRÖM: Don't talk so much, sir! But be on your way and act! But act correctly, quickly, and without any capers! If you should find yourself inclined to desert us, remember there are two barrels in my pistols!

PECHLIN: What's that? You're threatening my life?

ANCKARSTRÖM: I am risking mine! . . . Go, quickly!

PECHLIN: No, now I'm not joking any more—I want to get out of this!

ANCKARSTRÖM: You'll not get out of this . . .

PECHLIN: To think I could let myself be fooled and by such youngsters! . . .

ANCKARSTRÖM: Forward, and don't look back! . . . Forward!

PECHLIN: Oh well! You are right; there is only one way . . . but . . . I do not want to be discovered . . . not on the scaffold . . .

ANCKARSTRÖM: Think of Hästesko . . . (*Looks at his watch*) At this moment his head is falling, for he wanted to rescue his poor little country from going under because of a law-breaker and to save a comedian's bad financial affairs.

(ALL *involuntarily look at their watches.*)

PECHLIN: Now! . . .

HORN (*puts his hand over his heart*): Now his head fell!

RIBBING: I felt it, too! . . .

PECHLIN (*seriously*): I heard it . . . Your faith is great, my young friends, and it has strengthened me in my decision, which now is . . . irrevocable! . . . Farewell, Klas Horn, dreamer! . . . farewell, Ribbing, nobleman! . . . farewell, Anckarström, Brutus, brutal Brutus! [42] (*Leaves*)

(*Silence*)

ANCKARSTRÖM: There is nothing to add! . . . I ask you as friends to witness my will! (*Takes out a paper*) In favor of my wife and children! . . . Now I'll have to strike out the name of the youngest!

HORN: Your sorrow is ours . . .

ANCKARSTRÖM: Do not pity the one who has died . . .

(HORN *and* RIBBING *sign their names.*)

ANCKARSTRÖM: And so! . . . The day after tomorrow!

HORN and RIBBING and ANCKARSTRÖM (*grasp each others' hands*): The day after tomorrow!

CURTAIN

ACT IV

At Drottningholm. The large room in China Castle.[43] *The doors at the back towards the park are open. The* KING *is sitting by a frame embroidering. The* QUEEN *is reading a book.*
BADIN *and* PAPILLON *can be seen out on the lawn.*

KING: Well, so we got peace!

QUEEN: Which peace?

KING: With Denmark, of course . . . and with it peace in the family!

QUEEN: Oh! (*Continues reading*)

KING: Tell me, how many cross stitches are equivalent to a diamond stitch?

QUEEN: I don't understand that sort of thing! . . . How did you ever get started embroidering, sire?

KING: My mother taught me, and afterwards I got pleasure out of it! I think very clearly when I embroider, and then I feel that I have the strings in my hand. (*Pause*) You despise handiwork, don't you?

QUEEN: Pretty much!

KING: And *I* learned it primarily to lend respect to woman's work! Making sacrifices is rewarding! . . . Badin!

(BADIN *enters.*)

KING: Tell the musicians that they may begin! . . . Then tell Baron Armfelt to come here!

(BADIN *goes out.*)

QUEEN: Which musicians are they?

KING: Bellman and his friends!

QUEEN: I don't like his nasty songs!

KING: He has beautiful ones, too! And today, in your honor, it will be a particularly melodious one. Just listen!

(*Back of the stage,* BELLMAN's *"Böljan sig mindre rör"* [44] *is sung by soprano, alto, tenor, and bass voices to the accompaniment of French horn, oboe, flute, mandolin, and lute.*)

(QUEEN *gets up and goes.*)

KING: Why are you leaving, madame?

QUEEN: Because I don't want to see Baron Armfelt!

KING: You have a very sure instinct for making my friends feel your antipathy . . .

QUEEN: Instinct?

KING: Papillon! . . .

(PAPILLON *enters.*)

KING: Take this frame away!

(PAPILLON *carries the frame out to the right.*)

QUEEN: When does the fete start?

KING: It is already started, but since it is a country fete, we're dispensing with all court formalities and etiquette for the day!

QUEEN: All etiquette! And the usual orgies begin at dark?

KING: Yes!

QUEEN: Then I'll go back to the city!

KING: I don't believe the commandant will let down the drawbridge again today!

QUEEN: No? . . . We'll see! (*Goes*)

(*Pause.* KING *throws himself into a chair.* ARMFELT *enters.*)

KING: Report! . . . quickly! . . . Where is the Dalecarlian regiment?

ARMFELT: Here! Everywhere about!

KING: In the palace, too?

ARMFELT: Everywhere! In the palace basement, in the chapel, in Canton,[45] in the Gothic Tower!

KING: Have Fersen and De Geer come?

ARMFELT: No!

KING: Not come? . . . They must come!

ARMFELT: They're too cunning! And where there aren't any secrets, it isn't hard to be cunning!

KING: Then it won't go today!

ARMFELT: It will go tomorrow in the national hall then!

KING: Everything can fail!

ARMFELT: Oh, you do have doubts?

KING: I am not certain! . . . Have you seen Pechlin?

ARMFELT: He is down in the summer theater strolling with Horn and Ribbing!

KING: I have invited them myself!

ARMFELT: But how could you invite Anckarström?

KING: Anckarström? Is he here?

ARMFELT: He showed his invitation and insisted he had received the invitation himself at Horn's Huvudsta!

KING: What's that? I didn't see him! But I felt him! So he was standing on the veranda! . . . What daring! . . .

ARMFELT: What is there between you and Anckarström to cause this boundless hatred? . . .

KING: Have you seen Schröderheim?

ARMFELT: He's like a winter fly, since he's divorcing his wife.

KING: And she's like a wasp without a stinger!

ARMFELT: They say she's pregnant!

KING: That, too! Then she'll leave me in peace for a while, I hope!

ARMFELT: Why don't you arrest the conspirators?

KING: What good would that do? . . . Besides . . . I'd have to arrest too many—all the way from the lower nobility up . . .

ARMFELT: Well, so what?

KING: Find Anckarström and ask if I may speak with him!

ARMFELT: Is that wise?

KING: I want to talk with him . . . without witnesses!

ARMFELT: Are you thinking of charming him?

KING: I want to know how my opponents regard the matter!

ARMFELT: A rehearsal for tomorrow's performance!

KING: I want to hear their motives and arguments . . .

ARMFELT: To be able to answer them tomorrow!

KING: If he can persuade me that I am wrong . . . well!

ARMFELT: He can't! But if he could! . . . Duke Charles was almost persuaded that the men of Anjala were right!

KING: There is a difference between Charles and me! . . . Go now! . . . If you want to listen to the conversation, do it . . . from in there!

ARMFELT: Good luck! (*Goes*)

(KING, *alone, sits by the open doorway at the back.*)

(*Just outside appear the* THREE GRACES *led by* MEGAERA.[46] *They stop in front of the* KING *and stare at him.*)

KING (*applauds*): Bravo! Graces . . . *A bas!* Megaera! . . .
When did Beauty and Delight choose the wild revenge
For the leader at a rural fete in green groves,
Where only Flora and Cupid see their nests,
To hide their feats of love under the flowers?

MEGAERA (*Lady Schröderheim*):
When the prince became tyrant and the ruler despot!

KING:
Oh, if you felt the tender power that love wields,
Your lord's too great mildness you would disdain!

MEGAERA:
Oh, great Caesar, beware the Ides of Mars! [47]

KING:
Mars bears no fear for me, for war
Always became my rescue when peace failed.
But Venus in conjunction with Mars,
There lies the danger!

MEGAERA: Beware the Ides of Mars, Caesar!

(GRACES *and* MEGAERA *lift their hands threateningly and go.*)

KING: That was Lady Schröderheim as Megaera!

(TAUBE *appears outside.*)

KING: Taube!

TAUBE (*on the stairs outside*): Your Majesty!

KING: How is Schröderheim's divorce coming?

TAUBE: Well! Not too well . . .

KING: Why not?

TAUBE: She's demanding an unreasonable settlement . . . or alimony!

KING: But she's the one who's guilty, and *he* is to pay alimony!
Superb!

TAUBE: And then she demands that her unborn child is to be legitimate!

KING: He's to pay the mistress of other men and then acknowledge
another man's child as his own legitimate offspring! Well, that's

really something . . . Start over again, and bring her into criminal court!

TAUBE: It's a sad affair . . .

KING: Most of all for Elis! She isn't so prejudiced that she can be ashamed!

TAUBE: That wives have fun would do, I suppose, but they want to keep their social standing, too . . . and get their sins sanctioned . . .

KING: That would do, too, but when they want their husbands to bear the shame for their beastliness . . . Make the trial short! Good-bye!

(TAUBE *goes.* KELLGREN *and* THORILD *walk by in deep discussion.*)

KING: Stop! Are you still arguing about the pope's beard? Or about unrhymed verse? . . . And you haven't gone to England, Master Thorild! Go to Paris, Master, where there's more to be learned! Go to Paris!

(KELLGREN *and* THORILD *go on.* LILJENSPARRE *outside*)

KING: Well, Liljensparre, is everything ready for tomorrow?

LILJENSPARRE: Everything, Your Majesty! But Olof Olsson is sick.

KING: There, damn it! I suppose he has eaten too much at the corruption breakfasts, the pig! *Passez!*

(LILJENSPARRE *goes on.* MUNCK *appears outside.* KING *shoves his chair back so that he cannot be seen.* MUNCK *glances about for the* KING *and then goes on.*)

(BELLMAN, HALLMAN, *and* KEXELL *outside*)

KING: Horace!

BELLMAN: Augustus!

KING: Thanks for your song!

BELLMAN: Thanks for your gold!

KING: Yours is better!

BELLMAN (*recites*):

Europe, admire a monarch so noble,
So royal, so learned, and in virtues so strong!

Who would not kiss your sceptre, your hand?
Who would not live and die in your land?
We'll follow you,
We'll honor you,
And unto death will our love be honest and true . . .
Our gentle king, long may he live!
(*They go.*)

PECHLIN (*enters quickly, very much excited*): Your Majesty!

KING: What lie is it this time?

PECHLIN: Listen to me, and believe me, sire! . . . this one time!

KING: Never again!

PECHLIN: But when I'm telling the truth!

KING: You're lying at your best!

PECHLIN: Sire, your life is in danger!

KING: It always is! As long as there are roofing tiles, slipshod horses, and bodies of water!

PECHLIN: They intend to murder you!

KING: Intend! Haven't they been up to that as long as I can remember? Haven't they murdered my honor and my wife's? Didn't they murder my child in his mother's womb? What's left for them?

PECHLIN: Your life, Your Majesty! As truly as I am standing here . . . and I can name them . . .

KING: So can I—Pechlin, number one!

PECHLIN (*on his knees*): No, no, no! . . . Then I would not be here! . . . Listen to me!

KING: On your way, old fool; the noose is waiting for you!

PECHLIN: In heaven's name . . .

KING: Do you have anything to do with heaven?

(ARMFELT *and* ANCKARSTRÖM *can be seen outside.*)

PECHLIN: He's the one!

KING: Armfelt?

PECHLIN: No, the other one!

KING: Chatterbox, go!

PECHLIN (*leaves unwillingly*): It *is* he!

   (ARMFELT *stops outside; gestures to* ANCKARSTRÖM *to enter.*
ANCKARSTRÖM *enters.* KING *signals to* ARMFELT *that he is to go.*)

   (*The* KING *and* ANCKARSTRÖM *observe each other for a while
silently.*)

ANCKARSTRÖM (*impatient, but self-controlled*): Your Majesty has
summoned me!

KING: Yes, I have! . . . About your name a certain nimbus of the
vapor of fame has been condensing lately, and you have become
a sort of spokesman for those who are dissatisfied! It is in your
capacity as their representative that I ask you to state the views
which give you a kind of pedestal! To the point! What do you
want of me? What have I done to you? Why do you hate me?

ANCKARSTRÖM: You know that yourself, Your Majesty!

KING: No, on my honor! . . . Anckarström, do you consider yourself a so-called man of the people?

ANCKARSTRÖM: Yes!

KING: Listen! When you faced death recently because of treasonous
talk, I spared your life; but the mob, whose spokesman you were,
spat on you, and mistreated you right on the street!

ANCKARSTRÖM: What did that matter? Do you believe, Your Majesty, that my ideas of right and wrong can be changed in the
slightest by an ignorant mob's naive behavior on one single occasion?

KING: Then it's right in the abstract you're working for?

ANCKARSTRÖM: The right, which can be objective in spite of personal
antagonisms—yes! . . . and personal interests!

KING: Can you state in one word the object of your hatred?

ANCKARSTRÖM: One word? . . . Absolutism!

KING: Do you like majority rule then?

ANCKARSTRÖM: Yes! Because many eyes see more than two; many
wills satisfy more desires and needs!

KING: You know what *you* want, at least!

ANCKARSTRÖM: Yes!

(*Pause*)

KING (*bluntly*): What do you intend to do if I change the form of government?

ANCKARSTRÖM: A person doesn't tell that sort of thing!

KING (*tortured, pained*): Do you know that I intend to give the commoners greater liberty than they have now?

ANCKARSTRÖM: Yes, I know that!

KING: How . . . can you know that?

ANCKARSTRÖM: How? That is beside the point; but even if you return a little of all that you've taken, there'll always be a remnant of the theft left!

KING: Theft?

ANCKARSTRÖM: Yes!

KING: You're what you always were, Jacob! . . . And your hands are Esau's! [48] . . . still!

(BADIN *appears at the door at the back with a letter.*)

KING: Give it to me!

(BADIN *comes up, delivers the letter, goes.*)

KING (*reads the letter and studies* ANCKARSTRÖM. *Thereupon he tears the letter to pieces*): You may go!

(ANCKARSTRÖM *is leaving.*)

KING: Wait!

(*Pause*)

KING: I wronged you once, Jacob! . . . long ago!

ANCKARSTRÖM: I have forgotten *that!*

KING: But never forget that I have granted you your life!

ANCKARSTRÖM: That life I am also ready to give . . . for a great cause!

(*Pause*)

KING: If my friends were like my enemies, I could go far!

(*Shouts of hurrah and jubilation outside*)

KING (*rises*): What is that?

ARMFELT (*enters hastily*): Now it's all crazy!

KING (*to* ANCKARSTRÖM): You may go!

(ANCKARSTRÖM *goes.*)

KING: What is it?

ARMFELT: The latest news from Paris! . . . The Bastille[49] has been taken and burned down! The mob has brought the king from Versailles to Paris!

KING: As a prisoner?

ARMFELT: Yes! . . .

KING: And that's why my guests are celebrating, in my Versailles? [50]

ARMFELT: Have you heard what they're singing?

KING: No!

SONG (*outside*):
Dansons la Carmagnole!
Vive le son! Vive le son!
Dansons la Carmagnole!
Vive le son du canon!

KING: What is that?

ARMFELT: It's called "The Carmagnole"! . . .

KING: They shall get cannons, tomorrow! . . . Is everything ready?

ARMFELT: Everything! But . . . Olof Olsson is dead, as you know!

KING: Dead! I heard he was ill! . . . Oh well! Let's use his corpse! Listen . . . he shall be buried in Riddarholm Church just as Olof Håkonsson was! Fersen, De Geer, and the others will be invited to the funeral! If they do not come, they will have the mob at their windows; and if they come, the mob will be after them anyway! . . . Can't a rumor be spread that he was poisoned or something like that?

ARMFELT: Now you are cynical, Gustav!

KING: Yes, now I am cynical! Just as cynical as . . . the others!

ARMFELT: The Bastille has fallen . . . and Gustav III becomes an absolute monarch!

KING: Yes! That he does! But I have made the revolution myself!

ARMFELT: What a paradox! What a trick!

KING: Now we shall go to look at the people!

ARMFELT: And then?

KING: We shall dance!

ARMFELT: You are divine at any rate!

KING: Nonsense!

ARMFELT: Yes, people admire you, though they despise you!

KING: And they hate me, though they love me! That makes sense!

ARMFELT: They have to take you as you are!

KING: And I am what I have become! I have not made myself! . . . But, listen, since Fersen and De Geer haven't come, you may dismiss the Dalecarlian regiment!

ARMFELT: It won't be easy to do that without its being noticed, but I'll try!

KING: Noticed or unnoticed, but they have to leave so as not to stir up bad blood!

ARMFELT: Good! It shall be done . . . preferably before they get drunk!

KING (*listening*): To think they are singing "La Carmagnole" at Drottningholm Palace! . . . Am I not a liberal? Who can deny that?

ARMFELT: Shall I close the doors?

KING: No, let them stand open . . . The people shall see that their King has confidence . . .

ARMFELT: In the Dalecarlian regiment?

KING: And that he has no secrets . . . and no fear . . . et cetera! . . . *Sortie!* (*Goes out to the right.* ARMFELT *exits to the left.*)

(SCHRÖDERHEIM *comes in from the back and glances about as if he were looking for someone. Sits down tired on a chair and waits.* LADY SCHRÖDERHEIM, *masked and costumed as* MEGAERA, *enters; also acts as if she were looking for someone. Catches sight of* SCHRÖDERHEIM; *intends at first to leave, but decides to stay*)

SCHRÖDERHEIM (*sadly*): Let your mask fall, Anne Charlotte!

LADY SCHRÖDERHEIM (*takes off her mask*): Elis!

SCHRÖDERHEIM: Yes, it is Elis! . . . (*Silence*)

LADY SCHRÖDERHEIM: You are tired? . . .

SCHRÖDERHEIM: Yes, we are all tired of this carnival which is to be followed by a Holy Week with a long, long Good Friday.

LADY SCHRÖDERHEIM (*weakly*): Why didn't you talk it over with me, Elis, before you applied for a divorce?

SCHRÖDERHEIM: Child, I have been talking to you for thirteen years, but you haven't let yourself be talked to; besides, it isn't I who have done this!

LADY SCHRÖDERHEIM: It is the King who's getting his revenge?

SCHRÖDERHEIM: Yes! And his getting revenge implies that he has been wronged. Why did you interfere with his marriage?

LADY SCHRÖDERHEIM: Is it admirable to get revenge?

SCHRÖDERHEIM: Is it admirable to wrong anyone?

LADY SCHRÖDERHEIM: What have you accused me of?

SCHRÖDERHEIM: I? I have accused you of nothing! . . . But you! That was nasty, because it was a lie!

LADY SCHRÖDERHEIM: I said that you had neglected me! That is true!

SCHRÖDERHEIM: Anne Charlotte! When I married you, I married you to have a wife and a home! Well, we were husband and wife at first, and I didn't neglect getting a child! When I sat with our daughter, you were out . . . you were never at home. And when you stated definitely that you did not want any more children . . . well, I accepted that, since I respected your freedom . . . in that matter. But when you wanted me to be your lover or whatever it's called, then I said no! . . . because I had vowed to be your husband.

LADY SCHRÖDERHEIM: I could never understand the distinction!

SCHRÖDERHEIM: No, you didn't! . . . I looked upon marriage as a union of two good friends of opposite sex, who had children together . . . I respected you as a wife and loved you as a wife; that's why I didn't want to consider you as my mistress! . . . Well, our little girl died; so I was absolutely alone at home. Then

I left! . . . So you, who neglected your home, husband, and child, you accuse me of neglect! That is nice! And the more you wronged me, the more furious you became!

LADY SCHRÖDERHEIM: We should have been divorced long ago!

SCHRÖDERHEIM: Yes, my friend! We should have! But you didn't want to, because it was through me as state secretary that you had got your position at court, and you didn't want to lose that.

LADY SCHRÖDERHEIM: Lose?

SCHRÖDERHEIM: Yes, don't you know that you have been banished from court?

LADY SCHRÖDERHEIM: Have I?

SCHRÖDERHEIM: Yes, you have! The court chancellor has already made out the papers!

LADY SCHRÖDERHEIM: That is your revenge!

SCHRÖDERHEIM: No, I tell you! It is a natural consequence of your actions, your unlimited arrogance particularly. I don't avenge myself, because I'm the only one who has understood you! You weren't made for the home but for the street; that isn't your fault, no more than I deserve to bear the dishonor you have brought upon yourself!

LADY SCHRÖDERHEIM: I am banished from court, this court, whose ornament I've been!

SCHRÖDERHEIM: Well! Now there's another younger, more beautiful, and wittier ornament for the court!

LADY SCHRÖDERHEIM: Younger?

SCHRÖDERHEIM: Yes, you're thirty-five, my friend, and she's nine-teen!

LADY SCHRÖDERHEIM: I don't want to live any longer!

SCHRÖDERHEIM: See! That's how I talked for thirteen years, but I had to put up with my misery! Now it's your turn!

LADY SCHRÖDERHEIM: That pleases you!

SCHRÖDERHEIM: No, because it makes me sad to see you lose your beauty; yes, because I can breathe, when I see there is justice in this world!

LADY SCHRÖDERHEIM: Was there justice for you, too?

SCHRÖDERHEIM: Yes! . . . otherwise I wouldn't dare to talk as I do! I got mine, old girl! I am in half disfavor, and am completely ruined!

LADY SCHRÖDERHEIM: Elis . . . I am very unhappy!

SCHRÖDERHEIM: I still more! . . . so I understand your unhappiness! . . . Has he deserted you?

LADY SCHRÖDERHEIM: Yes!

SCHRÖDERHEIM: I can't weep exactly! But . . . and now?

LADY SCHRÖDERHEIM: I've rented *one* room in the suburbs, and I'll hide myself there until . . . the day comes . . .

SCHRÖDERHEIM: Poor Anne Charlotte! . . . Gustav's sun is setting . . . and we'll be in the shadows . . . It *was* a sun, but it has to be night sometimes, too, of course! . . . Good night, my friend!

LADY SCHRÖDERHEIM: Good night, Elis! (*Silence*) Say *one* word!

SCHRÖDERHEIM: Well, what? What? . . . Am I to say "Thank you for all the beauty and the goodness that you brought into my life". . . ? I was ugly myself, I know, but then a husband doesn't need to be handsome! . . . I forgive you the evil and cruelty . . . It was my duty to put up with and to overlook, and I did, but I did not have the right to live in disgrace . . .

LADY SCHRÖDERHEIM (*looking into a mirror*): Am I ugly?

SCHRÖDERHEIM: Don't ask me!

LADY SCHRÖDERHEIM: Yes, you, the only one who can say it!

SCHRÖDERHEIM: Well then, you know you've never been considered a beauty . . .

LADY SCHRÖDERHEIM: No, I didn't know that! . . .

SCHRÖDERHEIM: Heavens, I thought . . .

LADY SCHRÖDERHEIM: On with the mask! Out of the garden of Eden! Down into oblivion! Now I see that I am terribly ugly! Maybe I wasn't witty either?

SCHRÖDERHEIM: Yes, you were glib, could say good equivocal bits and make poor malicious remarks, but you weren't intelligent, because when you interfered in matters of state and I was to straighten out something for you, you became distrait and got a headache . . . yes!

LADY SCHRÖDERHEIM: You never dared to say that before!

SCHRÖDERHEIM: I didn't want to, because your charm lay just in this self-adoration which the men's flattery supported . . . You see, child, everything a gentleman tells a lady is completely value-less; it isn't a lie, but it resembles a poem . . . For that reason Lady Schröderheim became merely a poem composed by ardent men!

LADY SCHRÖDERHEIM: There isn't much left of me now!

SCHRÖDERHEIM: No, there isn't anything left of Lady Schröderheim, because now begins Mrs. Stapelmohr, the continuation of Miss Stapelmohr . . .

LADY SCHRÖDERHEIM (*stretches out her arms towards the out-of-doors*): I don't exist any more, and yet I am standing here any-way . . . standing on my own grave . . . like a cross on my own grave . . . and with my mask in my hand . . . unmasked . . . because the comedy is over, and no one applauds! (*Lets her arms sink, then puts on her mask and goes out at the back*)

(SCHRÖDERHEIM *alone. Gets up and walks about with his hands behind his back speaking inaudibly to himself. Then the beating of drums can be heard.* BADIN *enters.*)

SCHRÖDERHEIM: What's up?

BADIN: Yes, what's up? . . . The park is to be cleared, because a crowd of uninvited people have in some unknown way got in; women from Stockholm alleys, men in costumes that look like disguises . . . There's talk of the conspirators, you know, Mr. Secretary! . . .

SCHRÖDERHEIM: What are you saying? Badin, you are probably the only friend the King has; open his eyes . . . show him that there is danger . . . persuade him . . .

BADIN: My lord, the King knows there is danger . . . He slept last night in the large bedroom with guards in the room! And all the same he jumped up every time the clock struck! . . . Finally he got up on a chair and broke the mechanism to pieces!

SCHRÖDERHEIM: So he finally believes that it's serious?

BADIN: Yes, it's serious now, but he mustn't show he believes it is!

SCHRÖDERHEIM: Do you know if the Dalecarlian regiment is still here?

BADIN: No, they have already marched off!

SCHRÖDERHEIM: Who gave the orders?

BADIN: The King himself!

SCHRÖDERHEIM: Good heavens! . . . Badin, find the King, stay with him, watch over him . . . Warn him! Quickly! . . . Run!

BADIN: I will! . . . I will run! (*Goes out at the back*)

(SCHRÖDERHEIM *wanders about as before talking to himself; finally he goes out to the left.*)

(HALLDIN *enters from the back, pale as a ghost. Looks about; takes up a package of brochures, which he places on chairs and tables about the room. As he is about to leave,* FERSEN *and* DE GEER *appear at the back.* HALLDIN *conceals himself behind a screen.*)

FERSEN: So we're here just the same! A daring venture that can succeed!

DE GEER: I haven't understood the purpose of this feat of daring, Fersen!

FERSEN: You haven't! . . . Well, since we're going to be arrested anyway, it had better happen today than tomorrow! If it happens today, it is a tactical error . . . We'll have the sympathy of the public tomorrow!

DE GEER: What's happening is incomprehensible! But the nobility defends liberty, while the lower estates defend tyranny!

FERSEN: Or . . . the tyrant defends the people, even the mob . . .

HALLDIN (*back of the screen*): That's why he is an enlightened despot!

FERSEN: Who spoke?

HALLDIN (*back of the screen*): One who believes neither in enlightened despots nor liberty-loving counts!

DE GEER: Who are you?

HALLDIN (*back of the screen*): No one; only a voice!

FERSEN: *Diable!*

(HALLDIN *comes out with a mask over his face; goes out at the back*)

FERSEN: Who was it?

DE GEER: Don't know!

FERSEN: Apparently there's a masquerade here the whole year round, but that mask . . . Do you believe there is a conspiracy, De Geer?

DE GEER: They're lying most when they tell the truth here at court . . . so that nowadays I know nothing!

FERSEN: And the King! He was taught to lie as a child—especially during the unsuccessful coups d'état . . . I was along then! And since then he has lied so much he doesn't know who he is himself, and as he jokes about everything he can't tell the difference between a joke and what's serious.

DE GEER (*picks up a brochure from a chair*): What's this—a lampoon? . . . No, good lord!

FERSEN: What's it about?

DE GEER: Yes! It's the old story with new additions.

FERSEN: About . . . the Queen?

DE GEER: And the prince! (*Throws the brochure into the fire*) But he is a human being with human feelings, all the same . . . That is ugly!

FERSEN: When he admits the mob, then . . . And *they* are his friends! . . . Just look! There's Pechlin!

DE GEER: *Our* friend!

FERSEN: Follower rather! A dirty sort!

DE GEER: Certainly not quality! . . . But how serious he looks, and frightened! I have never seen that before!

FERSEN: Pechlin afraid? Then . . . things have gone far!

PECHLIN (*enters, serious*): Good evening, gentlemen!

FERSEN: What's up now?

PECHLIN: No one knows! . . . Are we alone?

DE GEER: Not so sure! I thought there was a noise back of the secret door over there!

FERSEN: Don't speak so loudly then! . . .

PECHLIN (*softly*): The King has won the three lower estates and the national marshal[51] as well!

DE GEER: Then we have absolutism!

FERSEN (*angry*): Again! Again! . . . Isn't there any Fredrikshald[52] then?

PECHLIN: But . . . there is one hope!

DE GEER: What?

PECHLIN: We might be able to buy off the clergy!

FERSEN: That I don't believe!

DE GEER: What's their price?

PECHLIN: Fifty thousand *riksdaler!*

DE GEER: We don't have that much!

FERSEN: The archbishop can't be bought. I acquit him of that!

PECHLIN: I don't believe in it, either! There's only one thing left! One!

DE GEER: Which is?

PECHLIN: To make the King a prisoner! (*Silence*)

DE GEER: Where?

PECHLIN: Here!

FERSEN: When?

PECHLIN: Now! . . . He'll be here soon! (*Silence*) Most likely that is the only way!

DE GEER (*slowly, emphatically*): Maybe!

FERSEN (*sharply*): Maybe! (*Silence*)

PECHLIN: He's coming! . . . Then I'll go . . . and . . . see what we can do! . . . Keep him here for a while, gentlemen! (*Goes out to the left*)

FERSEN: Absolutism!

DE GEER: There is somebody back of the secret door!

FERSEN: Maybe . . . the ones who were going to arrest us!

DE GEER: He or we! . . . Now's the time!

FERSEN: He or we! (*Silence*)

DE GEER: Do you hear a clock ticking in the next room?

FERSEN: No, but I hear the King's red heels crushing grains of sand and stepping on the nailheads of the floorboards!

DE GEER: Can you tell if he is armed or not?

FERSEN: (*grasping his sword*): He has a sword, but I can disarm him with a feint on top of a false tierce parade . . .

DE GEER: He is a poor fencer, with his sword, but he's a dandy one, with his tongue!

FERSEN: Listen! . . .

DE GEER: If only there weren't that secret door! . . .

FERSEN: He's talking with someone! . . . and now he has stopped . . . The silk lining of his coat is rustling . . .

DE GEER: If you can hear that, you have . . .

FERSEN: At this moment the immediate destiny of Sweden and that of the dynasty is being decided!

DE GEER: The fate of the dynasty has already been settled! . . .

FERSEN: It has become cloudy! Just think if it should rain! Then the fete will be ruined . . .

DE GEER: And the park is being cleared . . . Do you think Pechlin can do anything?

FERSEN: He's usually not at a loss . . . See there!

KING (*enters from right without noticing* FERSEN *and* DE GEER; *speaks to someone outside*): Well, since Fersen and De Geer haven't chosen to accept the invitation, but have stayed at home . . . we'll postpone the matter until tomorrow! (*Waits for a reply that cannot be heard*)

KING (*as before*): No, that won't do! (*As before*) Oh? Well, we can talk about that later! Not now! (*Pause*) No, I am busy. (*Turns about. Sees the two and cannot conceal his amazement and anger. Loses his poise; picks up a brochure from a chair, forms it into a fan and fans his face, without having had time to see what the content of the brochure is*) So! (*Pause*) You come a little late, gentlemen . . . when you have been invited by a King.

FERSEN: Your Majesty! Since the National Estates are meeting tomorrow, we had . . . (*Gets stuck*)

DE GEER: We had intended to use the precious time to . . . (*Gets stuck*)

KING: How did you happen to change your minds so quickly?

FERSEN: An important letter from my son[53] in Paris . . .

KING: What does he write?

FERSEN: The Bastille has been captured and burnt down!

KING: I know that! . . . Would you close the doors, Count Fersen? It's beginning to rain.

(FERSEN *does not move; looks about for a servant*)

KING: Close the doors, Count Fersen!

(FERSEN *does not move.* KING *rings violently. Pause.* KING *rings again.*)

(ARMFELT *enters from left.*)

KING (*gets up, goes up to* ARMFELT, *and takes him aside. Speaks softly*): Is the Dalecarlian regiment still here?

ARMFELT: No, they marched out along Lov Island! Why, didn't you say they should?

KING (*strikes himself on his forehead*): Oh! . . . Are the burghers' officers here?

ARMFELT: No! . . . You didn't want to invite them!

KING (*as before*): Are there any people left in the park?

ARMFELT: No, they have fled because of the rain!

KING: Look at those two! What do you think they are up to?

ARMFELT: They're looking towards the door as if they were expecting someone . . . and they have their fencing swords!

KING: I can believe that. (*Draws himself towards the right-hand door as if he were frightened*) Here is something! . . . I can hear steps outside! Spurs and swords! . . . (*He opens the right-hand door and signals.*)

(*Three* GUARDS, BADIN, PAPILLON *enter—armed, from the right.*
PECHLIN, HORN, RIBBING *enter from the back. The two parties observe each other for a moment with questioning and threatening
expressions.*)

KING (*to* FERSEN, DE GEER, PECHLIN, HORN, *and* RIBBING): You may go,
gentlemen! We'll meet tomorrow!

FERSEN *and* DE GEER: Tomorrow! (*They and theirs go out at the back
closing the doors behind them.*)

KING (*dismisses all but* ARMFELT *with a gesture. Sits down with the
brochure still in his hand*): What was that?

ARMFELT: It did look strange!

KING (*reads absent-mindedly in the brochure. His face changes, and
he collapses*): Leave me! But watch the doors!

ARMFELT: Do you want to be alone?

KING: Yes! . . .

ARMFELT: It's the lampoon?

KING: Yes! Have you seen it?

ARMFELT: I have read it! . . . It's horrible!

KING: Think of it. They have stolen my son . . . How can he be
successor to the throne after this? . . . It is terrible!

ARMFELT: I will leave you!

KING: It is horrible! . . . But I cannot do anything about it!

ARMFELT: No! Nothing! (*Goes out at the left*)

(KING *gets up. Walks about, collects the brochures which he
throws into the fire. Then he stops—crushed—by the windows at
the back and taps with his fingers on the panes, with his back to
the audience. The secret door now is opened.* ANCKARSTRÖM *steps
out and lifts his pistol. But simultaneously the* QUEEN *has come
in from the left reading a letter, and stops between the* KING *and*
ANCKARSTRÖM, *just as he is about to fire.* ANCKARSTRÖM *draws back
and shuts the door.*)

KING (*turns around*): Madame! it was you? . . . Ha! I thought . . .
(*Puts his hand over his heart*)

QUEEN: Sire? . . . (*Looks at him searchingly*) Are you ill?

KING: I? No! . . . I was alone . . . I'm looking for someone . . . Excuse a somewhat strange question—would you want to keep me company this evening?

QUEEN: If you could put up with my . . .

KING: You want to? Really? . . . You know, it seems to me as if I had escaped a great danger and as if you had saved me!

QUEEN: Sire!

KING: Or as if a great danger lay ahead of me . . . Keep me company, and let us talk about anything but tomorrow! You know what is going to happen tomorrow!

QUEEN: I don't believe anyone knows that!

KING: You mean the outcome! Very well put! . . . No one knows that . . . except me!

QUEEN: Sire!

KING: Madame! I was born with a caul and with Caesar's luck . . .

QUEEN: Caesar's luck . . . Wasn't there someone called Brutus?

(ANCKARSTRÖM's *face appears at a window at the back, but the* QUEEN *stands again before the* KING.)

KING: Bravo, madame! There really was someone whose name was Brutus!

QUEEN: And as long as Caesar followed his queen's good advice . . .

KING: The queen is the strongest piece in the game and has the function of protecting the king . . . Don't you want to protect me?

QUEEN: That I always do, sire!

KING: Not always! . . . "Wasn't there someone called Brutus?"— that is superb! Superb! Madame! (*Gives the* QUEEN *his hand to lead her out to the right*)

CURTAIN

Notes on

'Gustav III'

THE TIME

BETWEEN THE death of Charles XII at Fredrikshald in 1718 and the accession of Gustav III in 1771, Sweden achieved greatness culturally—through men like Linné, Swedenborg, and Celsius, to mention only three of its best known scientists—and passed through, politically, what might be called the most shameful and humiliating period in its history. The treaties of 1720 and 1721 had ended the wars of Charles XII but had almost stripped Sweden of its territorial gains of the preceding century and a half. The Swedes abolished absolutism and set up instead a more democratic system of parliamentary rule which under the able direction of the leading statesman Arvid Horn gave the country a breathing space until he was forced out of power in 1738. From 1739 to 1771, Sweden's history is the history of strife between the two parties called the Hats and the Caps, unwarranted involvement in wars, corruption, bribery, and, through bribery, control of Swedish affairs of state by the Russians, the French, the English, and the Danes. It was a period when the Russians could name the successor to the Swedish throne and could determine the selection of a consort for the Swedish crown prince.

When Gustav came to the throne, he had no real power; the country was close to anarchy. In August, 1772, he carried through what has become known as the Revolution of 1772. It provided a constitutional monarchy with the power to legislate divided equally between the king and the Estates; it gave the Estates the right to raise taxes, and gave the Estates alone the power to start an offensive war; it eliminated foreign intervention and bribery; it served as the beginning of one of the most colorful and brilliant periods in the history of Swedish culture.

Supported in part by subsidies from France—its one friend in all

266

Europe, Sweden was able to bring appreciable order out of domestic chaos and strengthen its defenses against Russia and other enemies. Under the leadership of Gustav, monetary reforms, the farmer's right to buy and sell where and when he wanted to, the elimination of torture, the humanization of criminal laws, and, even for some years, the freedom of the press contributed to making Gustav known internationally as one of the most enlightened monarchs of his time, a man whom Voltaire and Rousseau and their followers praised highly.

No other Swedish king has been as interested in the theater and in literature as Gustav III, and no other Swedish king has been so ambitious to make his court as brilliant as any in Europe. Gustav liked the splendor, pomp, and ceremony of Versailles; he tried to make Drottningholm, Haga, Gripsholm, and his other royal palaces the centers of culture and festivity, not only for his own pleasure but to elevate his countrymen culturally. That he succeeded appreciably is testified to by such matters as the court theaters at Drottningholm and Gripsholm, the development of the royal opera and the theaters in Stockholm, the Swedish Academy which he founded in 1786, the development of Swedish fine arts which he encouraged, and the encouragement of brilliant writers, only a few of whom Strindberg mentions in his play.

But Gustav III forgot that Sweden was financially poor and could not afford to let him realize all his ambitious plans for his country. Moreover, his reforms were not always wisely planned and wisely carried out. In his attempt to control the consumption of liquor and to bring additional funds into the national treasury, for example, he established what amounted to a liquor monopoly, which failed to achieve either goal but instead increased drinking, and cost the government dearly financially. He, moreover, built up a tremendous debt, which he was in no real position to pay.

The nobility particularly resented Gustav; he had, for all practical purposes, reduced its parliamentary power to the level of the burgher's, the clergy's, and the yeomen's; by so doing, he had deprived the aristocrats of large sources of income.

In 1788 aware of Catherine the Great's plans to bring Sweden under Russian control and seeking a way out of his personal difficulties, Gustav seized or created a border incident as a pretext for beginning a war against Russia (the constitution required that the Estates declare war if it were not defensive). Aristocratic officers conspired at Anjala farm in Finland to force the king to make peace and to abide by the constitution. Gustav's rescue came in the Danish declaration of war; hastening back to Sweden, Gustav III—like Gustav Vasa before him—went to Dalarna, raised a people's army, hurried to Gothenburg, then in danger from an invading Danish-Norwegian army, set up its defenses, and, with the aid of the Prussian and English ambassadors, forced Denmark to agree to peace.

Summoning an assembly of the Estates, Gustav III and the three lower estates passed the Act of Unity and Security, which made the king almost absolute and extended the privileges of commoners at the expense of the nobility. It is on the eve of this meeting of the Estates that Strindberg has chosen to present Gustav.

The aristocratic conspirators did not succeed in eliminating the king until March 16, 1792, when he was assassinated by Anckarström at a masquerade ball at the royal opera. Anckarström had, however, tried to find opportunities to kill him before that, according to Strindberg's sources.

THE CHARACTERS

The eldest son of King Adolf Fredrik and Queen Lovisa Ulrika, *Gustav* was born on January 13, 1746. Physically weak but handsome, endowed with an excellent memory and a quick mind, Gustav was from the beginning considered exceptionally gifted. Brought up by tutors selected by the Estates, exposed to the antagonisms between his parents and the people in power, and involved too early in the intrigues at court, Gustav developed his natural charm until very few even of his opponents could withstand it, his ability to conceal what he thought and felt to the point of secretiveness, his acting ability, and his extraordinarily active imagination. He was exposed to the theater from his early childhood. The major facts of his career include his marriage to the Danish princess Sophia Magdalena who was the choice of neither Gustav nor his parents but of the Estates acting under Russian and Danish pressure; his successful revolution of 1772; his idealistic and patriotic programs for the advancement of Sweden and its people; the birth in 1778 of Crown Prince Gustav Adolf—gossip said the child's father was

THE SWEDISH HOUSE OF HOLSTEIN-GOTTORP

Adolf Fredrik (1751-1771)
m.
Lovisa Ulrika of Prussia

1. Gustav III   2. Charles XIII   3. Fredrik   4. Sophia
   (1771-1792)   (1809-1818)   Adolf   Albertina
   m.   (the last reigning
   Sophia   member of the
   Magdalena   house)
   of Denmark

Gustav IV Adolf
(1792-1809)
m.
Fredrika of Baden

Gustav, Prince   Sophia Magdalena
of Vasa   m.
                      Leopold of Baden

                      Grand Duke Frederik of Baden
                              m.
                      Louise of Prussia

                      Victoria
                         m.
                      Gustav V
                      (House of Bernadotte)

The dates are for reigns.

Adolf Fredrik Munck; the break with his mother who believed the
gossip; trips abroad to France, Italy, Germany, Denmark, and Russia;
his development of the royal opera and the Swedish theater (he himself
wrote good plays for the stage); his often unwise spending of his own
and the nation's money; his love of pomp and ceremony; his favorites;
his estrangement of the nobility; his involvement in wars with Russia
and Denmark; and perhaps above all, his genuine patriotism. Assassinated by Anckarström at a masked ball in 1792, Gustav has continued

to be the subject of debate. There is still no generally accepted interpretation of this charming, colorful, gifted monarch who affected his people's history profoundly. Esaias Tegnér, one of the great romantic poets, said: "His [Gustav's] inner spirit (was) as rich as his exterior was many-colored and varying . . . His great soul had room not only for the plans of a hero and a statesman but also for the attractions of art and the joy of life. He was a Hercules' club, entwined with leaves and roses, he was like the diamond, the firmest of all precious stones, but all the same the one whose surface plays with the richest and most beautiful colors."

Baron Gustav Mauritz Armfelt (1757-1814) became a member of the royal lifeguards in 1774, displeased Gustav III because of his frivolity and ambition, secured permission to go abroad, stayed in Paris until 1780 when the king visited Spaa, and there made his peace with him. From 1780 until the king's death in 1792, Armfelt was the leading (and spoiled) royal favorite. Given one honor and one official post after the other, Armfelt distinguished himself by his loyalty to the king and by his military and political ability. In 1788, the brilliant, arrogant and handsome Armfelt was made Commander of the Volunteers' Corps raised in Dalarna. From 1811 to 1814, he was in the service of the Czar of Russia. Armfelt has been called the Alcibiades of the North.

Elis Schröderheim (1747-1795), the son of Bishop Georg Clas Schröder of Karlstad—Gustav III's tutor in Christianity, was a childhood playmate of Gustav and from 1778 to 1786 an intimate friend and loyal supporter of the king. In 1782 he was made state secretary in the department of civil affairs. As such, he contributed financially to the king's income by selling pastorates, an old practice which was driven to such excess that the estate of the clergy protested against it in 1786. The protest was effective to the extent that clerical appointments were removed from Schröderheim's control. A good-natured, witty person who knew that the king could not bear boredom, Schröderheim did much to make Gustav's court a court dedicated primarily to pleasure and entertainment. In 1776, Schröderheim had married Anna Charlotta von Stapelmohr, whose physical attractiveness, playful wit, and extramarital affairs made her one of the most talked about women in court circles. SB (IX, 414) says: "She was like him [her husband], liked by many, but hardly respected by anyone."

Baron Carl Fredrik Pechlin (1720-1796), the son of the Holstein minister to Sweden, entered the Swedish military service in 1733 and became a Swedish baron in 1751. An able military man and an active participant in parliamentary and other political intrigues, General Pechlin was, as SB says (IX, 423), the man suspected above all others by Gustav III. "He [Pechlin] knew how to cover his tracks so well that no one could secure legal evidence against him just as he could never be made to confess anything [illegal or treasonous] . . . Pechlin was undeniably a daring and cunning man, exceptionally able to see through and lead others, sharp-sighted, calm and collected in making his plans, and just as merciless in executing them as untroubled by his conscience in his choice of means." From the king's assassination in 1792 until Pechlin's death, he was imprisoned in Varberg Fortress.

Count Klas Fredrik Horn, the son of Count Fredrik Horn—"*Gustavs vän*" ("Gustav's friend") and one of the king's major supporters in the Revolution of 1772, was an idealistic enthusiast about the ideas of the French Revolution who saw in Gustav III the main obstacle to their realization in Sweden. Unlike Anckarström, Horn was opposed to killing the king. Meetings of the conspirators were held, as Strindberg says, at Huvudsta, Horn's estate near Stockholm. Arrested after the assassination, Horn was deprived of his noble rank and his rights as a Swedish citizen, and permanently exiled.

Count Adolf Ludvig Ribbing, the son of Count Fredrik Ribbing—a member of the national council, belonged to one of the distinguished families of the high nobility. Count Adolf had resigned as captain in the guards when a younger man was promoted above him. SB (IX, 241) attributes his hatred of the king to this fact, to the king's prevention of his marriage plans, and to his estate's general hatred for the king. Count Horn, the conspirator, was one of Ribbing's childhood friends. As a conspirator, Ribbing originally opposed the plan to kill the king but finally decided to support Anckarström fully. Ribbing's punishment was loss of Swedish citizenship and rank and permanent exile.

Captain Jacob Johan Anckarström, the assassin of the king, had been one of the king's pages and a member of the royal guards, from which he resigned in 1783. What the original cause of Anckarström's hatred of the king was is uncertain although speculations about Gustav's behavior with some of his young and attractive pages were not flattering to the king. His resentment of the king was based, however, not only on personal matters but on his objection to the king's private extravagance and public actions such as the war against Russia, the Act of Unity and Security, and the curtailment of the aristocrats' privileges. Anckarström finally succeeded in assassinating the king at the masked ball at the Royal Opera on March 16, 1792; the captain was arrested the following day; on April 11, he was condemned to the loss of all property and privileges, to be placed in the stocks on a public square for three days for public punishment by the executioner, the consequent loss of his right hand, decapitation, and being broken on the wheel. He was executed on April 27.

Count Fredrik Axel von Fersen (1719-1794) was from 1755 on one of the outstanding figures in Swedish political life. The leader of the Hat Party until the Revolution of 1772, Fersen proved sensible and practical and tried to curb the excesses of his fellow party members. After the revolution, Gustav III failed to win Fersen for his cause, and Fersen—without any final break with the king—was one of the most effective opponents of proposals to increase the king's power and of most of the proposals made by Gustav in the various meetings of the Estates up until and including that of 1789.

Baron Carl De Geer (1747-1805), one of the wealthiest men in Sweden, was one of Gustav's major opponents in the Estates. Like most of the other leaders among the nobility, De Geer in spite of his declared patriotism and lofty ideals was more interested in protecting the privileges of the nobility than he was in protecting the interests of the Swedish people.

Count Adolf Fredrik Munck (1749-1831), the son of a colonel, began his career at court as a page. He became a favorite of both Queen Sophia Magdalena and King Gustav when in 1776 he managed their reconciliation and their assumption of matrimonial life. Whether Munck was the father of Crown Prince Gustav Adolf or not—as gossip had it and as many Swedes including the queen mother Lovisa Ulrika believed —has never been proved. The heaping of honors and other rewards on Munck would indicate gratefulness on the part of each of the mismated and fundamentally incompatible royal couple. He was, as Strindberg says, a member of the temporary regency in 1788-1790 while

Gustav was at the front and he did have charge of the making of counterfeit Russian rubles for use in invaded Russian territory. Munck was
unwise enough to use some of the counterfeit coins for his own benefit.
After the assassination of Gustav III, Munck was tried, convicted, and
sentenced to make good all the counterfeit money he had put into
circulation, to leave the country, to change his name, and to see to it
that news of his "death" arrived shortly. If these conditions were ful-
filled, he was to continue to receive his salary for life. He spent the rest
of his life in Italy; in 1800, interestingly enough, Gustav IV Adolf
granted him a pension. Munck was handsome, secretive, ambitious for
both rank and money, arrogant on occasion, and not too careful about
his methods of getting what he wanted.

Baron Carl Edvard Taube, originally a lieutenant in the army, was
at the request of his brother, Baron Evert Taube, granted a pastorate
as the quickest means of making his fortune. SB (IX, 257): "and so the
ex-lieutenant became within a few years court chaplain and *pastor
primarius* of Stockholm."

Nils Henrik Aschan Liljensparre (1738-1814) was the first chief of
police in Stockholm and organized the Swedish police system. Exceptionally able and efficient, Liljensparre became one of the most famous
European experts in his field. He was ennobled in 1786.

Olof Olsson, a farmer from Östergötland and the manager (*arren-
dator*) of one of Count Fersen's estates, had been a member of the
parliament several times before he was selected speaker of his estate by
King Gustav in the assembly of 1789. Olsson died on March 13, 1789,
while he was holding this position; at the king's expense, Olsson was
buried with great ceremony in Riddarholm's Church, the burial place
of most Swedish royalty.

Johan Henrik Kellgren (1751-1795), a neoclassicist and one of the
greatest Gustavian poets and critics, wrote the texts for Swedish operas
sketched by Gustav III. His poems are among the best in Swedish literature, a literature particularly rich in poetry.

Thomas Thorild (1757-1808), one of the great Gustavian writers, was
idealistic and enthusiastic about ideas behind the French revolution in
their literary, as well as in their social and political, applications. Freedom, equality, and brotherhood were his favorite themes. He spent some

time in England, which he had supposed was the most advanced country politically and socially in Europe. Strindberg's quotations illustrate the abrupt, enthusiastic qualities of his prose style.

Carl Michael Bellman (1740-1795), one of the greatest lyric poets of all time and certainly the greatest of the many gifted Swedish writers during the Gustavian Period, wrote innumerable songs which he set to music, either his own or others. The two cycles, the *Songs of Fredman* and the *Epistles of Fredman,* include his greatest works. His songs still sung and loved throughout Scandinavia, Bellman occupies a place in Swedish culture roughly comparable to that of Burns in Scotland's. The queen's objections to Bellman's songs rest in the fact that many of them deal frankly with the amorous, drinking, and gambling activities of unfortunates in Stockholm.

Carl Israel Hallman wrote comedies which became very popular. SB (IX, 347): "Even as a sixty-year-old, Hallman—according to Thorild's account—was a happy Anacreonistic old man, a patriarch of the comic, with a head as beautiful as that of a Greek statue. Besides, he was a regular customer in the taverns. If he got any money, he invited his friends to eat and drink with him; if he didn't have any, they invited him."

Olof Kexell (1748-1796), a poverty-stricken writer and government employee, was primarily known for his popular dramas, his humorous writings, his minor difficulties with the law, and his good nature and friendliness.

Badin (*ca.* 1744-1832) the Negro who according to one of Strindberg's sources—Crusenstolpe's *Morianen*—was "given" to the then crown princess Lovisa Ulrika in the late 1740's by a Dane who had settled in Stockholm. Influenced by Rousseau's theories of education, Lovisa Ulrika used Badin as an experiment in natural education; for several years the boy was allowed to do what he wanted to without being in the slightest danger of discipline. The results proved so distressing that the queen ultimately found it necessary to place him under discipline. Badin became the friend and confidant of the members of the royal family, married twice but had no children. According to all available sources, Badin was a highly intelligent, loyal addition to a court dominated by a royal family badly torn with family and political troubles.

Queen Sofia Magdalena (1746-1813), the daughter of King Fredrik V of Denmark and his queen Louise, was the unfortunate victim of her high birth from her early childhood. Arrangements were then made for her eventual marriage to Prince Gustav of Sweden. In spite of his parents' objections and his own disinclination for the match, the official engagement was publicly announced in both capitals in 1766, and the marriage took place in the same year. The marriage of the melancholy, introverted, stiff-mannered, shy but physically attractive Sofia Magdalena and the lively Swedish crown prince who was her opposite in almost every way proved most unhappy. Incompatible by nature, the royal couple were not helped to any adjustment in marriage by Gustav's brilliant mother, Queen Lovisa Ulrika, who disliked, despised, and rendered uncomfortable her unfortunate daughter-in-law. Gossip, as Strindberg says, ascribed the paternity of Sofia Magdalena's oldest son and only child to survive infancy, to her favorite, Adolf Fredrik Munck. In general, Queen Sofia Magdalena's life was a lonely, unhappy one. Her son's latest biographer, Sten Carlsson, says in his *Gustav IV Adolf* (p. 17): "She is without question one of the most colorless of the queens in our history."

Lady Anne Charlotte Schröderheim (died, 1792) born von Stapelmohr, was well known at court and in Stockholm society for her physical attractiveness, her quick and stinging wit, and for extramarital love affairs. She was the object of lively gossip, and, according to Strindberg's sources, was one of the relatively few people who were not subject to King Gustav's charm.

ACT I

1. Holmberg owned not only the book store but also the printshop in which *The Stockholm Post* was published. When Halldin's attack on the liquor law in 1779 and its pernicious effects appeared in that newspaper, Halldin and Holmberg were arrested and tried. Halldin was sentenced to death but was pardoned by the king; Holmberg, however, had to serve his sentence—imprisonment for fourteen days on bread and water.

2. Queen Sofia Magdalena escaped occasionally from her isolation at court by driving with her favorite lady-in-waiting, Baroness Virginia

Charlotta Manderström to public inns such as Clas-on-the-Corner (*Clas på Hörnet*).

3. In 1788, Gustav used a border incident as an excuse to declare war on Russia—illegally, in that the constitution provided that an offensive war could be begun only with the consent of the four estates. Shortly after the opening of the war, a substantial number of officers mutinied at Anjala in Finland and demanded that peace with Russia be secured and the Estates be convened. From this embarrassing situation, Gustav was saved by the Danish declaration of war against Sweden. As Strindberg says, Gustav went to Dalarna in the tradition of Gustav Vasa and there secured volunteers for the Danish War. With these volunteers, Gustav hastened to Gothenburg then in peril of falling into the hands of the Danes and released the city from danger. Shortly afterwards the English and Prussian ambassadors forced the Danes to agree to a truce and evacuation of their army from Sweden. Gustav then summoned the 1789 meeting of the Estates during which he forced through an act of unity and security which for almost all practical purposes made him an absolute monarch. The war with Russia was resumed culminating in the great naval victory of Svensksund and ending in 1790 with the Treaty of Värälä. Of the Anjala men, only Colonel Hästesko was condemned to death and executed (on September 8, 1790) in Stockholm; Major Jägerhorn, who was also condemned to death, succeeded in escaping from the country. Usually Gustav's treatment of traitors and other enemies was humane and merciful.

4. The liquor law for which Gustav was held responsible was the statute of 1775, which forbade private distillation and sale of liquor and set up instead government distilleries. The king's statute had a two-fold purpose: to control the consumption of liquor and to increase the national income. The practical results were unfortunate because the ideal of controlling consumption was soon forgotten; it soon became almost a patriotic duty to drink, and the government lost money on the project.

5. In 1766, the Estates established freedom of the press in a statute which specifically prohibited the publication of (1) attacks on the Christian religion and on the national constitution and (2) libelous or immoral works. In 1774, Gustav III confirmed the statute enthusiastically; later in his reign—in 1779 as a result of violent protests against the liquor law—Gustav felt it was necessary to further restrict the

freedom of the press until eventually it was only a nominal freedom.

6. Charles XI, who reigned from 1660 to 1697, was an absolute monarch. Among other things, he confiscated crown lands and other property which earlier rulers—particularly Queen Christina—had given to her favorites and other noblemen.

7. See note 3.

8. Gustav's "disastrous private affairs" were primarily financial and political. His love of pleasure and his vanity caused him, as his enemies said, to waste national revenue on expensive court festivals, theatrical and operatic programs, foreign travels, extensive building programs, and on political-financial projects conceived in enthusiasm but executed haphazardly.

9. SB (IX, 425) says that during the war with Russia, Gustav III—in imitation of Fredrik II of Prussia—had had counterfeit rubles made at Drottningholm under Count Munck's direction for use in invaded Russian territory. See the note on Munck, page 272.

10. Marquis de Mirabeau (1749-1791) was one of the leading men in the French National Assembly of 1789. Fairly conservative, de Mirabeau proposed giving the assembly the right to legislate and to tax and the king the right to veto. One of Strindberg's favorite ideas is that historical events are international rather than narrowly national in scope and significance. Hence, his many references to such contemporary events as the French Revolution and Washington's election to the presidency.

11. Djurgårn (*Djurgården*) was then a suburb with inns and taverns as its special attractions for poverty-stricken literary men like Hallman, Kexell, and Bellman.

12. Until the Revolution of 1772, the country was alternately controlled by the two political parties, popularly called the Hats and the Caps.

13. Olof Håkansson (1695-1769), a farmer from Blekinge, had been vice-speaker of his estate at the meeting of the Estates in 1731 and from the meeting of 1738 on had been the most powerful member and usually the speaker until his death during the parliament of 1769.

14. With the possible exception of Anckarström, the listed aristocrats belonged to some of the most distinguished noble families.

15. *Camphio* (*cambio or campio*) the card game of Italian origin

which corresponds to modern Swedish "kille," was one of the most popular of the card games of the Gustavian period.

16. SB (V, 154) quotes Queen Christina's autobiography: "When I was born, I was covered with hair all the way from my head to my knees, so that only my face, arms and legs were free."

17. Grisslehamn is a small port northeast of Stockholm. Haga on the outskirts of the capital was one of Gustav III's favorite residences.

18. This Bellman song deals with a group of Stockholmers playing *trisette,* an Italian card game then popular. The first and title line can be translated: "I already foretell and believe it'll be a grand slam."

ACT II

19. Haga is the royal park and palace which lies on the shore of Brunnsviken, a body of water to the north of Stockholm and possibly in earlier days a bay (*vik*) of Lake Mälare. In 1771, Gustav III bought the property in order to build a royal villa there. The king's pavilion was built in 1785; the palace proper was never completed. The park—in the English manner—was completed, however. The present palace or the queen's pavilion was built during the reign of Gustav IV Adolf.

20. Johann Friedrich Struensee (1737-1772) was a German doctor, personal physician of King Christian VII of Denmark, the lover of the queen Caroline Matilda, and for his last two years absolute ruler of Denmark. In 1772, conspirators succeeded in removing him from power; he was tried and executed. The English-born queen, the daughter of George II of England, was imprisoned in 1772, divorced, and exiled to Hanover. The popular belief that Munck was Queen Sofia Magdalena's lover and the fact that he was given one office after the other makes the Danish story a striking parallel.

21. Shortly after his successful revolution in 1772, Gustav III proposed divorcing Sofia Magdalena. SB (IX, 387) says that she received the news that the revolution had succeeded with amazement and tears, and that the king took her reaction as an indication of both her stupidity and her hatred for him. His councillors' defense of the queen's good nature, intelligence and devotion to her husband, their assurance that his neglect may have caused her to weep when she heard that he had become anything but a figurehead, and the danger of trouble with

her native land caused the king to give up whatever plans he had for a divorce.

22. Prisoners of state were frequently confined in the fortress at Varberg in the province of Halland.

23. Anders Liidberg of Stockholm was the speaker of the Burghers' Estate in 1789.

24. Per Zacharias Ahlman was the efficient secretary of the Farmers' Estate and a loyal supporter of the king.

25. After the disastrous Russian-Swedish War of 1741-1743, the people of Dalarna and other provinces rose in rebellion and about five thousand armed rebels, mainly Dalesmen and including the provincial regiment, marched on Stockholm, encamped on Norrmalm's (now Gustav Adolf's) Square, and demanded the election of the Danish prince Fredrik as crown prince, the punishment of the unsuccessful generals, and various reforms. The Dalesmen opened fire on the regular troops; in the ensuing struggle, many rebels and soldiers lost their lives or were wounded, and the rebel army was finally routed. Many of the Dalesmen were severely punished.

26. In 1520, Gustav Vasa appealed to the people of the western province of Dalarna (literally, the Dales; usually referred to in English as Dalecarlia) for support against the Danes and, after some hesitation on their part, got it. Three years later, Sweden was free of its unpopular and unsatisfactory union with Denmark-Norway and Gustav Vasa was king of Sweden. The people of Dalarna proved as enthusiastic and able supporters of Gustav III when he went to them and appealed to them as his ancestor had done for help against the Danes and other enemies of the homeland.

27. Anckarström's wife was the daughter of a Russian government official.

28. Carl Gustaf Nordin (1749-1812) and Olof Wallquist (1755-1800) were two of the most powerful and influential leaders in the estate of the clergy; as such, they were instrumental in getting that estate to support the king in one meeting of the Estates after the other. From 1787 on, Wallquist was bishop of Växjö, and Nordin was bishop of Härnösand from 1805 on.

29. SB (VIII, 342) says: The Secret Committee on February 4, 1766, declared the agreement with the Danish king fifteen years before for

the marriage of his daughter, Princess Sofia Magdalena, and Gustav—
then five years old—was binding. In spite of the protests of Gustav's
parents, King Adolf Fredrik and Queen Lovisa Ulrika, the marriage
contract was drawn up and the engagement publicly announced in both
Stockholm and Copenhagen. The Empress Elizabeth of Russia interfered frequently in Swedish national affairs—at the peace conference
in Åbo following the unfortunate Russian-Swedish War of 1741-1743,
one Russian condition for a fairly favorable peace was that Sweden
elect Elizabeth's relative Adolf Fredrik of Holstein-Gottorp crown
prince. Only after Gustav's revolution of 1772 did Russian rulers lose
a determining voice in domestic Swedish affairs.

30. See note 21.

31. Georg Heinrich von Görtz, Charles XII's adviser and minister of
finances in the closing years of his reign, was executed—without a fair
trial—on February 20, 1719. His financial accounts were examined over
a nine-year period, with the unexpected conclusion that the Swedish
government was actually indebted to Görtz instead of having several
million coming to it. The debt was not paid to the Görtz heirs until
Gustav III in 1776-1777 arranged to settle the debt of over 70,000 *riksdaler*.

32. Many of the changes which have made Sweden "a model for a
world" have antecedents in reforms during Gustav III's reign. Among
them are the humanization of the treatment and punishment of crim-
inals, the abolition of torture, and the provision for a measure of protection of servants against their masters.

33. During the election of members to the Estates in 1789, clubs
were organized by the king's adherents to secure the election of members favorable to the king's program. Strindberg suggests what some
of the means used were not only for securing the election of royalist
candidates but also for influencing the Estates.

ACT III

34. Gustav's coup d'état was to force through the meeting of the
Estates in 1789 an amendment to the constitution which made him
almost an absolute monarch. This Act of Unity and Security not only
curtailed the privileges of the nobility but gave the right to initiate

legislation and to control administration and the power to declare war and make peace treaties to the king.

35. Göran Persson(*ca.* 1530-1568), was the favorite and counsellor of Erik XIV.

36. Christian, the last of the union kings, in 1520 had executed a large number of Swedish aristocrats in the Blood Bath of Stockholm and elsewhere, and in 1600, Duke Charles, later Charles IX, was primarily responsible for the beheading of several aristocrats at Linköping. Erik Göransson Tegel (*ca.* 1560-1636), the son of Göran Persson, was the prosecutor in the trial at Linköping.

37. Karlberg was then a royal palace outside Stockholm; since 1792, it has been the military academy for the training of army officers.

38. Carl Fredrik Mennander was archbishop from 1775 until his death in 1786. Gustav III considered Elis Schröderheim as a possible successor to Mennander, but finally decided upon Uno von Troil.

39. The tongue-tip trilled *r* rather than the uvular *r* is still considered the standard Swedish *r*.

40. Duke Charles, Gustav's oldest brother, was admiral of the fleet with its main station at Karlskrona.

41. Sulla (138-78 B.C.) was the Roman dictator who limited the power of the people's representatives and converted the Roman senate into an aristocratic tool of government.

42. Brutus (*ca.* 79-42 B.C.) was one of Caesar's murderers and a champion of freedom.

ACT IV

43. China Castle is a little pleasure palace constructed at Drottningholm by King Adolf Fredrik and Queen Lovisa Ulrika in 1763-1766. It is, as the name suggests, built in Chinese style, an expression of the then tremendous interest in the Orient.

44. See the note on Bellman under "Characters." "Böljan sig mindre rör" ("Quiet the billows are") is one of the exquisite songs in Bellman's *Bacchi tempel.*

45. Canton and the Gothic Tower are two of the show places at Drottningholm, not far from the palace proper.

46. Most of the people at his court shared Gustav's enthusiasm for

the theater. The three graces in classic mythology are Aglaia (Brilliance), Euphrosyne (Joy), and Thalia (Bloom). Megaera was one of the Furies, the punishers of men's misdeeds.

47. In the Roman calendar, the Ides of March fell on the fifteenth of March. Gustav was assassinated on March 16, 1792. On occasion, poets called Gustav Augustus or Caesar. The Bellman tribute below is an indication of Gustav's friends' and followers' opinion of him as a person and as a king. The poem is among Bellman's less happy works.

48. The Biblical elder brother of Jacob who was deprived of his birthright.

49. The Bastille, a national prison in Paris, was stormed and destroyed by the French revolutionists on July 14 and 15, 1789.

50. Gustav considered Drottningholm his Versailles.

51. The national marshal was speaker of the estate of the nobility. In the crucial assembly of the Estates in 1789, Count Charles Emil Lewenhaupt was the national marshal; he was then sixty-eight years old, had never had any claims to either great intelligence or abilities, and was for that reason a willing tool of the king in the estate that above all others opposed the king's plans to extend his powers.

52. Charles XII was killed at Fredrikshald in Norway on November 30, 1718.

53. Fersen's son, Count Axel Fersen, was the officer in Paris who became the friend of the members of the French royal family, perhaps the lover of Marie Antoinette, and the man who tried unsuccessfully to save the lives of the royal family by getting them across the French border to safety.

Committee on Publications
The American-Scandinavian Foundation